Student Study Guide

Criminal Justice
Today

Test #4 87

Rachel
#431-5409

Sharon Jett
635-4939

Student Study Guide

Steven Chermak

EIGHTH EDITION

Criminal Justice Today

An Introductory Text
for the Twenty-first Century

Frank Schmalleger, Ph.D.

Professor Emeritus
The University of North Carolina at Pembroke

PEARSON

Prentice
Hall

Upper Saddle River, New Jersey 07458

Executive Editor: Frank Mortimer, Jr.
Associate Editor: Sarah Holle
Marketing Manager: Tim Peyton
Editorial Assistant: Barbara Rosenberg
Managing Editor: Mary Carnis
Production Liaison: Barbara Marttine Cappuccio
Production Editor: Janet Bolton
**Director of Manufacturing
  and Production:** Bruce Johnson
Manufacturing Manger: Ilene Sanford
Manufacturing Buyer: Cathleen Petersen
Cover Image: David Young-Wolff, Stone/Getty Images
Printing and Binding: Banta Harrisonburg
Copy Editor: Maine Proofreading Services

Pearson Prentice Hall™ is a trademark of Pearson Education, Inc.
Pearson® is a registered trademark of Pearson plc
Prentice Hall® is a registered trademark of Pearson Education, Inc.

Pearson Education LTD.
Pearson Education Australia PTY, Limited
Pearson Education Singapore, Pte. Ltd.
Pearson Education North Asia Ltd.
Pearson Education Canada, Ltd.
Pearson Educacion de Mexico, S.A. de C.V.
Pearson Education—Japan
Pearson Education Malaysia, Pte. Ltd.
Pearson Education, Upper Saddle River, New Jersey

10 9 8 7 6 5 4 3 2 1
ISBN 0-13-184494-6

Contents

To the Student

Dear Criminal Justice Student:

I hope you will take a few minutes to read this letter since it may be my only chance, as the author of your textbook, *Criminal Justice Today*, to tell you the best way to use my book and the student study guide that accompanies it. I'd also like to tell you why I think it's important for you to be successful in your introductory course.

When I wrote *Criminal Justice Today*, I hoped to create a textbook that would accomplish the following goals.

1. Introduce beginning criminal justice students and others interested in the field to the basic concepts and terminology they would need to intelligently analyze the process of American criminal justice as it unfolds daily on street corners, in courtrooms, and in correctional settings across the country.
2. Be the most current source to prepare students to work in the criminal justice system of the twenty-first century.
3. Provide a realistic conceptual framework that students could feel comfortable adopting and that would guide their thinking about the American criminal justice system of today and of the future.

There is, however, a "higher purpose" in studying criminal justice—and it has to do with why you should want to be especially attentive to your instructor, to your textbook, to this study guide, and to the study of the subject matter of this course. Think of your course as a study in justice, and view your professor as a guide to justice issues in the modern world. Use your textbook, in combination with this study guide, other course materials, and the lectures your instructor provides, as a tool to evaluate the American criminal justice system relative to your understandings of fairness and of right and wrong. If you do that, you will achieve the highest purpose I had in mind when I wrote *Criminal Justice Today*: You will be firmer in your understanding of the fact that "injustice anywhere is a threat to justice everywhere," and you will be a better citizen as a result.

To get the most out of *Criminal Justice Today*, I urge you to give serious attention to the theme of my book (which is discussed in the first chapter). Use the theme as a tool for analyzing the concepts and ideas you encounter in the chapters that follow. Pay special attention to the lofty ideal of social justice that is discussed in Chapter 1, and think seriously about what *justice* means to you in specific situations in everyday life. Ask yourself, as you read the textbook, whether justice is being done in the day-to-day practice of American criminal justice—and if it is not, how the criminal justice system can be improved.

If you have suggestions about improving *Criminal Justice Today* or any of our supplements, please don't hesitate to contact me. Likewise, if there are features you would like to see added to the next edition, I'd be happy to hear directly from you. Please write to me at:

The Justice Research Association
P.O. Drawer 23557
Hilton Head Island, SC 29925
e-mail: author@cjtoday.com

As you set out to study the American criminal justice system, my thoughts and best wishes for success go with you. Enjoy your course!

Sincerely,

Frank Schmalleger, Ph.D., Director
The Justice Research Association

Introduction

This short introduction to the *Student Study Guide* discusses two important issues. First, I briefly provide some thoughts on why the study of criminal justice is important. Second, I share with you some basic tips on how to study.

Why Study Criminal Justice?

I'm working on a research project with a colleague at Indiana University. We are members of a group called the Indianapolis Violence Reduction Partnership. Since 1997, individuals from local, state, and federal law enforcement agencies, local prosecutors, a U.S. attorney, and individuals working in the corrections field have been meeting bi-weekly to identify the causes of violent crime in Indianapolis, suggest solutions to respond to violent crime, and then implement these solutions. My role in the project is to bring a relevant theoretical and research understanding to the project. In addition, I have the opportunity to evaluate what works and what doesn't work in criminal justice. This project relates well to what you will be studying in this class. We have examined the causes of crime in Indianapolis, have tried to develop better measurements to identify the crime picture, have implemented law enforcement strategies, have worked with court officials to change the way cases are processed, and have attempted to involve correctional agencies in the response to violence.

In addition, this project helps me show why the study of criminal justice is such an important topic. First, the study of criminal justice is important because crime, and society's response to crime, are among the greatest challenges facing every country. In Indianapolis, the Violence Reduction Partnership started meeting because we are concerned about the number of homicides. The homicide rate was increasing dramatically and criminal justice practitioners believed that extraordinary steps had to be taken in order to respond to the problem. Indianapolis is like every other city in the United States—despite the good news that has been displayed prominently in the news media that crime and violent crime is going down, crime is still a major public concern. What can we do to reduce crime? How can we respond to violent crime? How can we eliminate gang and drug activity? In cities and towns, in suburban and rural areas, crime is a significant social problem, and the primary institution responsible for responding to it is the criminal justice system.

The second reason why criminal justice is such an interesting topic is that the successes and failures of the system affect everybody. The amount of crime and violence in a community affects quality of life. For example, an incredible number of financial and personnel resources are expended to respond to crime. The components of the criminal justice system are primarily public-funded institutions. When money has to be spent on additional criminal justice resources to respond to crime, there is less money for other government and community programs. In addition, the existence of crime and feelings of insecurity melt the bonds that we have with other people in the community. When people don't feel safe, they prefer not to go out at night or mingle with others in the community. They are less likely to trust and help each other. If the criminal justice system can respond more effectively to crime, it can strengthen community bonds.

Third, criminal justice is an exciting topic because you already know a great deal about it. You have probably had positive and negative experiences with the criminal justice system. Perhaps you have gotten a ticket or have been arrested for other reasons. It is also likely that you have asked for police assistance. One of the best three-digit numbers known to the public is 9-1-1. This is because people know that when they need assistance, this number is probably the best one to call to get a fast response. In addition, one of the things you will realize as you read the textbook is that you have already heard about many of the cases discussed. The September 11, 2001 terrorist attacks, the Columbine shooting, the Oklahoma City Bombing, and the O.J. Simpson murder trial (among many, many others) are discussed to illustrate specific criminal justice points. Moreover, you already have opinions about many of the topics discussed: Should we have a death penalty? Should we build more prisons? Should we have long sentences for drug offenses? Should we loosen the procedural constraints on police when gathering evidence? You will be able to use your knowledge and opinions to react to the criminal justice issues presented and explored in the textbook.

How to Study

Each chapter of the *Student Study Guide* includes two learning tips. The topics include taking tests, reading comprehension, taking notes, study habits, and strategies for active learning. Each tip is a short description of simple steps you can take to improve your performance. It would be beneficial if you perused these tips frequently and used them as foundations to learning. In addition, the rest of this introductory section describes five general study strategies you can rely on for success in college:

   I. Effective Time Management
  II. Focused In-Class Performance
 III. Reading to Learn
 IV. Efficient Test Preparation
  V. Using University Resources

I. Effective Time Management

Most research on learning indicates that undergraduate students should spend three hours outside of class studying for every one hour in class. This means that if you are currently enrolled for 15 hours of course credit, you can expect to spend 45 hours outside of class completing the required coursework! I think you will appreciate the need for effective time management even more when you consider the outside activities you participate in, the number of hours you work, and other opportunities you have to enjoy your college experience. Don't worry. It is possible to balance study obligations with the activities that pull you away from studying. The key to finding this balance is effective time management. Here are four suggestions you can use to achieve study goals and to make good use of your time.

1. *Set long-term and short-term priorities.* Buy a calendar, if you haven't already, and put it in a prominent place in your room. Mark the dates of all tests, projects, or assignments due. Also, set priorities every day. Make a list of what you need to accomplish and stick to it.

2. *Establish a daily routine.* It is important that you study every day. Pick a time when you are rested, energized, and focused and make good use of it. Find a location that is quiet where you can work without interruptions.

3. *Plan well and be realistic.* If you work a lot of hours or if you have other obligations, then you may want to reduce the number of courses you enroll in. Also, rely on the "student grapevine" to discover information on the amount of work required for certain classes and specific professors. Take a few "easy" classes with a few "hard" classes.

4. *Review frequently.* Review your notes immediately after class or as soon after as possible. Review them again right before the next class session. These short (10 to 15 minutes) sessions save a lot of time in the long run.

II. Focused In-Class Performance

It is very important that you attend class and concentrate while there. Do not fall into the trap of relying on a friend's set of notes. Even if your professor gives you the notes for the class, attend class and personalize them. Here are three more suggestions that will help.

1. *Learn to concentrate.* Try not to get distracted in class; stay focused on the materials being presented. Let me share an anecdote with you. I once had a student visit during my office hours very upset because she had received low C's on the first two tests. What was upsetting her was that she said she studied a lot, attended class,

and did the reading. I asked to see her notes. She had gotten some of the main points from lecture, but she also had multiple doodles on every page. Although her artwork was outstanding, I suggested that she needed to stop daydreaming and focus on the lecture materials. I asked her to sit in the front of the class and I looked over her notes after every lecture for a couple of weeks. This simple solution resulted in a significant improvement in her performance.

2. *Be prepared for lecture.* Be physically and mentally alert when attending lecture. Try not to be fatigued, hungry, or distracted. Complete the reading assignment before attending class. This will help you identify important points made in lecture. Review your notes from the prior class as a warm-up to the materials about to be presented.

3. *Take good notes.* Pay close attention to the professor's teaching style to identify how he or she highlights key points. Listen carefully and then select the key points of the lecture. Make sure your notes are well organized, and be sure to leave enough space to add information or study hints.

III. Reading to Learn

One of the best learning resources you have at your disposal is the textbook. It is nearly impossible for a professor to cover every important piece of information in the textbook. Professors pick and choose points of emphasis, and expect students to take complete advantage of all of the information in the textbook. The following suggestions may help you do so.

1. *Overview and preview.* Spend some time looking over the materials contained in the entire textbook, and read the table of contents. Then preview each chapter prior to reading it. Also before reading each chapter, skim it; read sections, preview the headings and subheadings, and peruse the tables and graphs. Then read the introduction and summary before actually reading the chapter. This overview and preview will give you some perspective on the information in the book and the way it is organized.

2. *Select the main points.* One of the most difficult skills to develop is how to identify and highlight the most important information in a chapter. Try to prioritize the information in a section, and break it down into main points and supporting points. Underlining or highlighting the main points will help you remember them. Be an active reader. Try to be engaged in the reading material by reacting to it and mentally challenging what was written. This will help streamline the material into your long-term memory.

3. *Use the Student Study Guide.* The student study guide is a good reference that provides you with many opportunities to test whether you have really comprehended the materials. The SSG is designed to help you learn terms, cases, and ideas presented in the textbook. In addition, it puts the issues discussed in the textbook in a broader perspective, allowing you to understand the application of these ideas to practical criminal justice situations.

The chapters of the study guide correspond directly with the chapters of the textbook. Each section of the SSG will help you learn the information presented in the textbook. For example, it might be helpful if you read the learning objectives and chapter summary in the SSG before reading the chapter in the textbook, and then read them again after finishing the chapter. These two sections provide an overview of the key issues to be looking for when reading the textbook and to be reviewing when studying for exams. The SSG also has a section on key terms and key cases, giving you quick access to many of the main ideas of a chapter. The crossword puzzles and word search puzzles at the end of each chapter will test your understanding of the key terms and key cases. The SSG also includes a chapter outline and space for you to take notes on the readings or lectures. Try to answer the practice test questions without looking in the book. Remember that the textbook will be closed when you are taking an actual examination. Finally, when you complete the student activities and the APB exercise, be sure to refer to issues that are addressed in the textbook.

IV. Effective Test Preparation

Taking tests is among the most stressful of all college activities. It is important that you recognize that the sources of test anxiety include society's heavy emphasis on grades, time pressures, and the mystery of not knowing how well you are going to do. The three following strategies can reduce this anxiety.

1. *Preparation.* Taking good notes, reading to learn the textbook, and staying on schedule are the first ingredients for test success. In addition, try to find out as much as possible about the test before taking it. Read the syllabus closely for clues. Attend review sessions, if possible, but don't expect to be told what the questions are going to be. Use review sessions as opportunities to ask questions and test how well you are prepared for the examination. You should always attend the class immediately prior to the examination date. Often there are opportunities to ask questions about the examination and a professor might make slight adjustments on what will be covered because of lack of time. Review sessions, talking to former students, and attending the class right before the exam will help you predict what will be on the examination.

2. *Don't panic.* Patience is always a good virtue, including when you are taking an examination. Before you write anything, think about the question and think about the answers. When you are not sure about an answer, eliminate as many answers as possible before you guess. Make sure to pace yourself so that you have enough time to answer all questions and time to review questions.

3. *Use study strategies that fit the instructor and the type of examination.* Multiple-choice, short-answer, and essay examinations are significantly different. Each type of examination tests your understanding and comprehension of the material, but in slightly different ways. Multiple-choice and short-answer questions require considerably more memorization and identification of specific terms, cases, and key names. Essay questions require a large amount of information and facts, as well as a more global understanding of the subject.

It is also important that you realize that all professors are slightly different in their expectations about what should be known. Try to learn as much as possible about a professor before taking an examination he or she prepared. If you are having difficulties finding out any information, it is best to be overprepared for the first examination. You can alter your study strategy as you learn more about his or her testing style. The best way to adapt your test preparation to match a professor's test style is to do a self-evaluation after each examination. Identify the questions that you answered incorrectly. Did most of your incorrect answers come on questions that were covered in lecture? In certain sections of the textbook? Or about specific terms or cases? Once you have completed this self-evaluation, you will be able to change your study strategies to improve your test performance.

V. Using University Resources

Universities have an incredible number of resources that can enhance your classroom performance. For example, your university may have a writing center staffed by individuals trained to help with all stages of the writing process. Your library also has many resources and individuals willing and eager to help you succeed in college. Make an effort to learn about the resources as soon as possible and put them to use. Go back through orientation materials or surf your university's webpage for information and note the services that might help you.

Your instructor is also a valuable resource. Obviously, she or he is the best person to provide you assistance with your performance in this class. Don't be afraid to go to office hours if you are having problems or schedule an appointment for assistance. Over time you can build a good relationship with an instructor and then rely on that person for information about potential majors, internship possibilities, and career opportunities.

Using the Student CD

Scenarios

Each chapter on the CD-ROM found in the back of your textbook contains an interactive multimedia scenario based on an actual U.S. Supreme Court case. Each scenario contains rich audio and graphics that illustrate the different events that happen in each case. After listening to the audio and viewing the graphics in each segment, you will be asked questions that call for a decision. The scenarios are designed to improve your justice-related decision-making skills by putting you in the role of a decision maker such as a police officer, a parole officer, or a judge. They are not intended to be legal interpretations of specific cases or of laws. Each scenario also contains background material, legal highlights of the case upon which it is based, a "what really happened" section, and information on related cases. After you play through an entire scenario and answer all of the questions, an interactive decision timeline will become active at the bottom of the screen. The timeline has areas that show decision-point text when clicked—so that you can see what decisions "real" criminal justice officials made and why, and alternative decisions they could have made and why.

Quiz Games

Each chapter of the CD-ROM contains a practice quiz in the form of a match game that is intended to help you assess your understanding of the course material. These chapter-specific vocabulary-building games focus on the key terms listed at the start of each chapter and should help you remember crucial concepts and associated definitions.

Exercises

Each CD-ROM chapter contains an exercise that consists of 10 multiple-choice and 10 true-or-false questions. You can answer the questions and hit the check button to see how you scored. These exercises are also intended to help you assess your understanding and comprehension of the course material.

Glossary

The terms in the disc-based glossary parallel the definitions of important terminology used in the book. You can use the disc-based glossary to find the definitions of key terms.

Web Link

If you want to browse the Internet while using the *Criminal Justice Today* CD-ROM, click on the Web link button in the bottom left of the main program screen. This window contains hot links that will take you to important criminal justice-related websites.

Student Study Guide

Criminal Justice Today

chapter 1

What Is Criminal Justice?

LEARNING OBJECTIVES

After reading this chapter, you should be able to:

- Identify the theme on which this textbook builds

- Highlight the differences between the individual-rights and public-order perspectives

- Explain society's need for a system of order maintenance, and detail the role of law within that system

- Describe the personal sacrifices necessitated by public order

- Expound upon the relationship of criminal justice to social justice and other wider notions of equity and fairness

- Explain the structure of the criminal justice system in terms of its major components

- Describe the differences between the conflict and consensus models of the criminal justice system

- Describe the process of American criminal justice, including the stages of criminal case processing

- Explain the meaning of due process of law, and identify where due process guarantees can be found in the American legal system

- Explain how multiculturalism and diversity present special challenges to, and opportunities for, the American system of criminal justice

[1]

Chapter Summary

Chapter 1 accomplishes five objectives. First, it describes the major theme of the book. Second, it discusses whether the criminal justice process functions as a system. Third, it provides an overview of the textbook and the criminal justice process. Fourth, it explains the differences between criminology and criminal justice. Finally, it explains how multiculturalism presents unique challenges and opportunities for the criminal justice system.

The author describes the major theme that will be revisited throughout the textbook. This theme, individual rights versus public order, provides a framework for thinking about difficult criminal justice issues. This framework involves balancing individual rights (i.e., the right of individuals to be protected from overzealous and intrusive government agents) against community interests (i.e., the right of society to feel secure from crime). Individual rights and community interests are delicately balanced in our **criminal justice system**. When a movement is made to expand individual rights, such as in the 1960s, community interests are affected. Conversely, and more recently, as community interests have expanded, individual rights have been limited. To help put these "shifts of the pendulum" in perspective, this chapter discusses a series of celebrated cases such as the Oklahoma City bombing and the September 11 attacks. The way one balances these two competing interests evolves around each person's conception of justice. What is fair? Can the system be fairer? Everyone—including politicians, victims, defendants, police officers, prosecutors, and judges—attempts to balance individual and community interests, which affects how justice is applied. Individuals who prefer to protect freedoms and liberties are called **individual-rights advocates**. Individuals who believe that the interests of society should take precedence over liberties are called **public-order advocates**. It is important to realize that (1) understandings of justice are different for everyone and (2) our definitions are molded by our life experiences.

The criminal justice system is the mechanism in place for meting out justice when violations of criminal law occur. Yet does the criminal justice system function as a system? Supporters of a **consensus model** of justice say yes. This model argues that the system is predictable, that there is a high level of cooperation among agencies and individuals in the system, and that the components of the system—police, courts, and corrections—operate without conflict. Conversely, the **conflict model** of criminal justice views the operation of these components from a different perspective. Supporters of this model argue that the goals of criminal justice agencies and the individuals working within them differ and that the system's processes are affected by outside influences such as political pressure, informal arrangements, media coverage of high-profile cases, and discretion.

Both models have some value in helping us understand the operation of the criminal justice system. There are times when the agencies of criminal justice work closely together, representing a consensus model. For example, when criminal justice crises arise, such as when the federal building in Oklahoma City was bombed or the World Trade Center and the Pentagon were attacked, all components were focused on similar goals. However, at other times the goals of each agency conflict. For example, a prosecutor may want police officers to crack down on juvenile crime. Police officers, however, may feel that other crimes, perhaps drunk driving, should take priority.

The author provides an overview of the book and introduces you to the stages in the justice process. It is important that you familiarize yourself with these stages. In general, the criminal justice process starts when a citizen (victim or witness) calls the police to report a crime. The police are responsible for conducting the **investigation**, making an **arrest** (if they can establish probable cause), and **booking** the suspect. The court process begins when this suspect appears before a judge at the **first appearance**. Here, the judge decides what should be done with the suspect pending the outcome of the case. A **grand jury** or **preliminary hearing** will then be conducted to determine whether the criminal justice process should continue. An **information** can result from a preliminary hearing, and an **indictment** can result from a grand jury hearing. The suspect then will be arraigned on the charges. A trial will be held, and if the person is found (or pleads) guilty, then **sentencing** occurs. It is then the responsibility of the corrections component of the criminal justice system to carry out the sentence.

This chapter also discusses Herbert Packer's two models of the criminal justice system. The first model is the **crime control model**, which prioritizes efficiency in order to maintain social order. In contrast, **Packer's due process model** prioritizes individual rights and protecting innocent citizens.

Key Concepts

Arraignment: Strictly, the hearing before a court having jurisdiction in a criminal case, in which the identity of the defendant is established, the defendant is informed of the charge and of his or her rights, and the defendant is required to enter a plea. Also, in some usages, any appearance in criminal court prior to trial.

Bail: The money or property pledged to the court or actually deposited with the court to effect the release of a person from legal custody.

Booking: A law enforcement or correctional administrative process officially recording an entry into detention after arrest and identifying the person, the place, the time, the reason for the arrest, and the arresting authority.

Civil Justice: The civil law, the law of civil procedure, and the array of procedures and activities having to do with private rights and remedies sought by civil action. Civil justice cannot be separated from social justice because the kind of justice enacted in our nation's civil courts is a reflection of basic American understandings of right and wrong.

Concurrent Sentence: One of two or more sentences imposed at the same time, after conviction for more than one offense, and served at the same time. Also, a new sentence for a new conviction, imposed upon a person already under sentence for a previous offense, served at the same time as the previous sentence.

Conflict Model: A criminal justice perspective that assumes that the system's components function primarily to serve their own interests. According to this theoretical framework, justice is more a product of conflicts among agencies within the system than it is the result of cooperation among component agencies.

Consecutive Sentence: One of two or more sentences imposed at the same time, after conviction for more than one offense, and served in sequence with the other sentence. Also, a new sentence for a new conviction, imposed upon a person already under sentence for a previous offense, which is added to the previous sentence, thus increasing the maximum time the offender may be confined or under supervision.

Consensus Model: A criminal justice perspective that assumes that the system's components work together harmoniously to achieve the social product we call *justice.*

Crime: Conduct in violation of the criminal laws of a state, the federal government, or a local jurisdiction, for which there is no legally acceptable justification or excuse.

Crime-Control Model: A criminal justice perspective that emphasizes the efficient arrest and conviction of criminal offenders.

Criminal Justice: In the strictest sense, the criminal (penal) law, the law of criminal procedure, and the array of procedures and activities having to do with the enforcement of this body of law. Criminal justice cannot be separated from social justice because the kind of justice enacted in our nation's criminal courts is a reflection of basic American understandings of right and wrong.

Criminal Justice System: The aggregate of all operating and administrative or technical support agencies that perform criminal justice functions. The basic divisions of the operational aspects of criminal justice are law enforcement, courts, and corrections.

Criminology: The scientific study of the causes and prevention of crime and the rehabilitation and punishment of offenders.

Due Process: A right guaranteed by the Fifth, Sixth, and Fourteenth Amendments of the U.S. Constitution and generally understood, in legal contexts, to mean the due course of legal proceedings according to the rules and forms established for the protection of individual rights. In criminal proceedings, due process of law is generally understood to include the following basic elements: a law creating and defining the offense, an impartial tribunal having jurisdictional authority over the case, accusation in proper form, notice and opportunity to defend, trial according to established procedure, and discharge from all restraints or obligations unless convicted.

Due Process Model: A criminal justice perspective that emphasizes individual rights at all stages of justice system processing.

Grand Jury: A group of jurors who have been selected according to law and have been sworn to hear the evidence and to determine whether there is sufficient evidence to bring the accused person to trial, to investigate criminal activity generally, or to investigate the conduct of a public agency or official.

Indictment: A formal, written accusation submitted to the court by a grand jury, alleging that a specified person has committed a specified offense, usually a felony.

Individual Rights: The rights guaranteed to all members of American society by the U.S. Constitution (especially those found in the first ten amendments to the Constitution, known as the *Bill of Rights*). These rights are especially important to criminal defendants facing formal processing by the criminal justice system.

Individual-Rights Advocate: One who seeks to protect personal freedoms within the process of criminal justice.

Information: A formal written accusation submitted to the court by a prosecutor, alleging that a specified person has committed a specific offense.

Justice: The principle of fairness; the ideal of moral equity.

Multiculturalism: The existence within one society of diverse groups that maintain unique cultural identities while frequently accepting and participating in the larger society's legal and political system. Multiculturalism is usually used in conjunction with the term *diversity* to identify many distinctions of social significance. *Adapted from*: Robert M. Shusta et al., *Multicultural Law Enforcement*, 2d ed. (Upper Saddle River, NJ: Prentice Hall, 2002), p. 443.

Preliminary Hearing: A proceeding before a judicial officer in which three matters must be decided: (1) whether a crime was committed, (2) whether the crime occurred within the territorial jurisdiction of the court, and (3) whether there are reasonable grounds to believe that the defendant committed the crime.

Probable Cause: A set of facts and circumstances that would induce a reasonably intelligent and prudent person to believe that a particular other person has committed a specific crime. Also, reasonable grounds to make or believe an accusation. Probable cause refers to the necessary level of belief that would allow for police seizures (arrests) of individuals and full searches of dwellings, vehicles, and possessions.

Public-Order Advocate: One who believes that under certain circumstances involving a criminal threat to public safety, the interests of society should take precedence over individual rights.

Social Control: The use of sanctions and rewards within a group to influence and shape the behavior of individual members of that group. Social control is a primary concern of social groups and communities, and it is their interest in the exercise of social control that leads to the creation of both criminal and civil statutes.

Social Justice: An ideal that embraces all aspects of civilized life and that is linked to fundamental notions of fairness and to cultural beliefs about right and wrong.

Trial: In criminal proceedings, the examination in court of the issues of fact and relevant law in a case for the purpose of convicting or acquitting the defendant.

USA PATRIOT Act of 2001: A federal law (Public Law 107-56), enacted in response to terrorist attacks on the World Trade Center and the Pentagon on September 11, 2001. The law, officially titled The Uniting and Strengthening America by Providing Appropriate Tools Required to Intercept and Obstruct Terrorism Acts, substantially broadens the investigative authority of law enforcement agencies throughout America and is applicable to many crimes other than terrorism.

Victimology: The scientific study of crime victims and the victimization process. Victimology is a subfield of criminology.

Warrant: In criminal proceedings, a writ issued by a judicial officer directing a law enforcement officer to perform a specified act and affording the officer protection from damages if he or she performs it.

Learning Tips

Taking Notes

Each chapter of this study guide includes a Chapter Outline. Each entry of the outline has note-taking space to make it convenient for you to enter appropriate comments from your instructor's lecture related to specific topics in the chapter. This feature will help you organize your notes for easy review and study.

The Syllabus

Students tend to look at a course's syllabus once or twice at the beginning of the semester and then disregard it. Try to use the syllabus as a guide to organizing your semester, preparing for each class, and gaining insight into what the instructor considers important in the class. Many instructors include a brief overview of the course that could provide the key for essay or short-answer questions, including definitions, later in the semester.

CJ Today on the World Wide Web

A wealth of study help is available at your fingertips. Go online to http://cjtoday.com to access the dynamic CJ Today website. You'll find links to study aids tailored to each chapter in the text, Web Extras and Library Extras, crime and justice news, and the Prentice Hall Cybrary. In addition, there is a career center, as well as message boards to discuss criminal justice issues with other students. Give it a try—click on the URL above to enter the home page for *Criminal Justice Today*.

Other Web links to organizations and agencies related to the material in Chapter 1 include:

WEB SITE TITLE	URL
American Civil Liberties Union	http://www.aclu.org
Justice for All	http://www.jfa.net
Preventing Crime: "What Works, What Doesn't"	http://cjcentral.com/sherman/sherman.htm
United States Department of Justice	http://www.usdoj.gov
Bureau of Justice Statistics	http://www.ojp.usdoj.gov/bjs
National Criminal Justice Reference Service	http://www.ncjrs.org
Terrorism Files	http://www.terrorismfiles.org
National Center for Victims of Crime	http://www.ncvc.org
Office for Victims of Crime (OVC)	http://www.ojp.usdoj.gov/ovc
Violence, Public Heath, and the Media	http://www.annenberg.nwu.edu/pubs/violence

Student Activities

Activity 1

One of the most important issues faced by the criminal justice system is how best to respond to terrorism. Since the attacks of September 11, the public believes that terrorism is a significant threat in the United States. What do you think? Answer questions in the space provided below. You may want to look at the following websites for background information: The Prentice Hall Cybrary, at http://www.cybrary.info, has an extensive collection of articles on terrorism posted; also the National Criminal Justice Reference Service, at http://www.ncjrs.org, has information on terrorism.

1. Is terrorism a serious problem in this country? Why or why not?
2. What ten things can the criminal justice system do to respond to terrorism?
3. Of the ten items you cited, which one do you think might be most effective? Why?
4. Why is it so difficult to respond to terrorism?

_____

_____

_____

_____

_____

_____

Activity 2

What is your definition of justice? Consider the facts of the following case:

Dale and Mike Parak were twin brothers and best friends. They spent their entire lives looking out for each other's interests. When growing up, the two were inseparable. They played sports together, double-dated frequently, and attended the same university. They grew closer as they aged, they got married at about the same time, and eventually both were divorced. After they retired from their jobs, they decided to live together to save money and because they still enjoyed each other's company.

When he was 70 years old, Mike was diagnosed with cancer. Doctors predicted that he had about six months to live. The brothers, however, agreed that Mike should not suffer. Mike and Dale wrote and signed a note stating that they decided to commit suicide. Dale broke 20 tranquilizers into Mike's evening meal and watched as he ate it. Yet when Dale checked on Mike one hour later, Mike was still alive. Dale panicked. He took a .38-caliber revolver from his desk and shot Mike, killing him instantly. Dale then went into the kitchen and took a handful of tranquilizers. He did not die. He awoke the next morning as somebody pounded on the front door. It was a neighbor who, seeing that Dale was dazed and confused, decided to call an ambulance and the police.

The responding police officer conducted an investigation, and Dale was arrested and charged with the murder of his brother Mike. The prosecutor, although noting it to be a difficult case, pursued the case because she thought no citizen had the right to decide when someone should die. Dale Parak pleaded guilty to first-degree manslaughter and was sentenced to five years in a maximum-security prison. (Note that this was the lowest sentence that could be given to a defendant convicted of his crime.)

1. According to the definition of justice you provided, was this sentence just? Why or why not?
2. If you were the prosecutor in this case, would you have charged Dale Parak? Why?
3. If you were the judge in this case, how would you have sentenced Dale Parak? Why?

_____

_____

_____

_____

_____

_____

Activity 3

An effective way for you to understand the conflict of goals that is characteristic of the different criminal justice components is to talk to criminal justice professionals about their priorities and expectations. This assignment requires you to interview at least one representative of law enforcement, one of the court, and one of a corrections agency. For example, you could interview a police officer, a prosecuting attorney, and a correctional officer. Or you could interview a sheriff's deputy, a judge, and a probation officer. Any combination of representatives would be fine. Prepare questions in advance to find out about the background characteristics of these individuals, why they chose their careers, and the types of activities they do in a typical day. Finally, ask them about the organization's goals. For example, you could ask, What would you say are the five most important goals of this organization?

When you complete your interviews, discuss what you discovered in the space below. Did the three people you interviewed have the same goals? If so, were these goals prioritized in the same manner?

_____

_____

_____

_____

_____

_____

Activity 4

Crime and justice are subjects that are frequently presented on television. Prime-time television shows, soap operas, music videos, and cartoons often portray images of crime and criminal justice.

In the space below, list at least three television shows that you have seen that depict the police, courts, and correctional components of the criminal justice system (three television shows for each component). How do these shows present each component? Are the images positive or negative? What stages of the process are depicted? Do you think these images are fair representations of criminal justice? Why or why not?

_____

_____

_____

_____

_____

_____

Internet Activity

Visit the Prentice Hall Cybrary at http://www.cybrary.info. Choose a topic that is relevant to the material provided in Chapter 1. Describe the types of resources available on that topic.

_____

_____

_____

_____

_____

Distance Learning Activity

Visit the World Wide Web or the Prentice Hall Cybrary at http://www.cybrary.info to collect information on the criminal justice system's response to terrorism after the attacks at the World Trade Center and the Pentagon. Find at least one article that highlights individual-order concerns and one that highlights public-order concerns. After you have completed the assignment, participate in a class discussion to compare and contrast the findings from the different essays if your instructor asks you to do so.

_____

_____

_____

_____

_____

Student Study Guide Questions

True or False

_____ 1-1. A preliminary hearing involves a group of jurors selected from the community.

_____ 1-2. Expanding the rights of defendants to protect them from injustice would be most closely associated with a crime-control model of criminal justice.

_____ 1-3. The *Miranda* decision only requires that police personnel advise a person of his or her rights at the time of the arrest.

_____ 1-4. Parole differs from probation in that paroled offenders serve a portion of their prison sentences before being released.

_____ 1-5. Criminal justice is narrower than social justice because it is concerned only with violations of criminal law.

_____ 1-6. The consensus model of the study of criminal justice assumes that the system's subcomponents function primarily to serve their own interests.

_____ 1-7. Bail is a mechanism that defendants use to avoid advancing into the later stages of the criminal justice process.

_____ 1-8. Indictments are filed based on the outcome of a preliminary hearing.

____ 1-9. A concurrent sentence is a sentence that requires an offender who has been found guilty of more than one charge to serve one sentence after another is completed.

____ 1-10. Criminology is the application of scientific techniques to the investigation of a crime.

Multiple Choice

1-11. What decision(s) is (are) made at a suspect's arraignment?
   a. The suspect is required to enter a plea.
   b. The suspect is informed of the charges against him or her.
   c. The suspect is informed of his or her rights.
   d. All of the above are decisions made at arraignment.

1-12. Which of the following models assumes a systems model of criminal justice?
   a. due process model
   b. individual-rights model
   c. conflict model
   d. consensus model

1-13. Who would suggest that under certain circumstances involving criminal threats to public safety, the interests of society should take precedence over individual rights?
   a. a crime-control advocate
   b. a justice-ideal advocate
   c. an individual-rights advocate
   d. a public-order advocate

1-14. Who would support the full protection of personal freedoms and civil rights within the criminal justice process?
   a. a crime-control advocate
   b. a justice-ideal advocate
   c. an individual-rights advocate
   d. a public-order advocate

1-15. In the criminal justice process, a(n) _____ has to occur before a(n) _____.
   a. arraignment; preliminary hearing
   b. sentencing; trial
   c. arrest; first appearance
   d. booking; arrest

1-16. Upon being convicted of robbery and burglary, Jalen Arow is sentenced to seven years for the robbery and five years for the burglary. The sentence for burglary will be served right after the robbery sentence. This is an example of
   a. an unfair sentence.
   b. a discriminatory sentence.
   c. a consecutive sentence.
   d. a concurrent sentence.

1-17. Who is credited with creating the crime-control model of criminal justice?
   a. Earl Warren
   b. Jerome Skolnick
   c. Colin Ferguson
   d. Herbert Packer

1-18. A _____ is a group of jurors selected to hear the evidence and to determine whether there is sufficient evidence to bring the accused person to trial.
   a. jury
   b. public forum
   c. grand jury
   d. preliminary hearing

1-19. The conflict model of criminal justice
   a. assumes that the efforts of the component parts of the system are fragmented, leading to a criminal justice nonsystem.
   b. assumes that the movement of cases and people through the system is smooth due to cooperation among components of the system.
   c. assumes that all parts of the system work together toward a common goal.
   d. assumes police officers are the dominant actors in the criminal justice system.

1-20. A(n) _____ is a writ issued by a judicial officer directing a law enforcement officer to perform a specified act and affording the officer protection from damages if he or she performs it.
   a. indictment
   b. warrant
   c. pretrial release order
   d. information

Fill-In

1-21. Under certain circumstances involving criminal threats to public safety, _____ suggest that the interests of society should take precedence over individual rights.

1-22. The _____ is a perspective on the study of criminal justice that assumes that the system's subcomponents work together harmoniously to achieve that social product we call *justice*.

1-23. The crime-control model was first brought to the attention of the academic community by _____.

1-24. _____ are those who seek to protect personal freedoms within the process of criminal justice.

1-25. Jerome Skolnick's classic study of clearance rates provides support for the idea of a _____.

1-26. _____ is the step of the criminal justice process that occurs immediately after arrest.

1-27. _____ is an ideal that embraces all aspects of civilized life and that is linked to fundamental notions of fairness and to cultural beliefs about right and wrong.

1-28. _____ is a legal criterion residing in a set of facts and circumstances that would cause a reasonable person to believe that another person has committed a specific crime.

1-29. The money or property pledged to the court to effect the release of person from legal custody is called _____.

1-30. The _____ assumes that the criminal justice system's subcomponents function primarily to serve their own interests.

Crossword Puzzle

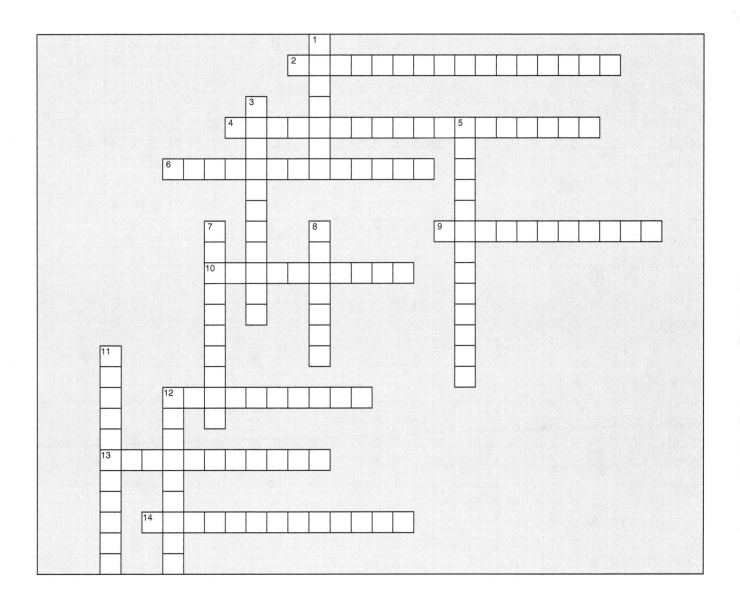

Across

2. Usually used in conjunction with diversity.
4. Also called the preliminary examination.
6. Provides the legal basis for an apprehension by the police.
9. The scientific study of the causes and prevention of crime and the rehabilitation and punishment of offenders.
10. Constitutional requirement of fairness and equity.
12. Type of sentence that runs at the same time as another sentence.
13. Type of sentence in which offenders are ordered to serve one sentence after another.
14. The federal law enacted in response to the terrorist attacks on the World Trade Center and the Pentagon on September 11, 2001.

Down

1. The principle of fairness.
3. The first appearance of the defendant before the court that has the authority to conduct a trial.
5. Scholar responsible for creating the crime control and due process models.
7. A grand jury returns an _____.
8. When a law enforcement official records an entry into detention after arrest.
11. Type of advocate that stresses the interests of society.
12. The model emphasizing a systems perspective.

Word Search Puzzle

```
H N C E A S R C C I G C R N E C C O N S E N S U S M O D E L
O E D N O I T A M R O F N I S S A I T C T N A E R B M I E S
M E C N E T N E S T N E R R U C N O C N J C R A M E S G O B
J Y A N L C O Y R L L S A S A B D I A N L I A B O G I L O A
I N D I V I D U A L R I G H T S A D V O C A T E R B L A C I
D M L R A I T L R U C A R O J E C O L E I N P P I O A C T M
A O A L M S E E G C I C S R O E V E S S S R O U E O R D I A
H O O E M T D V M O L A T O C U R K O S E T A B R E U E E A
T J L L Y C C R R M O N R I T U B S R L C T M L N Y T N L R
E L I E I G T I E I R R T N R T N U I N M E B I M C L I O S
T T O E D I O S U Y P S Y T I R T M N L N T T C C O U G B C
E J L C E O M L R S U C U O A C I O R R N I O O D Y C C T N
I T N R T E M U O J A C O V L N N C S I M N L R G A I R O A
U E N N B H J L L N N P O N A E N A N U F B E D S C T C U G
N N D I N D C A O P I C A R S E O E Y L U N O E L O L E U O
C O I G N D N U R R N M Y T I E Y O I T R E E R V U U R C T
D C U A G I R N A O T H I P R U C C O M F E D A C F M R F O
A R R E M T M Y M B E N N R R I T U I D T I N D L L I I A I
R G I I E N O S L A D A O R C M O N T R E R O V O M R E C E
I O R E T E L E R B I M S C O L V T U I I E U O E N N L D T
I C L L E M E I A L E C F D E R D C A K V I N C R M D R G E
A S C N N N I E E I B E T V M I L A C L E O A M E A O I R
N A J L C G T R U C U L R J T T I N N S T C S T S N I S A G
O C T L I I D U C A A H T I U E M R C S N N L E V E S L C E
V E R G V A C N I U E V R E I S V L C T N E C L N O T E O U
L V C S E R T H C S Y M L C C M T D S N I E I U O T J F M R
R M O N V R P S N E L C L N N A T I I I C E D G M C E B U T
S O N C A A G C P E V U F E I I O Y C L R L T U L B I N A I
T I I I A L R I N N O O C L Y S E I O E R I T M L C N E C I
E T U N U T C O T A T O N E M G R C C C B O O K I N G E R E
```

Arraignment
Bail
Booking
Concurrent Sentence
Conflict Model
Consecutive Sentence
Consensus Model
Crime
Crime-Control Model
Criminal Justice
Criminology

Grand Jury
Individual-Rights Advocate
Information
Justice
Multiculturalism
Preliminary Hearing
Probable Cause
Public-Order Advocate
Trial
USA PATRIOT Act

The Crime Picture

OUTLINE

Introduction
The Uniform Crime Reports
The National Crime Victimization Survey
Comparisons of the UCR and NCVS
Special Categories of Crime

LEARNING OBJECTIVES

After reading this chapter, you should be able to:

- Name and compare the two major national crime data-gathering programs in the United States today

- Explain what crime statistics can tell us about crime in America

- Describe some of the limitations inherent in statistical reports of crime

- Describe the FBI's Crime Index, and list the eight major crimes that make up that index

- Explain why crime statistics are generally expressed as rates instead of simple numerical tabulations

- Describe the two major categories of Part I offenses in the Uniform Crime Reports

- Explain the hierarchy rule, and discuss how it affects crime reporting

- Discuss the meaning of the term *clearance rate*

- Explain how the National Incident-Based Reporting System operates, and describe how it differs from the traditional Uniform Crime Reporting Program

- Identify the special categories of crime that this chapter discusses

Chapter Summary

Justin Stellar was standing at a bus stop when four teenagers approached him and asked for his wallet. Although he said he didn't want any trouble and gave them his wallet without resistance, one of the teenagers hit Justin in the head with a baseball bat. He was knocked unconscious and was rushed to the hospital for his injuries.

How would these crimes be classified by the criminal justice system? Chapter 2 in the text describes various crime classification instruments. For example, if Justin or the hospital reported this incident to the police, it could eventually be part of that department's annual uniform crime statistics submitted to the FBI. Or if Justin's household was one of the households selected for the **National Crime Victimization Survey (NCVS)**, then his victimization could be included as part of these victimization statistics (if he reported it to interviewers). If the teenagers were arrested, a prosecutor might charge the youths with **aggravated assault** and **robbery**. If the reported facts were more detailed and included the information that Mr. Stellar was an African-American male and the teenagers spray painted a racial epithet on his back while he was unconscious, this crime might be classified as a **hate crime**.

The two primary sources of data used to understand the crime picture in America are official statistics and victimization statistics. The most cited and well-known official source of data is the **Uniform Crime Reports (UCR)**, compiled annually by the FBI. There are approximately 16,000 police departments throughout the United States that voluntarily submit statistics on crimes reported to them. The FBI compiles these statistics and then reports the figures as either **Part I offenses** or **Part II offenses**.

The best-known source of victimization statistics is the **National Crime Victimization Survey (NCVS)**. This survey asks citizens directly about their victimization experiences, including characteristics of the perpetrator, the crime, and the incident. This survey includes information on six crimes: rape, robbery, assault, burglary, larceny, and motor vehicle theft.

Although both of these sources provide some general understanding of the crime problem, they have limitations. In developing the UCR, the FBI relies on the willingness of police departments to report and assumes that the information is accurately represented. But citizens do not report all crimes because, for a variety of reasons, they do not want to involve the police. Fear of retaliation, embarrassment, and belief that the police cannot do anything about it anyway are cited as reasons for not reporting crimes. These factors reduce the accuracy of UCR data. Victimization statistics might present a more accurate portrait of crimes not reported to the police, but this source of data has other limitations. Respondents, for example, might lie or exaggerate the circumstances of their victimization.

The text also provides general descriptions of the eight **index offenses** and interesting descriptive information about each offense category. **Murder, forcible rape, aggravated assault, robbery, larceny, burglary, motor vehicle theft**, and **arson** are discussed in detail. Murders, for example, do not occur frequently (compared to the other index offenses), but when they do, the police are able to clear a large percentage of them (approximately 65%). When a murder does occur, young males (18 to 24 years old) are most likely to have committed this type of crime.

This chapter also has a section on women and crime, discussing women as victims and offenders. Although women are not as likely as men to be victimized, they are more likely to be injured by crime and to be in fear of crime. Women are much less likely than males to commit one of the eight index offenses, although the rate at which women commit these types of crime is increasing rapidly.

The text also introduces other ways of understanding the crime picture. It discusses gun violence in the United States, highlighting major pieces of federal legislation enacted to regulate gun ownership. It examines the criminal justice system's interest in hate crimes, elderly crimes, drug crimes, and terrorism. It also discusses white collar, corporate, and computer crime.

Although statistics are important to a general understanding of crime, their value is tempered by their inability to indicate clearly how crime affects individuals. Was Mr. Stellar able to recover from his crimes physically? Psychologically? Emotionally? Was the criminal justice system responsive to his personal needs?

Key Concepts

Aggravated Assault (UCR): The unlawful, intentional inflicting, or attempted or threatened inflicting, of serious injury upon the person of another. While *aggravated assault* and *simple assault* are standard terms for reporting purposes, most state penal codes use labels like *first-degree* and *second-degree* to make such distinctions.

Arson: The burning or attempted burning of property, with or without the intent to defraud. Some instances of arson result from malicious mischief, some involve attempts to claim insurance monies, and some are committed in an effort to disguise other crimes, such as murder, burglary, or larceny.

Arson (UCR): The burning or attempted burning of property, with or without the intent to defraud.

Assault (UCR): An unlawful attack by one person upon another. Historically, *assault* meant only the attempt to inflict injury on another person; a completed act constituted the separate offense of battery. Under modern statistical usage, however, attempted and completed acts are grouped together under the generic term *assault.*

Bureau of Justice Statistics (BJS): A U.S. Department of Justice agency responsible for the collection of criminal justice data, including the annual National Crime Victimization Survey.

Burglary: By the narrowest and oldest definition, trespassory breaking and entering of the dwelling house of another in the nighttime with the intent to commit a felony.

Burglary (UCR): The unlawful entry of a structure to commit a felony or a theft (excludes tents, trailers, and other mobile units used for recreational purposes). For the UCR, the crime of burglary can be reported if (1) an unlawful entry of an unlocked structure has occurred, (2) a breaking and entering (of a secured structure) has taken place, or (3) a burglary has been attempted.

Clearance Rate: A traditional measure of investigative effectiveness that compares the number of crimes reported or discovered to the number of crimes solved through arrest or other means (such as the death of the suspect).

Computer Crime: Any crime perpetrated through the use of computer technology. Also, any violation of a federal or state computer-crime statute. Also called *cybercrime.*

Corporate Crime: A violation of a criminal statute by a corporate entity or by its executives, employees, or agents acting on behalf of and for the benefit of the corporation, partnership, or other form of business entity. *Source*: Michael L. Benson, Francis T. Cullen, and William J. Maakestad, *Local Prosecutors and Corporate Crime* (Washington, D.C.: National Institute of Justice, 1992), p. 1.

Crime Index (UCR): An inclusive measure of the violent and property crime categories, or Part I offenses, of the Uniform Crime Reports. The Crime Index has been a useful tool for geographic (state-to-state) and historical (year-to-year) comparisons because it employs the concept of a crime rate (the number of crimes per unit of population). However, the addition of arson as an eighth index offense and the new requirements with regard to the gathering of hate-crime statistics could result in new Crime Index measurements that provide less-than-ideal comparisons.

Crime Typology: A classification of crimes along a particular dimension, such as legal categories, offender motivation, victim behavior, or the characteristics of individual offenders.

Cyberstalking: The use of the Internet, e-mail, and other electronic communication technologies to stalk another person. *Source*: Violence Against Women Office, *Stalking and Domestic Violence: Report to Congress* (Washington, D.C.: U.S. Department of Justice, 2001).

Dark Figure of Crime: Crime that is not reported to the police and that remains unknown to officials.

Date Rape: Unlawful forced sexual intercourse with a female against her will that occurs within the context of a dating relationship. Date rape, or acquaintance rape, is a subcategory of rape that is of special concern today.

Forcible Rape (UCR): The carnal knowledge of a female forcibly and against her will. For statistical reporting purposes, the FBI defines *forcible rape* as "unlawful sexual intercourse with a female, by force and against her will, or without legal or factual consent." Statutory rape differs from forcible rape in that it generally involves nonforcible sexual intercourse with a minor. See also **carnal knowledge**.

Hate Crime: A criminal offense in which the motive is hatred, bias, or prejudice based on the actual or perceived race, color, religion, national origin, ethnicity, gender, or sexual orientation of another individual or group of individuals. Also called *bias crime*.

Identity Theft: A crime in which an imposter obtains key pieces of information, such as Social Security and driver's license numbers, to obtain credit, merchandise, and services in the name of the victim. The victim is often left with a ruined credit history and the time-consuming and complicated task of repairing the financial damages. *Source*: Identity Theft Resource Center website at http://www.idtheftcenter.org. Accessed April 4, 2002.

Larceny-Theft (UCR): The unlawful taking or attempted taking, carrying, leading, or riding away of property, from the possession or constructive possession of another. Motor vehicles are excluded. Larceny is the most common of the eight major offenses, although probably only a small percentage of all larcenies are actually reported to the police because of the small dollar amounts involved.

Motor Vehicle Theft (UCR): The theft or attempted theft of a motor vehicle. *Motor vehicle* is defined as a self-propelled road vehicle that runs on land surface and not on rails. The stealing of trains, planes, boats, construction equipment, and most farm machinery is classified as larceny under the UCR Program, not as motor vehicle theft.

Murder: The unlawful killing of a human being. Murder is a generic term which in common usage may include first- and second-degree murder, manslaughter, involuntary manslaughter, and other similar offenses.

National Crime Victimization Survey (NCVS): An annual survey of selected American households conducted by the Bureau of Justice Statistics to determine the extent of criminal victimization—especially unreported victimization—in the United States.

National Incident-Based Reporting System (NIBRS): An incident-based reporting system that collects data on every single crime occurrence. NIBRS data will soon supersede the kind of traditional data provided by the FBI's Uniform Crime Reports.

Organized Crime: The unlawful activities of the members of a highly organized, disciplined association engaged in supplying illegal goods and services, including gambling, prostitution, loan-sharking, narcotics, and labor racketeering, and in other unlawful activities. *Source*: The Organized Crime Control Act of 1970.

Part I Offenses: A set of UCR categories used to report murder, rape, robbery, aggravated assault, burglary, larceny, and motor vehicle theft, as defined under the FBI's Uniform Crime Reporting Program. Also called *major crimes*.

Part II Offenses: A set of UCR categories used to report data concerning arrests for less serious offenses.

Property Crime: A UCR offense category that includes burglary, larceny, auto theft, and arson.

Rape: Unlawful sexual intercourse, achieved through force and without consent. Broadly speaking, the term *rape* has been applied to a wide variety of sexual attacks and may include same-sex rape and the rape of a male by a female. Some jurisdictions refer to same-sex rape as *sexual battery*. See also **forcible rape; sexual battery**.

Robbery (UCR): The unlawful taking or attempted taking of property that is in the immediate possession of another by force or violence and/or by putting the victim in fear. Armed robbery differs from unarmed, or strong-arm, robbery with regard to the presence of a weapon. Contrary to popular conceptions, highway robbery does not necessarily occur on a street—and rarely in a vehicle. The term *highway robbery* applies to any form of robbery that occurs outdoors in a public place.

Sexual Battery: Intentional and wrongful physical contact with a person, without his or her consent, that entails a sexual component or purpose.

Stalking: Repeated harassing and threatening behavior by one individual against another, aspects of which may be planned or carried out in secret. Stalking might involve following a person, appearing at a person's home or place of business, making harassing phone calls, leaving written messages or objects, or vandalizing a person's property. Most stalking laws require that the perpetrator make a credible threat of violence against the victim or members of the victim's immediate family.

Transnational organized crime: Unlawful activity undertaken and supported by organized criminal groups operating across national boundaries.

Uniform Crime Reports (UCR): An annual FBI publication that summarizes the incidence and rate of reported crimes throughout the United States.

Violent Crime: A UCR offense category that includes murder, rape, robbery, and aggravated assault.

White-Collar Crime: Violations of the criminal law committed by a person of respectability and high social status in the course of his or her occupation. Also, nonviolent crime for financial gain utilizing deception and committed by anyone who has special technical and professional knowledge of business and government, irrespective of the person's occupation.

Learning Tips

Preclass Review

One way to give yourself a head start is to arrive at class early. Review the notes from the preceding class meeting, and review sections that were assigned. This will help you recall the focus of the previous class and get your mind prepared for the present class, and it may point out questions you intend to ask.

Office Hours

Very few students take advantage of posted office hours. As a consequence, very few students develop a relationship with the instructor, and most students are then hard-pressed to find a faculty member to write a recommendation letter or help with career advice as their college years draw to a close. Faculty members enjoy talking to students about specific courses and career opportunities in criminal justice. If you do go to an instructor's office hours, make sure you spend some time preparing in advance, creating a few questions on concepts from the class that might be unclear to you or exploring some facet of the class that interests you.

CJ Today on the World Wide Web

Web links to organizations and agencies related to the material in Chapter 2 include:

WEBSITE TITLE	URL
Sourcebook of Criminal Justice Statistics	http://www.albany.edu/sourcebook
Uniform Crime Reports	http://www.fbi.gov
NIBRS (coming UCR changes)	http://www.nibrs.search.org

WEBSITE TITLE	URL
Bureau of Justice Statistics	http://www.ojp.usdoj.gov/bjs
Bureau of Justice Assistance	http://www.ojp.usdoj.gov/BJA
FBI Hate Crime Statistics	http://www.fbi.gov/ucr/hatecm.htm
Fedstats	http://www.fedstats.gov
Violence Policy Center	http://www.vpc.org

Student Activities

Activity 1

Pick a newspaper that interests you. You could use your campus newspaper, a local city newspaper, or a national newspaper such as *USA Today*. In addition, most newspapers post articles on the Web.

Collect 30 crime articles from your newspaper. Read the articles you have collected, and then answer the following questions.

1. What types of crime are presented in the news?
2. What characteristics of crime victims are presented in the news? What characteristics of defendants are presented in the news?
3. Compare what you have discovered with the statistical information discussed in Chapter 2. Do the news media provide an accurate picture of crime in society?

_____

_____

_____

_____

_____

_____

Activity 2

Determine the number of index crimes reported to your university police department for each of the last five years. This information should be readily available to you from the police department, and it probably is posted on its website. Universities have been required to publish annual security reports since 1992. If you are having difficulties finding this information, check the Security on Campus website at http://www.campussafety.org. Click on the College and University Campus Crime Statistics link. Include in your statistics the number of murders, forcible rapes, aggravated assaults, robberies, burglaries, motor vehicle thefts, larcenies, and arson cases that have been reported each of the last five years. Answer the following questions, using these data, in the space provided below. Is your campus safe? Do the data show increases, decreases, or no change in the number of crimes committed on your campus? What types of things does your university do to make the campus safe for students?

_____

_____

_____

_____

_____

_____

Activity 3

Create a victimization questionnaire that you can use to determine the amount and types of victimization that occur on campus. Be sure to ask about the types of victimization experienced, the circumstances of each incident (where did the incident occur? what time?), and whether the student reported the incident to the police. In addition, collect demographic data so that you will be able to classify the responses by sex, age, and race. After you have completed the questionnaire, administer it to at least 50 students and then tabulate the results. What did you learn about victimization from the surveys? What types of victimization were reported? Were there differences by sex? Race? Age?

_____

_____

_____

_____

_____

_____

Activity 4

Read the articles posted at **Library Extra 2–5** and **2–8** at cjtoday.com, and then answer the following questions. What did you learn about violence against women in the United States? What are the major consequences of violence against women? How has the gender gap in crime changed over time?

LIBRARY extra

_____

_____

_____

_____

_____

_____

Activity 5

Visit the Prentice Hall Cybrary at http://www.cybrary.info. Click on Statistics. This section provides helpful information and interesting links to a variety of statistical data sources. Included here is a variety of crime statistics from throughout the world. For example, there is data from the British Crime Survey and the World Crime Survey. For this assignment, you are to collect crime data for any country of your choice other than the United States. In the space below, first discuss the amount and types of crimes in that country. Second, compare the crime picture of that country to what we have learned in this chapter about the United States according to the Uniform Crime Report statistics and National Crime Victimization Survey's data.

_____

_____

_____

_____

_____

Internet Activity

Visit the Prentice Hall Cybrary (http://www.cybrary.info) and use its search feature to find links to both the Uniform Crime Reports and the *Sourcebook of Criminal Justice Statistics*. Visit both sites in order to gather information about murder. How much information is available at these sites? What does it consist of? What are the similarities and the differences in the availability of information on the crime of murder between these two sites? Generally speaking, how do the two sites compare? Which one did you find most useful? Why?

_____

_____

_____

_____

_____

Distance Learning Activity

Read some of the following materials about new and promising strategies implemented to respond to juvenile homicide: (1) Blueprints for Violence Prevention (see section on model program descriptions) at http://www.ncjrs.org/html/ojjdp/jjbul2001_7_3/contents.html; (2) Gun Use by Male Juveniles (see section on promising gun strategies) at http://www.ncjrs.org/html/ojjdp/jjbul2001_7_2/contents.html; (3) Homicides of Children and Youth at http://www.ncjrs.org/pdffiles1/ojjdp/187239.pdf; (4) Youth Gang Homicides in the 1990s at http://www.ncjrs.org/txtfiles1/ojjdp/fs200103.txt; and (5) The Office of Juvenile Justice and Delinquency Prevention page at http://ojjdp.ncjrs.org/ojstatbb/index.html. After reading these materials, answer the following questions: What data about the juvenile homicide problem exist? Describe the major trends in the incidence of juvenile violence over the last ten years. What innovative strategies have been used to respond more effectively to the juvenile homicide problem?

_____

_____

_____

_____

_____

Student Study Guide Questions

True or False

___ 2-1. Rapes are significantly more likely than motor vehicle thefts to be reported to the police.

___ 2-2. Robbery is a crime against property; burglary is a personal crime.

___ 2-3. Violent crimes are generally more serious than property offenses.

___ 2-4. The NIBRS eliminates the need for the UCR hierarchy rule.

___ 2-5. The elderly are generally less likely to be victimized by violent and property crime.

____ 2-6. Although women are far less frequently victimized by crime than men, they are more likely to be injured by crime.

____ 2-7. Drug-related and other "victimless" crimes are all considered Part I offenses by the Federal Bureau of Investigation.

____ 2-8. Clearance rates refer to the proportion of crimes reported to the police.

____ 2-9. The National Crime Victimization Survey is compiled annually by the Bureau of Justice Statistics.

____ 2-10. Murder and aggravated assault are both considered Part I violent crime offenses.

Multiple Choice

2-11. Which of the following offense categories includes crimes such as larceny and arson?
    a. hate crime
    b. organized crime
    c. violent crime
    d. property crime

2-12. Which of the following agencies is responsible for compiling the Uniform Crime Reports?
    a. United States Marshals Service
    b. Office of Juvenile Justice and Delinquency
    c. Bureau of Justice Statistics
    ✓ d. Federal Bureau of Investigation

2-13. Which of the following is not one of the Uniform Crime Reports Part I offenses?
    ✓ a. drug possession
    b. motor vehicle theft
    c. murder
    d. rape

2-14. What is the reason rape victims give most often for not reporting the crime to the police?
    a. not worth the victim's time
    b. fear of reprisal
    ✓ c. fear of embarrassment
    d. police cannot do anything about it

2-15. Which of the following is not a problem with traditional Uniform Crime Reports statistics?
    a. Certain crimes are rarely reported to the police.
    b. When a number of crimes are committed in the same incident, only the most serious crime will be included in UCR data.
    c. Victims may believe that the police cannot do anything about a crime, so they do not report it to them.
    d. Certain types of crimes, such as victimless crimes, are not included in the UCR.
    e. All of the above are problems.

2-16. Which Part I offense is most likely to be reported by a victim to the police?
    a. robbery
    b. motor vehicle theft
    c. larceny
    d. rape

2-17. The National Crime Victimization Survey does not include information about which crime?
    a. robbery
    b. murder
    c. household larceny
    d. motor vehicle theft

2-18. The stealing of farm machinery would be classified under what category of the UCR?
a. burglary
b. robbery
c. larceny
d. motor vehicle theft

2-19. Megan Anderson unlawfully entered a computer services building and stole a laser printer. What crime did she commit?
a. aggravated assault
b. forcible rape
c. robbery
d. burglary

2-20. Which of the following is not a victimless crime?
a. gambling
b. motor vehicle theft
c. drug use
d. prostitution

Fill-In

2-21. _____ is the least reported of all violent index crimes.

2-22. _____ is intentional and wrongful physical contact with a person, without his or her consent, that entails a sexual component or purpose.

2-23. _____ is unlawful, forced sexual intercourse with a female against her will that occurs in the context of a dating relationship.

2-24. The type of assault that includes the use of a weapon or the need for medical assistance for the victim is called _____.

2-25. _____ are criminal offenses in which there is evidence of the perpetrator's prejudice based on the race, religion, sexual orientation, or ethnicity of the victim(s).

2-26. The most common of the eight major index offenses is _____.

2-27. _____ is the use of the Internet, e-mail, and other electronic communication technologies to stalk another person.

2-28. Sexual intercourse with a female who is under the age of consent—regardless of whether she is a willing partner—is called _____.

2-29. The index offense that is most likely to be reported by a victim to the police is _____.

2-30. The type of assault that is usually limited to pushing or shoving is _____.

Crossword Puzzle

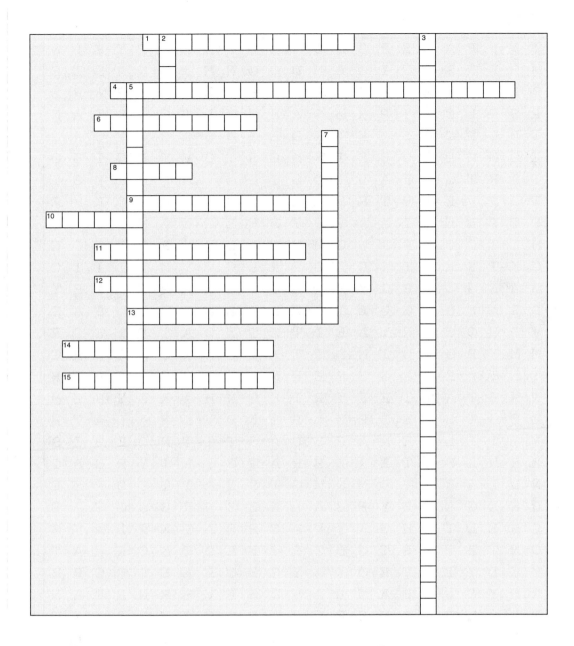

Across

1. The crime most likely to ruin a victim's credit history.
4. Agency responsible for collecting the National Crime Victimization Survey.
6. Another name for the Part I offenses of the UCR.
8. The burning or attempted burning of property, with or without the intent to defraud.
9. Number of crimes reported divided by the number of crimes solved.
10. The unlawful killing of a human being.
11. Also called cybercrime.
12. Crimes not reported to police are part of the

_____.
13. Burglary, larceny, auto theft, and arson.
14. The use of the internet to stalk a person.
15. _____ organized crime.

Down

2. Type of rape within the context of a relationship.
3. The new Uniform Crime Reports.
5. The FBI's source of national crime data.
7. Murder, rape, robbery and aggravated assault.

Word Search Puzzle

```
Y B E T R V S T A R F A A E R S D O T R L F U R O C Y E L N
A I E A R E S M H E R E T U I O B N D O O H M P R K A S T E
E E S M Y M U R A D C Y R E B B O R R E E N E B E I R S R E
O S T S D A O P S R L E A Y P R M G A H N H L T C D R T A N
S S K A Y C A T D U E C R I M E I N D E X N U L O O T O R B
F R M C N E R E O M M L A U E N T Y N C S Y O F T K U I G O
V S K K Y E Y T A R T G P E A U I O O T D M Y N F N L M O I
A C I Y Y A E T Y F V F N R T R S M H H E S A M R G O K M A
L Y R I R G A F T P L E E T A R P O Y S E E E E L N E T L N
P Y X T B G L H I T O O H H A U G M N E A D D Y R P O C O C
R N R G I R H U K T Y L R I T D L G E R E C C Y M T I I T C
U R R S R A O O A E G L O E C Y R R L O S I L A S M E I E Y
S I G A E V R D R A E U R G U L T C E E Y E A B Y O U S A S
L N D R T A T V S H O C R R Y A E I T K T X O A I Y I E C R
L E A C G T E M M X R G E U T N L T T R T C S R G G C T R T
O C R A U E T T L I R E E A S D R E H N V L T E S A F R T R
A E G A A D Y N M B T A T T E F T R I E E N H A K E Y R C M
N C G E E A T E C O T L A E I E D L B E F D V N H A L A T E
Y B N Y Y S G Y I T I L R E A A U L U A S T I T N D E B I S
M E N S A S G R R N K E E T E R L H R A T C Y R T Y R G A I
G T E E R A H N D I A E C V D N N M G T S N R T T C U R E E
G A O F R U T C N E G A N E Y E B A L R E S N R B S G G A E
D M O O G L R G S E L T A H T K Y V A C R E A L K R L N F S
O Y E U L T I O N T R T R E T G D T R T F E D T S O R H A T
G E N M S T R Y E L Y T A F E O X A Y C E C A E E L D C R R
T T R R A R H R H Y C L E E A U L A S D O P V B R N R E E N
A E U I C B M E A L L T L S M S R C O A L N S G Y R I A Y U
C D E A R A V I K A T Y C R N I B R S O Y C O H D R D B P F
G P M N N H I E O I S C I T N O Y M R T A V E M F L F E E E
N A T S G N I K L A T S R E B Y C R K Y O S E P A N R E G O
```

Aggravated Assault
Arson
Assault
Burglary
Clearance Rate
Computer Crime
Crime Index
Cyberstalking
Identity Theft

Larceny Theft
Motor Vehicle Theft
Murder
NCVS
NIBRS
Rape
Robbery
Stalking
Typology

The Search for Causes

LEARNING OBJECTIVES

After reading this chapter, you should be able to:

- List the various categories of theoretical approaches used to explain crime

- Describe the basic features of biological theories of crime causation

- Describe the basic features of psychological explanations for crime

- Describe the basic features of sociological theories of crime causation

- Identify two emergent theories of crime causation

Chapter Summary

Chapter 3 provides an overview of theories used to explain the causes of crime. It begins with an introduction to theory building in criminal justice, emphasizing the importance of research for testing hypotheses. The chapter is organized into nine general categories, and Table 3–1 is an extraordinarily useful tool for its summary of the characteristics of these theories and of the people most noted for their development.

Chapter 3 first discusses the criminological theories of the **Classical School**, including the works of **Cesare Beccaria** and **Jeremy Bentham**. The text discusses the five basic assumptions of classical theory:

1. Crime is caused by the individual exercise of free will;
2. Pain and pleasure are the two central determinants of human behavior;
3. Crime disparages the quality of the bond that exists between individuals and society;
4. Punishment is necessary to deter violators of the law and to serve as an example to others;
5. Crime prevention is possible through swift and certain punishment.

Theories in the **Biological School** search for physical or biological explanations of crime. Influenced by medical and technological advances, these theories have evolved over time. Compare the early biological theories of **Gall**, **Lombroso**, and **Sheldon** to contemporary biochemical theories. Gall argued that skull shape determined personality and behavior. Lombroso considered various parts of the body in his **atavistic** explanation for crime. Criminals, he argued, were throwbacks to earlier stages of evolution. William Sheldon used **somatotyping** (or body typing) to categorize each individual's physique by its **mesomorphic, endomorphic,** and **ectomorphic** characteristics. Sheldon found that juveniles with dominant mesomorphic physiques were most likely to commit crime. **Richard Dugdale** has considered biological inheritance as applied to criminal families in his examination of the Jukes's family tree and **Henry Goddard's** study of the Kallikaks.

Biological theories have advanced with medical technology. For example, chromosome theories look to internal gene structure to understand the causes of crime. The **XYY chromosome theory** was popular in the 1960s and early 1970s, but later studies question the ability of the XYY theory to predict criminal behavior. Other biological theories have examined the effects of chemical imbalances, hormones, and allergic reactions to food on criminal behavior.

Psychological explanations argue that criminal behavior results from inappropriately conditioned behavior or from abnormal, dysfunctional, and inappropriate mental processes. One thread of psychological theories presented in the text is **behavioral conditioning**. Another thread focuses on personality disturbances and diseases of the mind. People who believe in conditioning hold that the frequency of any behavior can be increased through rewards, punishments, and/or association with other stimuli. **Sigmund Freud** argued that personality was developed from the interaction of the id, the ego, and the superego. One source of criminal behavior is the ability of a person's superego to control his or her id.

Sociological explanations of crime examine the effects on behavior of environmental forces such as poverty, urban decay, and unemployment. For example, **Shaw and McKay's social ecology theory** argues that certain areas of a city—those with high rates of poverty, unemployment, and lack of schooling—are socially disorganized and likely to produce crime. **Merton**, borrowing the concept of **anomie** from **Emile Durkheim**, argued that since the means to achieve goals are not equally available to all groups, individuals are forced to use illegitimate means, such as crime, to accomplish goals. On the other hand, **subcultural** theories argue that the goals of various groups are different and some groups view committing crime as a legitimate goal. For example, **Marvin Wolfgang** and **Franco Ferracuti** found that murder was an acceptable goal for certain groups.

Chapter 3 also discusses **social process theories, conflict theories,** and some emerging theories such as **feminist criminology. Social process theories** explain deviant behavior by highlighting the process of interaction between individuals and society. **Conflict theories** consider law a tool of the powerful, which is used by the powerful to further their own interests. **Feminist criminology** emphasizes gender issues in criminology. None of these theories provides a definitive explanation of why people commit crimes. However, understanding how these theories explain the causes of crime is important because they have an impact on the development of criminal justice policy and the criminal justice system's response to crime.

Key Concepts

Anomie: A socially pervasive condition of normlessness. Also, a disjunction between approved goals and means.

Atavism: A condition characterized by the existence of features thought to be common in earlier stages of human evolution.

Behavioral Conditioning: A psychological principle that holds that the frequency of any behavior can be increased or decreased through reward, punishment, and association with other stimuli.

Biological School: A perspective on criminological thought that holds that criminal behavior has a physiological basis.

Broken Windows Thesis: A perspective on crime causation that holds that physical deterioration in an area leads to higher crime rates and an increased concern for personal safety among residents.

Chicago School: A sociological approach which emphasizes demographics (the characteristics of population groups) and geographics (the mapped locations of such groups relative to one another) and that sees the social disorganization that characterizes delinquency areas as a major cause of criminality and victimization.

Classical School: An eighteenth-century approach to crime causation and criminal responsibility that grew out of the Enlightenment and that emphasized the role of free will and reasonable punishments. Classical thinkers believed that punishment, if it is to be an effective deterrent, has to outweigh the potential pleasure derived from criminal behavior.

Conflict Perspective: A theoretical approach that holds that crime is the natural consequence of economic and other social inequities. Conflict theorists highlight the stresses which arise among and within social groups as they compete with one another for resources and for survival. The social forces which result are viewed as major determinants of group and individual behavior, including crime.

Constitutive Criminology: The study of the process by which human beings create an ideology of crime that sustains the notion of crime as a concrete reality.

Containment: The aspects of the social bond and of the personality that act to prevent individuals from committing crimes and which keep them from engaging in deviance.

Dangerousness: The likelihood that a given individual will later harm society or others. Dangerousness is often measured in terms of recidivism, or as the likelihood of additional crime commission within five years following arrest or release from confinement.

Deconstructionist Theory: One of the emerging approaches that challenges existing criminological perspectives to debunk them and which work toward replacing them with concepts more applicable to the postmodern era.

Defensible Space Theory: The belief that an area's physical features may be modified and structured so as to reduce crime rates in that area and to lower the fear of victimization that residents experience.

Deviance: A violation of social norms defining appropriate or proper behavior under a particular set of circumstances. Deviance often includes criminal acts. Also called *deviant behavior*.

Feminist Criminology: A developing intellectual approach that emphasizes gender issues in criminology.

Hypothesis: An explanation that accounts for a set of facts and that can be tested by further investigation. Also, something that is taken to be true for the purpose of argument or investigation. *Source: The American Heritage Dictionary and Electronic Thesaurus on CD-ROM* (Boston: Houghton Mifflin, 1987).

Interdisciplinary Theory: An approach that integrates a variety of theoretical viewpoints in an attempt to explain crime and violence.

Labeling Theory: A social process perspective that sees continued crime as a consequence of the limited opportunities for acceptable behavior that follow from the negative responses of society to those defined as offenders.

Life Course Perspective: An approach to explaining crime and deviance that investigates developments and turning points in the course of a person's life over time.

Moral Enterprise: The process undertaken by an advocacy group to have its values legitimated and embodied in law.

Neoclassical Criminology: A contemporary version of classical criminology that emphasizes deterrence and retribution and that holds that human beings are essentially free to make choices in favor of crime and deviance or conformity.

Peacemaking Criminology: A perspective which holds that crime-control agencies and the citizens they serve should work together to alleviate social problems and human suffering and thus reduce crime.

Phrenology: The study of the shape of the head to determine anatomical correlates of human behavior.

Positivist School: An approach to criminal justice theory that stresses the application of scientific techniques to the study of crime and criminals.

Postmodern Criminology: A brand of criminology that developed after World War II and that builds upon the tenets inherent in postmodern social thought.

Psychoanalysis: A theory of human behavior, based upon the writings of Sigmund Freud, that sees personality as a complex composite of interacting mental entities.

Psychological Profiling: The attempt to categorize, understand, and predict the behavior of certain types of offenders based upon behavioral clues they provide.

Psychological School: A perspective on criminological thought that views offensive and deviant behavior as the product of dysfunctional personalities. Psychological thinkers identify the conscious, and especially the subconscious, contents of the human psyche as major determinants of behavior.

Psychopath: A person with a personality disorder, especially one manifested in aggressively antisocial behavior, which is often said to be the result of a poorly developed superego. Also called *sociopath*.

Psychopathology: The study of pathological mental conditions—that is, mental illness.

Psychosis: A form of mental illness in which sufferers are said to be out of touch with reality.

Radical Criminology: A conflict perspective that sees crime as engendered by the unequal distribution of wealth, power, and other resources, which adherents believe is especially characteristic of capitalist societies. Also called *critical criminology; Marxist criminology.*

Rational Choice Theory: A perspective on crime causation that holds that criminality is the result of conscious choice. Rational choice theory predicts that individuals will choose to commit crime when the benefits of doing so outweigh the costs of disobeying the law.

Reaction Formation: The process whereby a person openly rejects that which he or she wants or aspires to but cannot obtain or achieve.

Research: The use of standardized, systematic procedures in the search for knowledge.

Routine Activities Theory: A neoclassical perspective which suggests that lifestyles contribute significantly to both the volume and the type of crime found in any society.

Schizophrenic: A mentally ill individual who suffers from disjointed thinking and possibly from delusions and hallucinations.

Social Development Theory: An integrated view of human development that points to the process of interaction among and between individuals and society as the root cause of criminal behavior.

Social Disorganization: A condition said to exist when a group is faced with social change, uneven development of culture, maladaptiveness, disharmony, conflict, and lack of consensus.

Social Learning Theory: A psychological perspective that says that people learn how to behave by modeling themselves after others whom they have the opportunity to observe.

Social Process Theory: A perspective on criminological thought that highlights the process of interaction between individuals and society. Most social process theories highlight the role of social learning.

Somatotyping: The classification of human beings into types according to body build and other physical characteristics.

Subculture of Violence: A cultural setting in which violence is a traditional and often accepted method of dispute resolution.

Supermale: A human male displaying the XYY chromosome structure.

Theory: A set of interrelated propositions that attempt to describe, explain, predict, and ultimately control some class of events. A theory gains explanatory power from inherent logical consistency and is "tested" by how well it describes and predicts reality.

Learning Tips

When to Study

While students tend to study favorite subjects first, difficult and boring subjects require more energy and creativity. Thus, subjects that are difficult or boring need to be addressed early when mental energy is high, saving more enjoyable coursework for later. However, if you find yourself continually avoiding a subject, this might indicate a serious trouble area. If this is the case, seek help from a professor or tutorial service.

Where to Study

Find a place where you will be alert, such as the library, and where there is good lighting and a low noise level. Regularly use this place to study until your mind and body are trained to recognize the area as your study place. Use this area exclusively for studying. Avoid watching television, eating, and socializing in your study place. Therefore, whenever you arrive at your study place, you will be able to focus your attention immediately.

CJ Today on the World Wide Web

Web links to organizations and agencies related to the material in Chapter 3 include:

WEBSITE TITLE	URL
Rand Corporation	http://www.rand.org
Human Genome Project	http://www.ornl.gov/TechResources/ Human_Genome
Crime Theory Page	http://www.crimetheory.com
Crime Times	http://www.crime-times.org
Biology, Behavior, and the Criminal Law	http://www.gruterinstitute.org/ news/vls.html
The Genocide Research Project	http://www.people.memphis.edu/ ~genocide
Western Criminology Review	http://wcr.sonoma.edu
American Society of Criminology	http://asc41.com

Student Activities

Activity 1

Chapter 3 begins by linking media images and criminal behavior. For example, it discusses the criticism that rap music and heavy-metal music poison the minds of our youth. Historically, rock and roll and other types of music have been criticized in a similar manner. Are crime, sex, and violence dominant themes in music? Be sure to provide examples. Do you believe that heavy-metal and rap music can cause juveniles to commit crimes? Why or why not?

_____

_____

_____

_____

_____

_____

Activity 2

Choose one of the theories discussed in Chapter 3. Assume that research has established that this theory has unequivocally identified the cause of crime. Now that you are certain about the cause of crime, what changes would you recommend in the criminal justice system and society to reduce the crime problem in the United States? Be sure to fully explain your theory, and then discuss what changes should be made in the criminal justice system. (*Hint:* The discussion in the text of each general type of theory and social policy would be helpful here. For example, if you were to argue that biological theories are definitive, the section on social policy and biological theories would be a helpful starting point for completing this assignment.)

_____

_____

_____

_____

_____

_____

Activity 3

Visit the website http://www.crimetheory.com and click on the Learning Section, and then Explorations in Criminal Theory. Choose one of the sections that explores a theory or theorist presented in Chapter 3. Which theory or theorist did you examine? Why did you choose him or her? What new information did you learn about that theory or theorist? Does this new information change your opinions of this theory? Are you more, or less, convinced of its validity?

_____

_____

_____

_____

_____

_____

Activity 4

When they occur, serial murders get more media attention than any other type of crime. Indeed, not only is serial murder a high-priority news topic, it is often the subject of movies and novels. Your assignment is to first locate at least ten newspaper articles about serial murder. You could use any newspaper database, such as Lexus-Nexus, to do this search. However, if you don't have direct access to a specific newspaper database, then search the Web. After you have collected these articles, answer the following questions. Why is serial murder so intriguing to news and popular media organizations? How do your articles present serial murder? What theories of serial murder are discussed in these articles?

_____

_____

_____

_____

_____

Internet Activity

Research serial killers on the Web. What kind of information is available? What are the best sites for such information?

Print out (or save to disk) the information on serial killers that you find on the Web. Prepare a notebook (or disk file) of this information, and include a section on individual serial killers throughout history. Your instructor may ask you to submit your notebook.

_____

_____

_____

_____

_____

_____

Distance Learning Activity

Visit the Crime Theory page. This webpage is located at http://www.crimetheory.com. Visit the Explorations link and complete one of the posted exercises. Submit a summary of what you learned about criminological theory by completing the exercise.

_____

_____

_____

_____

_____

Student Study Guide Questions

True or False

_____ 3-1. Anomie exists when there is a disjuncture between the goals of society and the means to achieve those goals.

_____ 3-2. Differential association theory was developed by Edwin Sutherland.

_____ 3-3. Techniques of neutralization are rationalizations that allow offenders to shed feelings of guilt for their behavior.

_____ 3-4. Cesare Lombroso is considered the founder of the Classical School of criminology.

_____ 3-5. Phrenologists study the shape of the skull to predict criminal behavior.

_____ 3-6. A basic assumption of the Biological School is that offensive and deviant behavior is the product of environmental forces.

_____ 3-7. Cesare Beccaria is considered the father of criminology.

_____ 3-8. Peacemaking criminology is one of the biological theories of crime.

_____ 3-9. Robert Merton's ritualist accepts both the goals and the means that society considers legitimate.

_____ 3-10. Ectomorphs have bodies that are characterized by thinness, fragility, and delicacy.

Multiple Choice

3-11. All of the following theorists are biological criminologists except
a. Cesare Lombroso.
b. William Sheldon.
c. Franz Gall.
d. Jeremy Bentham.

3-12. Atavism is
a. a condition characterized by an individual with a dysfunctional superego.
b. a condition characterized by features thought to be common in earlier stages of human evolution.
c. a term used to describe males with an extra Y chromosome.
d. a term used to describe ectomorphic body types.

3-13. Which school explains criminal behavior by looking at gene structure, hormones, and inheritance?
   a. Social-Psychological School
   b. Classical School
   c. Biological School
   d. Psychological School

3-14. Which school emphasizes the roles of free will and reasonable punishments?
   a. Sociological School
   b. Classical School
   c. Biological School
   d. Psychological School

3-15. Which of the following sociological theories argues that crime is most likely to occur in "zones of transition"?
   a. subcultural
   b. profiling
   c. anomie
   d. social ecology

3-16. _____ theory proposes that when an individual's bond to society weakens, the likelihood of crime increases.
   a. Labeling
   b. Differential association
   c. Containment
   d. Social control

3-17. Which of Sheldon's body types has a relative predominance of muscle, bone, and connective tissue?
   a. mesomorphs
   b. risomorphs
   c. endomorphs
   d. ectomorphs

3-18. According to Robert Merton, a(n) _____ accepts both the goals of society and society's acceptable means to achieve them.
   a. retreatist
   b. ritualist
   c. conformist
   d. innovator

3-19. Who would be considered a contemporary, or modern-day, biological theorist?
   a. Richard Herrnstein
   b. Sarnoff Mednick
   c. James Q. Wilson
   d. all of the above

3-20. All of the following theories can be considered social process theories except
   a. differential association.
   b. containment.
   c. social ecology.
   d. social control.

Fill-In

3-21. Who worked with Clifford Shaw to develop social ecology theory?

   _____

3-22. Who developed differential association theory? _____

3-23. Whose name is most widely associated with the field of psychology?

   _____

3-24. Who argued that crime results from social definition, through law, of unacceptable behavior? _____

3-25. Who applied anomie to criminology? _____

3-26. The author of *Sisters in Crime* is _____.

3-27. Who is the father of modern criminology? _____

3-28. _____ founded the Classical School of criminology.

3-29. _____ is the violation of social norms that define appropriate or proper behavior under a particular set of circumstances.

3-30. _____ is one theorist who has popularized peacemaking criminology.

Crossword Puzzle

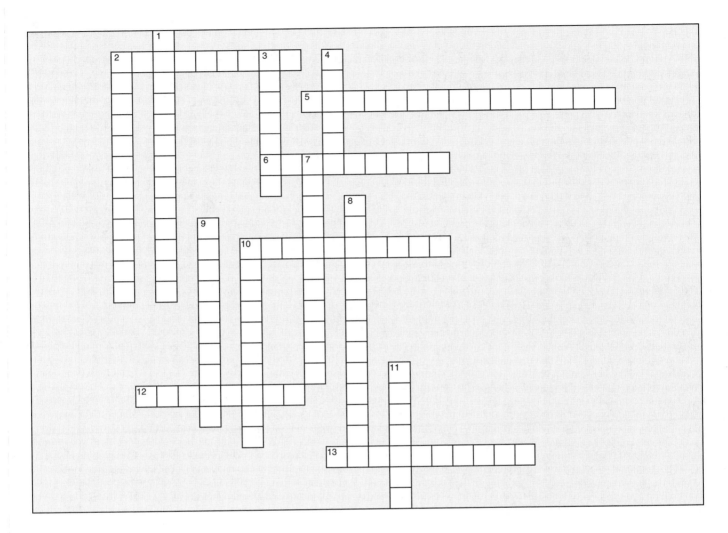

Across

2. Crime causation theory linked to the Enlightenment.
5. The process undertaken by an advocacy group to have its values legitimated and embodied in law.
6. A male believed to have an extra Y chromosome.
10. The study of the shape of the head to determine anatomical correlates of human behavior.
12. Theory that emphasizes gender issues in criminology.
13. Also called sociopath.

Down

1. Usually measured in terms of recidivism.
2. The type of criminology that studies the process by which human beings create an ideology of crime that sustains the notion of crime as a concrete reality.
3. The existence of features thought to be common in earlier stages of human evolution.
4. Without social norms.
7. A perspective which holds that crime-control agencies and the citizens they serve should work together to alleviate social problems and human suffering and thus reduce crime.
8. James Q. Wilson's thesis.
9. Something that is taken to be true for the purpose of argument or investigation.
10. An approach to criminal justice theory that stresses the application of scientific techniques to the study of crime and criminals.
11. Also called Marxist criminology.

Word Search Puzzle

```
S S L A C I G O L O I B S A R E Y I M S I E E I M O N H N F
L M O C O S N V A A O P M E E S I R P R E T N E L A R O M A
P I L M S O Y P B N E H C E C N E S T S C L A S S I C A L A
I O A C A E A G A F E M I N I S T C R I M I N O L O G Y S E
Y S I E D T D U O N G L O T L E R O E E E N E Y R P N E E R
O Y O R O R O L N L E E E C O G C E I G E E R E H C Y G O
G I F O R E O T I G O N B E L G B S U L L C V C S A O E I S
I Y N L O A O T Y Y T N R M A A E E I C P E I B E O R C H I
G O G A A C D O I P S O E H G O S E I M O E T Y A H C I O S
B U C O E T Y I G C I S C R N C C A C O V R C E R I T O R G
O F E C L I C L C E S N C Y H E G N K I S R E L C E E L I E
L A O V L O O D Y A G Y G A S P Y E T G N C P M H E L T N H
T N R O T N N Y G O L O N I M I R C L A C I S S A L C O E N
O S P I L F N I S E Y C E R C F E O L P N M R P Y L F O O L
A I A S P O T R M T N O R M S P I D I T D S E E R O E F R R
P E E C Y R N T Y I O T S I S S E N C G F L P N O S T I C S
L P O I R M S C S B R S U R M F E I I A E E E P E G U C O A
N A E L L A N D N I E C E G E I R I A C O R S E H S I C I S
I I I L V T I N E N S P E N I Y N E M C Y H R A T I T N I Y
L T N N M I S I S V T Y S V O V L O O O R I U C G S R N L L
T C S I O O F U N C I I L A I A E N L S N T O E N E S C I O
O S A R H N O I I S B A T A M T T M N O T A C M I H S V I E
M L F G P R A L L L Y A N R N A U H F E G N E A L T P N E S
A E N M E A F Y E E V S E C I A L T P C P Y F K E O E F E E
C C I G I N I S H I C P N N E I O I I E L O I I B P O Y Y I
E S N E O O P S S P U A M I E F R H L T E B L N A Y C P N M
S A T C E A S M A S M E L C N T E I C N S R I G L H O T C I
D E C R E E C P E N L R T O R A M T Y E N U A C H C I I L
Y T S E Y R O E H T Y S R T S C I P N L S I O S A F A O A T
O N S C H I Z O P H R E N I C E O O A E A P C C O O T S O N
```

Anomie
Atavism
Biological
Classical
Conflict Perspective
Constitutive Criminology
Containment
Dangerousness
Defensible Space
Deviance
Feminist Criminology
Hypothesis
Labeling Theory

Life Course Perspective
Moral Enterprise
Neoclassical Criminology
Peacemaking
Phrenology
Psychoanalysis
Radical Criminology
Reaction Formation
Research
Schizophrenic
Somatotyping
Supermale
Theory

chapter 4

Criminal Law

LEARNING OBJECTIVES

After reading this chapter, you should be able to:

- Explain the impact of common law on contemporary American criminal justice

- Discuss the nature of the rule of law, and describe its purpose in Western democracies

- Identify the various types of law, and explain the purpose of each

- List five categories of criminal law violations

- List the eight general features of crime

- Explain the concept of *corpus delicti*

- Discuss the four broad categories of criminal defenses that our legal system recognizes

- Explain the legal concept of insanity, and distinguish it from psychiatric explanations of mental illness

- Name at least five new and emerging innovative criminal defenses

- Distinguish between explaining a behavior and excusing it for purposes of the law

Chapter Summary

Imagine our society without laws. How would order be maintained? How would individuals be protected from harm? How would society be protected? Law provides these protections, insulating society from mass chaos. Chapter 4 discusses many areas of law including the nature and purpose of law, the rule of law, types of law, and general categories of crime.

Chapter 4 explains why we have laws. Laws are needed to prevent the victimization of innocent people. Laws also ensure that the philosophical, moral, and economic perspectives of those who created the laws are protected. They also uphold established patterns of social privilege and sustain existing power relationships. Laws can also promote change in society or help society adapt to change. For example, new laws have been created in response to the computer revolution. Many criminal laws were created to adapt to rapid social and technological changes.

The text also discusses different types of law. **Common law** is the traditional body of unwritten historical precedents created from everyday social customs, rules, and practice. **Criminal law**, which is the focus of this chapter, is concerned with offenses against society. The criminal justice processing machinery operates according to criminal law. Chapter 4 also distinguishes criminal law from civil law. **Civil law** provides legal guidance regulating the relationships between individuals. Sometimes criminal and civil cases overlap. An individual could be charged under criminal law but also sued in civil court by the victim. **Case law** involves the decisions of courts that provide guiding principles to future decisions, and **administrative law** is the body of law that regulates industry, business, and individuals.

Chapter 4 also provides a discussion of general categories of crime. Specifically, the text discusses five categories of violation: **misdemeanors**, **felonies**, **offenses**, **treason and espionage**, and **inchoate offenses**.

Finally, Chapter 4 discusses the general features of crime. Let's walk through a situation in view of the features discussed.

Facts: Joan killed her husband by stabbing him with a kitchen knife. Joan had been frequently subjected to beatings, some resulting in hospitalization, from her husband. Moreover, her husband had threatened to kill Joan on at least four prior occasions.

1. *Actus reus:* The first general feature of crime is that there has to be an act in violation of the law. Here, the act is murder. If Joan stabbed her husband and he survived, she could be charged with attempted murder. If Joan took steps to complete the murder but was unable to carry out her attempt, she could be charged with conspiracy to commit murder. If she approached an undercover police officer and asked him to commit a murder, she could be charged with solicitation to commit a murder.

2. *Mens rea:* A guilty mind is the second general feature that has to be established and is probably the most complex because it involves subjective evaluation of the mind. Should Joan be held to blame for this crime? Did Joan intend the consequences of her action?

3. **Concurrence:** The third element is the concurrence of the act and the intent. Joan's actions have to be linked with her intent.

4. **Harm:** The harm in this case, the death of another human being, is easily identified.

5. **Causation:** There has to be a link between the act and the harm. If Joan shot her husband and he survived for a month but then died of complications related to a cancerous brain tumor, it would be difficult to convict Joan of murder because the act (the shooting) would not be linked to the harm (the death).

6. **Legality:** There has to be a law on the books to punish someone for his or her behavior. Murder is well defined in our law books.

7. **Punishment:** Not only must there be a law on the books, but that law must provide a punishment for the crime. Statutory punishments for murder are among the severest punishments available to judges.

Even if each of the statutory elements can be established, a defendant has the opportunity to raise defenses that could excuse his or her actions. For example, Joan might argue that she committed the act in self-defense as a battered woman who thought her life was in danger.

The last part of Chapter 4 discusses several types of defenses, including alibi, justifications, excuses, procedural, and innovative. The **alibi defense** is very straightforward in that the defendant argues that he or she was nowhere near the crime when it happened. **Justification defenses** are used when the defendant admits to committing the act but claims it was necessary to avoid a greater evil. Examples include self-defense, necessity, and defense of home. **Excuse defenses** are used when a defendant claims that some personal condition or circumstance was such that he or she should not be held accountable. Examples include age, insanity, involuntary intoxication, and unconsciousness. **Procedural defenses** are defenses based on procedure, such as double jeopardy, collateral estoppel, selective prosecution, denial of speedy trial, and prosecutorial misconduct. **Innovative defenses** are similar to personal defenses but are unique and emerging defenses. Examples include black rage, urban survival syndrome, the abuse defense, premenstrual stress syndrome, and cultural defenses.

Key Concepts

Actus Reus: An act in violation of the law. Also, a guilty act.

Alibi: A statement or contention by an individual charged with a crime that he or she was so distant when the crime was committed, or so engaged in other provable activities, that his or her participation in the commission of that crime was impossible.

Alter Ego Rule: In some jurisdictions, a rule of law that holds that a person can only defend a third party under circumstances and only to the degree that the third party could act on his or her own behalf.

Attendant Circumstances: The facts surrounding an event.

Battered Women's Syndrome (BWS): I. A series of common characteristics that appear in women who are abused physically and psychologically over an extended period of time by the dominant male figure in their lives. II. A pattern of psychological symptoms that develops after somebody has lived in a battering relationship. III. A pattern of responses and perceptions presumed to be characteristic of women who have been subjected to continuous physical abuse by their mates. *Source: People* v. *Romero*, 8 Cal. 4th 728, 735 (1994); and *People* v. *Dillard*, 96 C.D.O.S. 3869 (1996).

Case Law: The body of judicial precedent, historically built upon legal reasoning and past interpretations of statutory laws, that serves as a guide to decision making, especially in the courts.

Civil Law: The branch of modern law that governs relationships between parties.

Class-Action Lawsuit: A lawsuit filed by one or more people on behalf of themselves and a larger group of people "who are similarly situated." *Source*: Gerald and Kathleen Hill, *The Real Life Dictionary of the Law* (Santa Monica, CA: General Publishing Group, 2000). Online version Web posted at http://dictionary.law.com/lookup2.asp. Accessed February 21, 2002.

Codification: The act or process of rendering laws in written form.

Common Law: Law originating from usage and custom rather than from written statutes. The term refers to an unwritten body of judicial opinion, originally developed by English courts, that is based upon nonstatutory customs, traditions, and precedents that help guide judicial decision making.

Compensatory Damages: Damages recovered in payment for an actual injury or economic loss.

Concurrence: The coexistence of (1) an act in violation of the law and (2) a culpable mental state.

Concurring Opinion: An opinion written by a judge who agrees with the conclusion reached by the majority of judges hearing a case but whose reasons for reaching that conclusion differ. Concurring opinions, which typically stem from an appellate review, are written to identify issues of precedent, logic, or emphasis that are important to the concurring judge but that were not identified by the court's majority opinion.

Corpus Delicti: The facts that show that a crime has occurred. The term literally means the "body of the crime."

Criminal Law: The branch of modern law that concerns itself with offenses committed against society, its members, their property, and the social order. Also called *penal law*.

Criminal Negligence: Behavior in which a person fails to reasonably perceive substantial and unjustifiable risks of dangerous consequences.

Cultural Defense: A defense to a criminal charge in which the defendant's culture is taken into account in judging his or her culpability.

Defense (to a criminal charge): Evidence and arguments offered by a defendant and his or her attorney to show why that person should not be held liable for a criminal charge.

Diminished Capacity: A defense based upon claims of a mental condition that may be insufficient to exonerate the defendant of guilt but that may be relevant to specific mental elements of certain crimes or degrees of crime. Also called *diminished responsibility*.

Double Jeopardy: A common law and constitutional prohibition against a second trial for the same offense.

Element (of a crime): In a specific crime, one of the essential features of that crime, as specified by law or statute.

Entrapment: An improper or illegal inducement to crime by agents of enforcement. Also, a defense that may be raised when such inducements have occurred.

Espionage: The "gathering, transmitting, or losing" of information related to the national defense in such a manner that the information becomes available to enemies of the United States and may be used to their advantage. *Source*: Henry Campbell Black, Joseph R. Nolan, and Jacqueline M. Nolan-Haley, *Black's Law Dictionary*, 6th ed. (St. Paul, MN: West, 1990), p. 24.

Excuse: A legal defense in which the defendant claims that some personal condition or circumstance at the time of the act was such that he or she should not be held accountable under the criminal law.

Ex post facto: Latin for "after the fact." The Constitution prohibits the enactment of *ex post facto* laws, which make acts committed before the laws in question were passed punishable as crimes.

Felony: A criminal offense punishable by death or by incarceration in a prison facility for at least one year.

Gross Negligence: The "intentional failure to perform a manifest duty in reckless disregard of the consequences as affecting the life or property of another." *Source*: Henry Campbell Black, Joseph R. Nolan, and Jacqueline M. Nolan-Haley, *Black's Law Dictionary*, 6th ed. (St. Paul, MN: West, 1990), p. 1003.

Guilty But Mentally Ill (GBMI): A verdict, equivalent to a finding of "guilty," that establishes that the defendant, although mentally ill, was in sufficient possession of his or her faculties to be morally blameworthy for his or her acts.

Inchoate Offense: An offense not yet completed. Also, an offense that consists of an action or conduct that is a step toward the intended commission of another offense.

Incompetent to Stand Trial: In criminal proceedings, a finding by a court that, as a result of mental illness, defect, or disability, a defendant is incapable of understanding the nature of the charges and proceedings against him or her, of consulting with an attorney, or of aiding in his or her own defense.

Infraction: A minor violation of state statute or local ordinance punishable by a fine or other penalty or by a specified, usually limited, term of incarceration.

Insanity Defense: A legal defense based on claims of mental illness or mental incapacity.

Jural Postulates: Propositions developed by the famous jurist Roscoe Pound that hold that the law reflects shared needs without which members of society could not coexist. Pound's jural postulates are often linked to the idea that the law can be used to engineer the social structure to ensure certain kinds of outcomes. In capitalist societies, for example, the law of theft protects property rights.

Jurisprudence: The philosophy of law. Also, the science and study of the law.

Justification: A legal defense in which the defendant admits to committing the act in question but claims it was necessary in order to avoid some greater evil.

Law: A rule of conduct, generally found enacted in the form of a statute, that proscribes or mandates certain forms of behavior. Statutory law is often the result of moral enterprise by interest groups that, through the exercise of political power, are successful in seeing their valued perspectives enacted into law.

Legal Cause: A legally recognizable cause. A legal cause must be demonstrated in court in order to hold an individual criminally liable for causing harm.

Mala in Se: Acts that are regarded, by tradition and convention, as wrong in themselves.

Mala Prohibita: Acts that are considered wrong only because there is a law against them.

Mens Rea: The state of mind that accompanies a criminal act. Also, a guilty mind.

Misdemeanor: An offense punishable by incarceration, usually in a local confinement facility, for a period whose upper limit is prescribed by statute in a given jurisdiction, typically one year or less.

M'Naghten Rule: A rule for determining insanity which asks whether the defendant knew what he or she was doing or whether the defendant knew that what he or she was doing was wrong.

Motive: A person's reason for committing a crime.

Natural Law: Rules of conduct inherent in human nature and in the natural order that are thought to be knowable through intuition, inspiration, and the exercise of reason, without the need for reference to created laws.

Offense: A violation of the criminal law. Also, in some jurisdictions, a minor crime, such as jaywalking, that is sometimes described as *ticketable*.

Penal Code: The written, organized, and compiled form of the criminal laws of a jurisdiction.

Political defense: An innovative defense to a criminal charge that claims that the defendant's actions stemmed from adherence to a set of political beliefs and standards significantly different from those on which the American style of government is based. A political defense questions the legitimacy and purpose of all criminal proceedings against the defendant.

Precedent: A legal principle that ensures that previous judicial decisions are authoritatively considered and incorporated into future cases.

Procedural Defense: A defense that claims that the defendant was in some significant way discriminated against in the justice process or that some important aspect of official procedure was not properly followed in the investigation or prosecution of the crime charged.

Procedural Law: The part of the law that specifies the methods to be used in enforcing substantive law.

Punitive Damages: Damages requested and/or awarded in a civil lawsuit when the defendant's willful acts were malicious, violent, oppressive, fraudulent, wanton, or grossly reckless. Also called *exemplary damages. Source*: Gerald and Kathleen Hill, *The Real Life Dictionary of the Law*. Accessed February 21, 2002.

Reasonable Force: A degree of force that is appropriate in a given situation and is not excessive. Also, the minimum degree of force necessary to protect oneself, one's property, a third party, or the property of another in the face of a substantial threat.

Reckless Behavior: Activity that increases the risk of harm.

Rule of Law: The maxim that an orderly society must be governed by established principles and known codes that are applied uniformly and fairly to all of its members.

Self-Defense: The protection of oneself or of one's property from unlawful injury or from the immediate risk of unlawful injury. Also, the justification that the person who committed an act that would otherwise constitute an offense reasonably believed that the act was necessary to protect self or property from immediate danger.

Stare Decisis: The legal principle that requires that in subsequent cases on similar issues of law and fact courts be bound by their own earlier decisions and by those of higher courts having jurisdiction over them. The term literally means "standing by decided matters."

Statutory Law: Written or codified law; the "law on the books," as enacted by a government body or agency having the power to make laws.

Strict Liability: Liability without fault or intention. Strict liability offenses do not require *mens rea.*

Substantive Criminal Law: The part of the law that defines crimes and specifies punishments.

Tort: A wrongful act, damage, or injury not involving a breach of contract. Also, a private or civil wrong or injury.

Treason: "A U.S. citizen's actions to help a foreign government overthrow, make war against, or seriously injure the United States." Also, the attempt to overthrow the government of the society of which one is a member. *Source*: Daniel Oran, *Oran's Dictionary of the Law* (St. Paul, MN: West, 1983), p. 306.

Key Cases

Ake v. *Oklahoma*: In this case, the United States Supreme Court held that the government must ensure access to a competent psychiatrist whenever a defendant indicates that insanity will be an issue at trial.

The Crown v. *Dudly & Stephens*: A famous case illustrating the necessity defense.

Durham v. *United States*: Provides the Durham rule for gauging insanity. This rule states that a person is not criminally responsible for his or her behavior if the person's illegal actions were the result of some mental disease or defect.

Ford v. *Wainwright*: In this case, the U.S. Supreme Court decided that prisoners who become insane while incarcerated cannot be executed.

Foucha v. *Louisiana*: The U.S. Supreme Court held that a defendant found not guilty by reason of insanity in a criminal trial could not be institutionalized indefinitely without showing that he or she was either dangerous or mentally ill.

U.S. v. *Brawner*: Provides the Brawner rule for gauging insanity. This rule places responsibility for deciding insanity with the jury. Juries are primarily guided by their own sense of fairness.

U.S. v. *Felix*: In this case, the U.S. Supreme Court ruled that the double jeopardy clause only applies to the prosecution of the same offense. Another offense or involvement in a conspiracy to commit that offense are not considered the same offense and thus would not be in violation of the double jeopardy clause.

Learning Tips

Binders

Use binders to take notes. They allow you to insert and remove pages. Therefore, you can easily add handouts, chapter notes, or notes from classmates and you can remove unnecessary information. Additionally, to review material, you can organize pages in a manner that allows you to recognize the overall strategy of lectures easily.

Memory Techniques

You can enhance your memory by creating associations. Your memory stores information in patterns that make sense to you. When you gather additional information, you will recall it more effectively if it is stored near similar information in your brain. For example, an important term in Chapter 4 is *tort*. A good way to remember this term is to associate it with civil law. Tort is a private or civil wrong; civil law regulates activity involving personal interests.

CJ Today on the World Wide Web

Web links to organizations and agencies related to the material in Chapter 4 include:

WEBSITE TITLE	URL
The Rule of Law	http://www.users.bigpond.com/ smartboard/btof/index18.htm
WashLaw Web	http://www.washlaw.edu
International Center for Criminal Law	http://www.icclr.law.ubc.ca
United States Attorney Office	http://www.usdoj.gov/ag
American Bar Association	http://www.abanet.org/crimjust/ home.html
American Prosecutor's Research	http://www.ndaa-apri.org/
Legal Law Help	http://www.legallawhelp.com/

Student Activities

Activity 1

Visit the link at **Library Extra 4–1**. Read an article posted in the law review journal and summarize the content of the article.

_____

_____

_____

REMEMBER

Chapter 1 discusses the stages of the criminal justice process. The key police stages include investigation, arrest, and booking. Court stages include first appearance, preliminary or grand jury hearing, and arraignment. Corrections include probation, parole, and prison. Law directly influences all of these stages.

_____

_____

_____

Activity 2

It would be helpful to refer to the text's discussion of the insanity defense before tackling this activity.

The insanity defense is one of the more controversial and complex defenses available to defendants. It is controversial because the public thinks that defendants are excused from punishment when found not guilty as the result of this defense. The complexity lies in the link it makes between the medical and legal professions.

Consider the legal implications of the following case: Tom Smith had recently escaped from a mental hospital when he was picked up by a concerned motorist. At a highway rest area, Tom killed the motorist by strangulation. He was charged with murder. On two prior occasions, Tom had been found not guilty by reason of insanity.

The medical implications are as follows: Tom has the IQ of about a ten-year-old child. He has a 30-year history of mental illness, dating back to his return from the Vietnam War. Tom suffers from posttraumatic stress disorder and is unable to recover from the horrors he experienced in war. He is delusional and strangled the motorist because the motorist listened to Grateful Dead rock music, which caused Tom to think he was the Antichrist.

The prosecution had no trouble establishing the elements of crime. The defense attorneys used an insanity defense (irresistible-impulse test), claiming that Tom belongs in a mental hospital, not a maximum-security prison. If you were the judge in this case, what would you decide? Should Tom be punished as a criminal or treated as a person with a mental illness? Be sure to explain your answer.

_____

_____

_____

_____

_____

Activity 3

An effective way for you to understand domestic violence and battered women's syndrome is to interview a domestic violence expert or a provider of victims' services. This activity requires you to contact such a professional in your community to discuss domestic violence and battered women's defense. Look in the telephone book for a shelter for abused or battered women, or contact the prosecutor's office for information on how to contact a provider of victims' services. A mental health facility is also a good resource. Complete an informational interview with this person to learn about domestic violence in your community. Ask about the extent of the problem and the types of resources available to domestic violence victims, and ask the person to comment on battered women's syndrome.

When you complete this interview, discuss what you discovered in the space below.

_____

_____

_____

_____

Activity 4

Presented below are several case descriptions. If you were a defense attorney asked to take each of these cases, what would you recommend as the best defense (refer to Table 4–3 in the book for assistance)?

1. Art Kapser and John Gelbor were good friends and coworkers. After work, Art and John went bowling. After John picked up a spare in the seventh frame, the two got into an argument on proper scoring of a spare. John punched Art in the face, knocking him to the floor and screaming, "If you don't shut up, I will kill you." Art left the bowling alley but returned with a .38-caliber revolver and shot John in the back, killing him instantly. Art was charged with murder. What could Art use as a defense?

2. Kellie Koser attended a college party. One of the partygoers handed her a beer. She drank it, although she did not know that the beer contained a sedative. She got tired quickly and decided to drive home. She fell asleep at the wheel and killed a bicyclist. She was charged with manslaughter. What could Kellie use as a defense?

3. Shelly Morrison and Todd Rutlow both drive the same model of pickup truck. Both trucks are black with white pinstripes, both have red fuzzy dice hanging from the rearview mirror, and both have a bumper sticker with the slogan "Peace is Possible." Moreover, both leave their keys in the ignition when they park. Shelly, after completing a long day of Christmas shopping, got into a black truck and drove away. She did not know it was Todd's truck. Police quickly apprehended Shelly and charged her with motor vehicle theft. What would you recommend as a defense?

4. Charles Shuter was charged with raping his 14-year-old daughter. The prosecutor also charged the mother with conspiracy to commit rape because she knew about the rape and bought condoms for her husband to use when committing the crime. The mother claims she did not contact the police because the husband threatened to kill her. What would you recommend as a defense for the mother?

5. When Marnee Diaz lost her job, she couldn't keep up with her bills. In order to put food on the table, she began robbing banks. What would you recommend as a defense?

6. Carol Smith is addicted to crack but enrolled herself in a drug-treatment program to control her addiction. An undercover police officer joined the same program to get information about drug suppliers. He got friendly with Ms. Smith and asked her to buy him some crack. She refused on four occasions. On the fifth occasion, however, she brought him one rock of crack cocaine. She was arrested for drug possession. What defense would you recommend?

7. Jason Jenser was a heavy drinker. Whenever he drank, he beat his lover, Bill. He frequently put a gun to Bill's head, threatened to kill him, and caused him numerous physical injuries. Bill wanted to leave, but Jenser threatened him with physical violence, so he stayed. That same evening, while Jenser was sleeping, Bill picked up a shotgun and killed him. What defense would you recommend?

Internet Activity

Visit law.com (http://www.law.com) and find the law dictionary that the site provides (*Hint:* click on Resources, then Other Resources). Enter each of the key terms (one at a time) at the start of Chapter 4 into the dictionary, and compare the definitions there with the definitions in the textbook (see the glossary). Write the definitions from the two sources side by side and compare them. What differences exist? What terms are in the textbook that are not in the online dictionary?

_____

_____

_____

_____

_____

_____

Distance Learning Activity

Visit the website for the *National Law Journal* or some other major industry legal publication. (National Law Journal page is at http://www.nlj.com, and Court TV On-Line is at http://www.courttv.com.) Submit a summary of one of the articles or cases posted on the website. If your instructor asks you to do so, share your summary with the other students in your class and participate in an online discussion about the issues that students wrote about.

_____

_____

_____

_____

_____

_____

Student Study Guide Questions

True or False

_____ 4-1. A basic distinction between criminal and civil law is that criminal acts injure individuals and society as a whole.

_____ 4-2. Misdemeanors are generally less serious than felonies.

_____ 4-3. Procedural law defines behaviors as criminal and specifies punishment.

_____ 4-4. The rule of law is also referred to as the supremacy of law.

_____ 4-5. Civil law is primarily concerned with assessing intent.

_____ 4-6. The Durham insanity rule states that a person is not guilty of a crime if, at the time of the crime, he or she didn't know what he or she was doing or didn't know that it was wrong.

_____ 4-7. Treason is the act of a U.S. citizen that helps a foreign government overthrow, make war against, or seriously injure the United States.

_____ 4-8. Procedural defense is based on discrimination by the justice system.

_____ 4-9. Contract law is the body of regulations created by governments to control the economic activities of industry, business, and individuals.

_____ 4-10. Insanity is a legal definition and not a psychiatric one.

Multiple Choice

4-11. Which of the following is generally considered the most serious?
   a. felonies
   b. misdemeanors
   c. offenses
   d. infractions

4-12. Which of the following is a procedural defense?
   a. duress
   b. mistake of fact
   c. double jeopardy
   d. infancy

4-13. Which type of law refers to a traditional body of unwritten legal precedents created through everyday practice and supported by court decisions?
   a. civil
   b. conflict
   c. common
   d. administrative

4-14. Murder, robbery, and drug offenses would all be defined as crimes under
   a. civil law.
   b. criminal law.
   c. common law.
   d. administrative law.

4-15. What type of law results from legislative action and is thought of as the "law on the books"?
   a. procedural
   b. administrative
   c. statutory
   d. substantive

4-16. Tax laws, health codes, and restrictions on pollution are examples of
   a. administrative law.
   b. procedural law.
   c. civil law.
   d. criminal law.

4-17. What is the Latin term that means "the body of the crime"?
   a. *actus reus*
   b. *mens rea*
   c. *stare decisis*
   d. *corpus delicti*

4-18. Which of the following is not an excuse defense?
   a. involuntary intoxication
   b. self-defense
   c. infancy
   d. insanity

4-19. Which of the following elements of crime means "guilty mind"?
   a. concurrence
   b. harm
   c. *actus reus*
   d. *mens rea*

4-20. A woman breaks into a home and, once inside, is cornered by the family dog, Spike, a Rottweiler. When the homeowner gets home and sees what Spike has in his control, she calls the police, who arrest the suspect. Based on these facts, the woman who broke into the home could be charged with
   a. conspiracy to commit burglary.
   b. nothing; she did not commit a crime.
   c. burglary.
   d. attempted burglary.

Fill-In

4-21. _____ governs relationships between parties.

4-22. A(n) _____ is an offense punishable by incarceration, usually in a local confinement facility, for a period of which the upper limit is prescribed by statute in a given jurisdiction, typically limited to a year or less.

4-23. The _____ holds that a person is not guilty of a crime if, at the time of the crime, he or she either didn't know what he or she was doing or didn't know that it was wrong.

4-24. A(n) _____ consists of an action or conduct that is a step toward the intended commission of another crime.

4-25. The _____ states that a person is not criminally responsible for his or her behavior if his or her illegal actions were the result of some mental disease or defect.

4-26. _____ is a procedural defense similar to double jeopardy.

4-27. _____ is the science and study of law.

4-28. A(n) _____ is an offense punishable by death or by incarceration for at least a year.

4-29. _____ literally means "guilty mind."

4-30. _____ is the part of the law that defines crimes and specifies punishments.

Crossword Puzzle

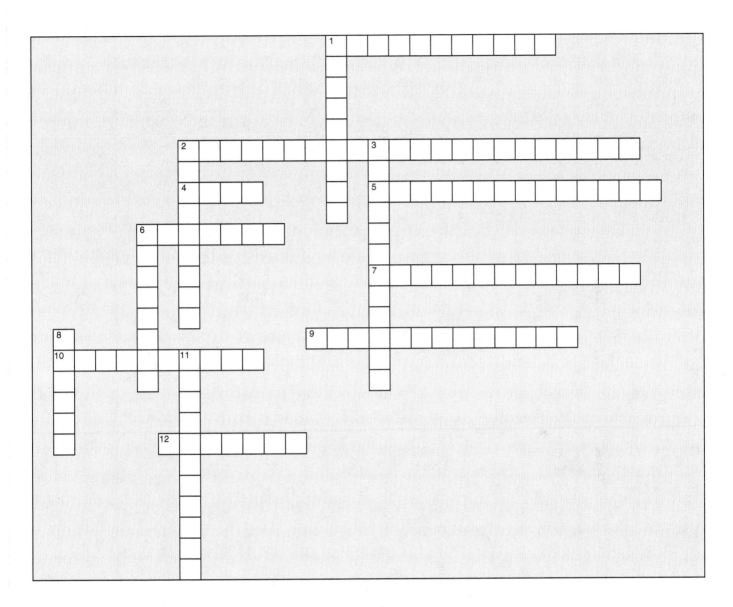

Across

1. The coexistence of an act in violation of the law and a culpable mental state.
2. The facts surrounding an event.
4. A private or civil wrong or injury.
5. The prohibition against a second trial for the same offense.
6. Judicial precedent.
7. The "body of the crime."
9. The science and study of the law.
10. An improper or illegal inducement to crime by agents of enforcement.
12. A guilty mind.

Down

1. Law originating from custom.
2. A guilty act.
3. The act or process of rendering laws in written form.
6. The branch of modern law that governs relationships between parties.
8. An offense punishable by incarceration in a prison facility for at least one year.
11. Less serious than a felony; more serious than an offense.

Word Search Puzzle

```
L E M U U E W L E C E F D P U I I L R S G E E E R R N S A I
S C O A M F P R T F E S C S R R N A N R S R Y C P F N I U V
L O T L C F D J U L N O N L U R F R N P C D R N M N C H E O
A T I N P F I D E N M C R E C I C I I D R E E E W A O L B
B E V C E A A R E P D W R A F R N O O A D T E G E C O C R C
B O E D N W I A E C A L L P E F N T P I W T N I O C E C R C
N E F E U E I N N L N N E A E A O O F O N N O L E O P A P I
E C B S U Y S R W A O E N N G N E E N R U E S G E D O X P I
S E W R H A M A E A U E R E O J A N T S O P A E E I W E L F
O A A E T M L U C E O A E R E E R L A A F R E N A F L Y O L
E O I O W E P U R N O L L L U C C N C T O S R I O I E A C U
A S R M S L T W O E C L B T T C A W I O I H T E N C U S D N
U Y I A O D T E F R W U R D E C N A A D D E C O F A C L S E
T D C M T I D L E E O P L N O R U O I L N E I N E T W S A T
N F J C N L E E L D E E E A C L E M C E L T M U I I O I M T
W A S E E N F E B C I D L X W E I G V B C I E A O O M C A D
I L T M O I Y D A P A I P Y C N D M O A E E V E E N X E P A
B N W U A O I Y N W B C E I I U O E R R E E E I P E I E E A
A A C E E F I H O I P D T S I P S F T I U T U E C W A N M T
L E O E L A S H S G L D H C E S N E F E D L A R U T L U C P
R H C N E O N P A L E E T E N I N C C U J D E E R L F A E D
U P N C C L T E E T D P D O R S R J U R I S P R U D E N C E
A T C E L C N G R C B R F E L O N Y G N A O I A T O M I A M
P R E D E R E T A E I E P E E E S N I W E R R O O R S N E L
M V R D I E A P N C E C W V I E E O O P A T E E E O R O A W
N L E O S F A R T A O E R D U L U S S A T L T R O T E J N A
F E E A U C Y O T B I D N U N E N T R A P M E N T E O U U U
N E E P I I D E D E T E I R O N A E M E D S I M F E W S L R
A N I T A U C U U E E N O I I S I M E B S E L A A D A N A E
W T Y O O A I C L N A T E A V T W A L F O E L U R S E O U M
```

Alibi
Alter Ego Rule
Case Law
Civil Law
Codification
Compensatory
Concurrence
Cultural Defense
Diminished Capacity
Double Jeopardy
Entrapment
Espionage
Excuse
Felony

Inchoate Offense
Infraction
Jurisprudence
Law
Misdemeanor
Motive
Negligence
Penal Code
Precedent
Reasonable Force
Rule of Law
Tort
Treason

Policing: History and Structure

LEARNING OBJECTIVES

After reading this chapter, you should be able to:

■ Summarize the historical development of policing in America, including the impact of the Prohibition era on American policing

■ Describe the nature of scientific police studies, and explain the significance they hold for law enforcement practice today

■ Describe the three major levels of public law enforcement in the United States today

■ Describe the nature and extent of private protective services in the United States today, and describe the role these services might play in the future

■ Explain the relationship between private security and public policing in America today

Chapter Summary

Chapter 5 begins with a discussion of the historical development of police departments in England and America. The text covers the historical evolution of policing in England because of similarities in its development to historical changes in American policing. An organized police response to social problems in England did not occur until the 1700s. Prior to that time, a posse, led by a **shire reeve** or *comes stabuli*, would respond to assist victims. The English police started to evolve in the 1700s when **Henry Fielding** became the magistrate of the Bow Street region of London. In 1829, under the guidance of **Sir Robert Peel**, the **New Police** (or the **Metropolitan Police**) was formed; it has been acknowledged as the world's first modern police force. Characteristics of the New Police force can still be found in English and American police forces. For example, the New Police operated under the belief that it was possible to discourage crime by patrolling the streets; the New Police wore uniforms to make themselves accessible to the public; and they structured their departments much the same as a military organization.

American policing evolved similarly, and early police departments, such as those organized in New York City, Boston, and Cincinnati, studied Peel's New Police when deciding structure and police response. However, police departments in the United States also addressed the special and unique concerns of the country, such as managing the Western frontier.

American police departments have evolved considerably over the years, relying recently on scientific research when deciding how to respond to crime most effectively. The text discusses important research studies, such as the **Kansas City Preventive Patrol Experiment**, that have had a tremendous impact on the current structure and philosophy of police departments. This experiment, conducted in the mid-1970s, tested (among other things) the effectiveness of preventive patrol in deterring crime and making citizens feel safe. The results from this study indicate that the number of officers on preventive patrol does not have a deterrent effect on preventable crimes and does not make citizens feel safe. These findings have forced police departments to alter how they use police officers on patrol and employ such innovative police strategies as directed patrol and split-force patrol.

Chapter 5 also provides a discussion of the decentralized structure of policing in the United States, highlighting differences among federal, state, local, and privately owned law enforcement agencies. Federal law enforcement agencies are responsible for enforcing federal laws. Although many agencies enforce federal law, the text describes in detail the best known: the **Federal Bureau of Investigation**.

Chapter 5 also discusses the responsibilities of state and local law enforcement agencies. State police agencies, whether centralized or decentralized, are responsible for patrolling state highways and conducting statewide criminal investigations. Officers who work for local law enforcement agencies have a more diverse job description than federal and state officers do. For example, the text discusses the diverse responsibilities of officers who work for the New York City Police Department. It also discusses the wide diversity in size and structure of local law enforcement agencies.

Chapter 5 concludes with a discussion of the growing private law enforcement industry. Indeed, the number of individuals employed in private security is higher than that in the other levels combined. Although the primary concern of the textbook is how local, state, and federal police respond to crime, discussion of private policing is important because of the growing influence of private security in criminal justice and the overlap of public and private security agencies.

Key Concepts

Bobbies: The popular British name given to members of Sir Robert (Bob) Peel's Metropolitan Police Force.

Bow Street Runners: An early English police unit formed under the leadership of Henry Fielding, magistrate of the Bow Street region of London.

Comes Stabuli: A nonuniformed mounted early law enforcement officer in medieval England. Early police forces were small and relatively unorganized, but made effective use of local resources in the formation of posses, the pursuit of offenders, and the like.

Directed Patrol: A police management strategy designed to increase the productivity of patrol officers through the scientific analysis and evaluation of patrol techniques.

Exemplary Projects Program: An initiative, sponsored by the Law Enforcement Assistance Administration, designed to recognize outstanding innovative efforts to combat crime and to provide assistance to crime victims.

Federal Law Enforcement Agency: A U.S. government agency or office whose primary functional responsibility is the enforcement of federal criminal laws.

Kansas City Experiment: The first large-scale scientific study of law enforcement practices. Sponsored by the Police Foundation, it focused on the practice of preventive patrol.

Law Enforcement Assistance Administration (LEAA): A now defunct federal agency established under Title I of the Omnibus Crime Control and Safe Streets Act of 1967 to funnel federal funding to state and local law enforcement agencies.

Municipal Police Department: A city- or town-based law enforcement agency; also known as *local police.*

New Police: A police force formed in 1829 under the command of Sir Robert Peel. It became the model for modern-day police forces throughout the Western world. Also called Metropolitan Police Force.

Night Watch: An early form of police patrol in English cities and towns.

Private Protective Services: Independent or proprietary commercial organizations that provide protective services to employers on a contractual basis.

Scientific Police Management: The application of social scientific techniques to the study of police administration for the purpose of increasing effectiveness, reducing the frequency of citizen complaints, and enhancing the efficient use of available resources.

Sheriff: The elected chief officer of a county law enforcement agency. The sheriff is usually responsible for law enforcement in unincorporated areas and for the operation of the county jail.

Statute of Winchester: A law, written in 1285, that created a watch and ward system in English cities and towns and that codified early police practices.

Sworn Officer: A law enforcement officer who is trained and empowered to perform full police duties, such as making arrests, conducting investigations, and carrying firearms. *Source*: Adapted from Darl H. Champion and Michael K. Hooper, *Introduction to American Policing* (New York: McGraw-Hill, 2003), p. 166.

Vigilantism: The act of taking the law into one's own hands.

Wickersham Commission: The National Commission on Law Observance and Enforcement. In 1931, the commission issued a report stating that Prohibition was unenforceable and carried a great potential for police corruption.

Learning Tips

Acronyms

To learn a series of facts, especially a lengthy series, use mnemonic acronyms. Acronyms are words that are formed through the first letters of a list of words. For example, ROR is an acronym for Released on Recognizance. Mnemonic devices can enhance the memorization of almost anything, from simple lists to a variety of criminal justice definitions.

REMEMBER

In Chapter 2, the text highlights two primary sources of national crime data. First, it discusses the Uniform Crime Reports. This source of data provides information on crimes reported to the police. Second, it discusses the National Crime Victimization Survey. This source of data asks a nationally representative sample of households about six types of crime.

Flash Cards

Flash cards are extremely beneficial for memorizing case names and definitions. Write key words, vocabulary, phrases, names, or theories on one side of the card, and write their meanings on the other. This is especially helpful for the numerous legal cases that are included in the text. Study with the flash cards at home, on the bus, while waiting for classes to begin, or whenever you have spare time.

CJ Today on the World Wide Web

Web links to organizations and agencies related to the material in Chapter 5 include:

WEBSITE TITLE	URL
Alcohol, Tobacco and Firearms	http://www.atf.treas.gov
Drug Enforcement Administration	http://www.usdoj.gov/dea
Central Intelligence Agency	http://www.odci.gov
U.S. Marshals Service	http://www.usdoj.gov/marshals
U.S. Secret Service	http://www.treas.gov/usss
U.S. Postal Inspection Service	http://www.usps.gov/websites/depart/inspect
U.S. Customs Service	http://www.customs.ustreas.gov
U.S. Coast Guard	http://www.uscg.mil
Citizenship and Immigration Services	http://www.uscis.gov
Law Enforcement Links	http://www.leolinks.com

Student Activities

Activity 1

The text discusses the 1931 Wickersham Commission. The recommendations of this commission have had an incredible impact on the criminal justice system. First, go to the library to find one of the commission reports. You will see that the report is a large volume but each report has a smaller section on the police. Review the section on policing, and then answer the following discussion questions.

Which commission report did you examine? What types of law enforcement problems are identified in that report? Are the problems similar to or different from problems experienced by law enforcement today? What recommendations are made in that report to reform policing?

_____

_____

_____

_____

_____

Activity 2

Assume that you have just been hired as the police chief of a small (about 45 officers) department. You were hired because you promised the mayor and city council that you could reduce the number of street crimes by using more officers on directed patrol. The city council has agreed to provide the department with funds to hire 16 more police officers to be used for this purpose. However, this money will be provided to the department only after you discuss how you will document whether directed patrol deters crime. Specifically, the city council wants you to design a research study, not unlike the

Kansas City Preventive Patrol Experiment, to evaluate the effectiveness of directed patrol. In the space provided below, discuss your research design, including how you would use the new officers in the study, length of time of the study, and beat selection. Be sure to read the discussion on the Kansas City Preventive Patrol Experiment in the book. In addition, it might be helpful to read publications about other research studies to get some ideas on how to design a study. You can read more about the National Weed and Seed Evaluation and the Kansas City Gun Experiment discussed in Chapter 5 at **Library Extra 5–1** and **Library Extra 5–3**.

LIBRARY
extra

_____

_____

_____

_____

_____

_____

Activity 3

In Chapter 5 the text discusses the important role that federal agencies play in law enforcement. The text highlights the activities of the Federal Bureau of Investigation but mentions that there are dozens of federal law enforcement agencies. This activity requires that you learn about the activities of a federal law enforcement agency other than the FBI. You can do this by visiting the website of a federal agency. Choose an agency. In the space provided below, compare and contrast the activities of the Federal Bureau of Investigation and the agency that you selected. In what ways are the law enforcement activities of that agency similar to the activities of the FBI? In what ways are they different?

_____

_____

_____

_____

_____

_____

Activity 4

Find out which law enforcement agencies have law enforcement responsibilities and duties in the county where the university you attend is located. List these agencies, their law enforcement responsibilities, and the level of policing they represent (for example, federal, state, local, or private). Do these agencies have responsibilities that overlap? What changes would you suggest to use their personnel resources more effectively?

_____

_____

_____

_____

_____

_____

Internet Activity

Visit a number of private security agency sites on the Web. (You can find such sites listed in the Cybrary, at http://www.cybrary.info.) Gather information on each agency, including things such as services offered, requirements for hiring, employment opportunities, table of organization, and so on. Assemble a notebook (or disk) containing the information you have gathered, organized by agency. Your instructor may request that you submit the material.

_____

_____

_____

_____

_____

Distance Learning Activity

Visit the websites of three different law enforcement agencies: one federal, one state, and one local. Use any search engine to research these agencies. Summarize the characteristics of the different agencies you selected. Also, assess the amount and type of information posted on the World Wide Web for each type of department.

_____

_____

_____

_____

_____

Student Study Guide Questions

True or False

____ 5-1. A centralized state law enforcement agency combines the tasks of major criminal investigations with highway patrol.

____ 5-2. More people are employed in private security than in all local, state, and federal police agencies combined.

____ 5-3. Early American police departments were structured according to the British model.

____ 5-4. _Comes stabuli_ is a Latin term that means "a uniformed leader of the county."

____ 5-5. Congress created the Federal Bureau of Investigation in 1980 because crime rates had increased dramatically in the previous decade.

____ 5-6. Early in his career, J. Edgar Hoover was personally responsible for apprehending the infamous criminal Jonathan Wild.

____ 5-7. Results from the Kansas City Preventive Patrol Experiment indicate that officers on preventive patrol deter crimes such as burglary and robbery and, therefore, citizens feel safe.

____ 5-8. Robert Peel is famous for his law enforcement activities on the Western frontier.

____ 5-9. The scientific police study undertaken in Newport News, Virginia, examined whether mandatory arrests can deter domestic violence batteries.

____ 5-10. Directed patrol is a police management strategy designed to increase the productivity of patrol officers through the application of scientific analysis and evaluation of patrol techniques.

Multiple Choice

5-11. Which of the following aspects of police work is the "backbone of policing"?
 a. management
 b. administration
 c. patrol
 d. investigation

5-12. Who is most closely associated with London's Bow Street Runners?
 a. Jonathan Wild
 b. Henry Fielding
 c. Sir Robert Peel
 d. Patrick Murphy

5-13. Which of the following was not characteristic of the "New Police"?
 a. They adopted a military administrative style.
 b. They occupied fixed posts throughout the city awaiting a public outcry.
 c. They believed that it was possible to discourage crime.
 d. They were uniformed.

5-14. Which of the following studies found that offenders who were arrested were less likely to commit repeat offenses than those handled in some other fashion?
 a. Newport News Problem-Oriented Policing Experiment
 b. Newark Foot Patrol Experiment
 c. Kansas City Preventive Patrol Experiment
 d. Minneapolis Domestic Violence Experiment

5-15. Which federal law enforcement agency has responsibility for maintaining the *Uniform Crime Reports*?
 a. U.S. Marshals Service
 b. U.S. Customs Service
 c. Federal Bureau of Investigation
 d. Drug Enforcement Administration

5-16. *Shire reeve* means
 a. police chief.
 b. attorney general.
 c. mounted officer.
 d. leader of the county.

5-17. The mission statement of which federal law enforcement agency includes law enforcement, counterintelligence, investigative support, law enforcement services, and direction, control, and administration?
 a. U.S. Marshals Service
 b. U.S. Customs Service
 c. Federal Bureau of Investigation
 d. Drug Enforcement Administration

5-18. A _____ is responsible for the operation of a county jail.
 a. sheriff
 b. uniformed patrol officer
 c. United States marshal
 d. state highway patrol officer

5-19. Who was responsible for starting the world's first modern police force?
   a. "Wild Bill" Hickok
   b. Richard Mayne
   c. Henry Fielding
   d. Sir Robert Peel

5-20. All of the following are reasons for the growth of private security in America except
   a. the fiscal crisis of the states.
   b. public police agencies requesting assistance from private agencies.
   c. an increase in fear of crime.
   d. an increase in crimes in the workplace.

Fill-In

5-21. The _____ was the study credited with beginning the tradition of scientific police evaluation.

5-22. The _____ is responsible for maintaining the "Ten Most Wanted" list.

5-23. The _____ was written in 1285, and it created a watch and ward system in cities and towns and codified early British police practices.

5-24. _____ means "leader of the county."

5-25. The first scientifically engineered social experiment to test the impact of the use of arrest on crime was the _____.

5-26. The _____ were also known as the Metropolitan Police.

5-27. _____ is a police management strategy designed to increase the productivity of patrol officers through the application of scientific analysis and evaluation of patrol techniques.

5-28. _____ means "mounted officer."

5-29. The study that found that vigorous enforcement of gun laws could reduce crime was the _____.

5-30. The federal law enforcement agency that compiles the *Uniform Crime Reports* is the _____.

Crossword Puzzle

Across

4. Examples include the FBI, DEA, and AFT.
6. Responsible for the operation of the jail.
7. The first large-scale scientific study of law enforcement practices.
9. A nonuniformed mounted early law enforcement officer in medieval England.
11. Independent or proprietary commercial organizations that provide protective services to employers on a contractual basis.
12. The leader of the Metropolitan Police Force.
13. A police management strategy designed to increase the productivity of patrol officers through the scientific analysis and evaluation of patrol techniques.
14. An early form of police patrol in English cities and towns.

Down

1. The sponsor of the Exemplary Projects Program.
2. The act of taking the law into one's own hands.
3. Also known as the Metropolitan Police Force.
5. Offically called the National Commission on Law Observance and Enforcement.
6. The law that created the watch and ward system in 1285.
8. Nickname for Petropolitan Police Force officers.
10. The leader of the Bow Street Runners.

Word Search Puzzle

```
E T E E T S N M F U C R P C T C E H S T E S N T S R T F M B
A S W I C K E R S H A M C O M M I S S I O N O T T F C I A D
S I E E R L E E P T R E B O R R I S T E R E K N I C E S R R
M L G C X E I S T A E M W I P S M I Y R T P U I O R E L G S
N G C E I U R H I N E S S H C T S L M I R E C P O M N E O R
A E E R B V N F F I R E H S L A F N I N E I O A W R L E R C
R H H E O N R O I P O F S S T C C P T E C E R G R R O I P R
E E S T N E M E G A N A M E C I L O P C I F I T N E I C S R
N S D S W R S R S I I T T B O T E L M T F X T I I F L E T E
A M A L B T E W E E S Y P E I L O N C F P H I T T B F C A
R A B S G A C R E R V T T B R E P E L V O I I N F E O A E I
I U I A S O P E R B A I O A C A M C C E N E E E W S W C J T
T I S E S I B A S Y N B T E T I P T H C R A H R O H S F O R
E I I T R C A E N C B O A C R U E R S R O F V E I O T R R M
E R F E M O N P R I N R O E E I T R E I W O C L B S R E P B
I I R E L C E M E E E I P C I T A E E A S N U C T W E R Y I
S E W H S E P S N F Y X T F M O O O O D E B R S B E E C R S
U U V R E R V E K I E R P I Y C C R I F A I O I O S T O A I
X T H I P N R A Y Y G F O P E T I R P T W O E M A E R T L A
S F I I G K C R T M S H E T N T E R S E E I R A O N U S P S
C I I D P E E I E C E N T R S C L S R S T B N R T C N I M T
O C V R V I C S Y B C N I W T I E I E E N A T C N G N U E T
I I R I L S W B R R N E E E A M H C N I E R V I H P E T X T
O E E E A E A R B S S W D I O T J E B E E C F I T E R E E O
A R C S T M N S S R A P E C H R C A C E B E I Y R E S I E P
S I N X I P C B V R A O E E P T E H N I E J S O O P R T E I
V A O A R B V H O T O L U C R T C T C E L F V H R S E L E E
K E I P A R I R R S M I A E T W C E A I T O P H N E S E R R
F I E X R T F O C P C C S G T W T N V C T T P L H M G E O S
E S A E S E L W T T T E W S T V D A L V I G I L A N T I S M
```

Bobbies
Bow Street Runners
Comes Stabuli
Directed Patrol
Exemplary Projects Program
Kansas City Experiment
New Police
Night Watch

Police History
Private Protective Services
Scientific Police Management
Sheriff
Statute of Winchester
Sworn Officer
Vigilantism
Wickersham Commission

chapter 6

Police Organization and Management

LEARNING OBJECTIVES

AAfter reading this chapter, you should be able to:

- Explain the basic purposes of policing in democratic societies

- List and discuss the five core operational strategies of today's police departments

- Define the term *police management*, and describe the different types of organizational structures typical of American police departments

- Identify the three styles of policing, and discuss differences in these approaches

- Describe community policing, and explain how it differs from traditional policing

- Explain police discretion and how it affects the practice of contemporary law enforcement

- Demonstrate why professionalism is important in policing today

- Identify some of the issues related to ethnic and gender diversity in policing, and suggest ways of addressing them

- Explain what a learning organization is, and describe how some police departments can benefit from becoming learning organizations

Chapter Summary

Chapter 6 discusses several areas of concern to the police organization. These areas include the police mission, operational strategies, managing police departments, policing styles, discretion and the officer, professionalism and ethics, ethnic and gender diversity in policing, and police departments as learning organizations.

Chapter 6 begins with a discussion of the police mission. In general, the basic purposes of policing include enforcing the law, apprehending offenders, preventing crime, preserving the peace, and providing services. This section also discusses how terrorism has impacted the police mission of federal, state, and local law enforcement agencies.

The mission of policing directly shapes the operational strategies departments use to accomplish their goals. Chapter 6 discusses the five core operational strategies of police departments: preventive patrol, routine incident response, emergency response, criminal investigation, and problem solving. These operational strategies highlight how police work in a democratic society. Importantly, this section also highlights the objectives, performance standards, and processes involved for each operational strategy.

Chapter 6 also discusses **police management**. Police management focuses on the administrative activities that control, direct, and coordinate police personnel, resources, and activities. This section discusses the general structure of police organizations and highlights the **chain of command**.

Police departments have unique policing styles formed in response to community and organizational factors. Three types of policing styles, developed by James Q. Wilson, are discussed in Chapter 6. First, police officers employed in **watchman style** departments are most concerned with maintaining order. These officers possess a considerable amount of discretion to resolve situations. Second, police officers in **legalistic style** departments are expected to enforce the letter of the law, meaning that their discretion to use a nonenforcement response is limited. Moreover, these officers are likely to ignore other disruptive behaviors. Third, officers in a **service style** department are most concerned with helping citizens rather than strictly applying the letter of the law. These officers would be familiar with community resources and use these resources to help solve community and individual problems.

Many police departments are moving to the service style, using what are popularly known as community policing strategies. **Community policing** is a strategy that calls for police departments to develop community relationships and solicit citizen assistance in solving problems. The current movement toward community policing has its roots in the **police-community relations** programs advocated in the 1960s, as well as in the **team policing** ideas of the 1970s. This chapter in the text discusses several examples of community-policing programs, such as Houston's DART program, Chicago's Alternative Policing Strategy, and Baltimore's Project Cope.

Chapter 6 also introduces the idea of **police discretion**. Despite the influence of departmental styles, individual officers possess an opportunity to make choices when enforcing the law. When "working the streets," officers are not directly supervised by superiors, providing them with discretion to informally or formally resolve incidents. The text describes potential factors that might influence the ways officers use discretion, such as the background of the officer, characteristics of the suspect, community interest, and pressures from the victim.

The author discusses key issues related to resolving many of the issues facing police departments in the section on **professionalism** and **ethics**. The accreditation of police departments, raising educational standards, and improving the recruitment and selection of officers are changes being made to address problem areas of policing.

The author concludes by discussing issues of ethnic and gender diversity in policing and police departments as learning organizations. Statistics show that the number of police from minority groups has dramatically increased but employment of women still lags significantly behind.

Key Concepts

Chain of Command: The unbroken line of authority that extends through all levels of an organization, from the highest to the lowest.

Community Policing: "A collaborative effort between the police and the community that identifies problems of crime and disorder and involves all elements of the community in the search for solutions to these problems." *Source*: Community Policing Consortium, *What Is Community Policing?* (Washington, D.C.: The Consortium, 1995).

CompStat: A crime-analysis and police-management process built on crime mapping that was developed by the New York City Police Department in the mid-1990s.

Crime Prevention: The anticipation, recognition, and appraisal of a crime risk and the initiation of action to eliminate or reduce it.

Crime Scene: The physical area in which a crime is thought to have occurred and in which evidence of the crime is thought to reside.

Crime-Scene Investigator: An expert trained in the use of forensics techniques, such as gathering DNA evidence, collecting fingerprints, photography, sketching, and interviewing witnesses.

Criminal Investigation: "The process of discovering, collecting, preparing, identifying, and presenting evidence to determine *what happened and who is responsible*" when a crime has occurred. *Source*: Wayne W. Bennett and Karen M. Hess, *Criminal Investigation*, 6th ed. (Belmont, CA: Wadsworth, 2001), p. 3. Italics in original.

Learning Organization: "An organization skilled at creating, acquiring, and transferring knowledge and at modifying its behavior to reflect new knowledge and insights." *Source*: David A. Garvin, "*Building a Learning Organization*," Harvard Business Review (1993), pp. 78–91.

Legalistic Style: A style of policing marked by a strict concern with enforcing the precise letter of the law. Legalistic departments, however, may take a hands-off approach to otherwise disruptive or problematic behavior that does not violate the criminal law.

Line Operations: In police organizations, field activities or supervisory activities directly related to day-to-day police work.

Peace Officer Standards and Training (POST) Program: The official program of a state or legislative jurisdiction that sets standards for the training of law enforcement officers. All states set such standards, although not all use the term POST.

Police-Community Relations (PCR): An area of emerging police activity that stresses the need for the community and the police to work together effectively and emphasizes the notion that the police derive their legitimacy from the community they serve. PCR began to be of concern to many police agencies in the 1960s and 1970s.

Police Discretion: The opportunity of law enforcement officers to exercise choice in their daily activities.

Police Ethics: The special responsibility to adhere to moral duty and obligation that is inherent in police work.

Police Management: The administrative activities of controlling, directing, and coordinating police personnel, resources, and activities in the service of preventing crime, apprehending criminals, recovering stolen property, and performing regulatory and helping services. *Source*: This definition draws on the classic work by O. W. Wilson, *Police Administration* (New York: McGraw-Hill, 1950), pp. 2–3.

Police Professionalism: The increasing formalization of police work and the accompanying rise in public acceptance of the police.

Police Subculture: A particular set of values, beliefs, and acceptable forms of behavior characteristic of American police. Socialization into the police subculture begins with recruit training and continues thereafter. Also called *police culture*.

Preliminary Investigation: All of the activities undertaken by a police officer who responds to the scene of a crime, including determining whether a crime has occurred, securing the crime scene, and preserving evidence.

Problem-Solving Policing: A type of policing that assumes that crimes can be controlled by uncovering and effectively addressing the underlying social problems that cause crime. Problem-solving policing makes use of community resources, such as counseling centers, welfare programs, and job-training facilities. It also attempts to involve citizens in crime prevention through education, negotiation, and conflict management. Also called *problem-oriented policing*.

Quality-of-Life Offense: A minor violation of the law (sometimes called a *petty crime*) that demoralizes community residents and businesspeople. Quality-of-life offenses involve acts that create physical disorder (for example, excessive noise or vandalism) or that reflect social decay (for example, panhandling and prostitution).

Response Time: A measure of the time that it takes for police officers to respond to calls for service.

Service Style: A style of policing marked by a concern with helping rather than strict enforcement. Service-oriented police agencies are more likely to take advantage of community resources, such as drug-treatment programs, than are other types of agencies.

Solvability Factor: Information about a crime that forms the basis for determining the perpetrator's identity.

Span of Control: The number of police personnel or the number of units supervised by a particular commander.

Staff Operations: In police organizations, activities (like administration and training) that provide support for line operations.

Strategic Policing: A type of policing that retains the traditional police goal of professional crime fighting but enlarges the enforcement target to include nontraditional kinds of criminals, such as serial offenders, gangs and criminal associations, drug-distribution networks, and sophisticated white-collar and computer criminals. Strategic policing generally makes use of innovative enforcement techniques, including intelligence operations, undercover stings, electronic surveillance, and sophisticated forensic methods.

Team Policing: The reorganization of conventional patrol strategies into "an integrated and versatile police team assigned to a fixed district." *Source*: Sam S. Souryal, *Police Administration and Management* (St. Paul, MN: West Publishing Co., 1977), p. 261.

Watchman Style: A style of policing marked by a concern for order maintenance. Watchman policing is characteristic of lower-class communities where police intervene informally into the lives of residents to keep the peace.

Learning Tips

Tests

Managing review time is essential for test preparation. Instant reviews, which should occur either directly after the class meeting or during your assigned readings, start the learning and memorization process. Weekly reviews should be more focused than instant reviews. Final reviews are the most in-depth reviews. They should be conducted within the week prior to the exam. Final reviews help demonstrate the big picture and further understanding of the information provided during the entire class. Used together, instant, weekly, and final reviews provide the foundation for successful test preparation.

Before the Test

Be sure to arrive early for exams. This will allow time for relaxation and general preparation. Avoid talking to other students about their test preparation. This will only cause more anxiety. Listen to all instructions while the exam is being distributed. As redundant as it may seem, read the directions twice. You may lose significant points for not following the simplest instructions. Before beginning, if necessary, take a minute to release all test anxieties and to relax your mind.

CJ Today on the World Wide Web

Web links to organizations and agencies related to the material in Chapter 6 include:

WEBSITE TITLE	URL
California Peace Officer Standards and Training	http://www.post.ca.gov
Community Oriented Policing Services (COPS)	http://www.cops.usdoj.gov/
The Community Policing Consortium (CPC)	http://www.communitypolicing.org
Copsonline	http://www.copsonline.com
Federal Law Enforcement Training Center	http://www.treas.gov/fletc
New York City Police Department (NYPD)	http://www.ci.nyc.ny.us/html/nypd
Singapore Police Force	http://www.spinet.gov.sg/pollink
A Treasury of Police Humor	http://www.policehumor.com

Student Activities

Activity 1

The text describes the Chicago Police Department's community policing program. Before beginning this assignment, read that section of the text again. This activity requires you to find information about one other police department's community policing program. There are several ways to do this. First, you could interview officers from the department you select. Second, you can visit the department's website. Most police departments have websites, and if they have a community-policing program, information will be posted on it. Third, there is a large body of research on community policing. You should be able to retrieve books or articles describing various community-policing programs from the library. A good book describing a few different approaches to community policing is *The New Blue Line* by David Bayley and Jerome Skolnick. Finally, you can learn from the community policing studies posted on the National Criminal Justice Reference Service page at http://www.ncjrs.org.

In the space provided below, compare and contrast what you found with the textbook's discussion of community policing in Chicago.

_____

_____

_____

_____

_____

REMEMBER

What theoretical school of thought would you use to explain police corruption? The text discusses how the application of differential association theory by Edwin Sutherland may help in understanding the amount and type of police corruption. However, many of the other theories discussed in Chapter 3 may also be relevant. Recall that Chapter 3 discusses the main premises of the Classical School, biological theories, psychobiological theories, psychological theories, sociological theories, conflict theories, the Phenomenological School, and other emergent theories.

Activity 2

Answer the following questions on police discretion in the space provided below.

Should police officers enforce the law equally in all situations? In what types of situations should police officers be allowed to not enforce the law? In what types of situations should they be required to fully enforce the law? Why does police discretion exist? What are its strengths and weaknesses?

_____

_____

_____

_____

_____

_____

Activity 3

In Chapter 6 the text describes individual police officer discretion as an important aspect of policing but also notes the dangers of having limited oversight of officers in most situations. Below are a number of examples in which police officers have to exercise discretion; this is not uncommon in police work. After each example, discuss how you, as a police officer, would respond to the situation. There are no right answers, but be certain to justify your response with an explanation.

1. You are dispatched to a low-income apartment complex. A man (his name is Arnold), who is homeless and addicted to crack, refuses to leave the entrance area to the building. He allows those living in the building to enter and does not bother most of them; however, a tenant has called to complain and would like him removed. It is midwinter and the temperature is below freezing. As the responding officer, how would you use your discretion to respond to this situation? Why?

2. While on random preventive patrol in a high-crime neighborhood, you notice two young children (you think they are about eight or nine years old) hanging around outside a drug store. When you approach them, they start acting very nervous (it is about eight o'clock at night). As you talk to them, a third kid, same age, comes out of the store followed by the cashier, who tells you that he has just tried to steal three candy bars. How would you respond to this situation? Justify your action.

3. While randomly patrolling a neighborhood, you observe a vehicle run a red light. While in pursuit, you also notice that the person is driving in a haphazard manner. After the person stops his vehicle, you discover that he is drunk. The person driving the car, however, is also your favorite uncle. How would you respond to this situation? How does your response differ from your responses to the previous two situations?

4. Your department has received a call from a citizen complaining that his next-door neighbors have been fighting for the last two hours (it is 3:30 A.M.). When you knock on the door and announce that you are the police, the fighting abruptly stops. A male, about 24 years old, opens the door, apologizes for the disturbance, and promises that they will be quiet. However, he will not allow you into the home to talk with the person that he was fighting with. How would you resolve this situation?

_____

_____

_____

_____
_____
_____

Activity 4

For this activity first read the short research report on police use of deadly force posted at **Library Extra 6–7**. This report discusses efforts to develop measures of what police actually do. After reading the report, summarize the findings in the space provided below.

LIBRARY extra

_____
_____
_____
_____
_____
_____

Internet Activity

Use the Cybrary (http://www.cybrary.info) to find descriptions of terrorism and policing studies on the Web. What kinds of studies did you find? What do they deal with? What were the findings or results of each of these studies? (*Hint:* you might want to first check the National Criminal Justice Reference Service at http://www.ncjrs.org.)

_____
_____
_____
_____
_____

Distance Learning Activity

In the space below, highlight the pros and cons of community policing. Some of the strengths and weaknesses are discussed in the textbook, but you should also visit additional websites containing community policing information. For example, see **Library Extra 6–5**.

LIBRARY extra

_____
_____
_____
_____
_____

Student Study Guide Questions

True or False

_____ 6-1. Legalistic police agencies are more likely to take advantage of community resources, such as drug-treatment programs, than are other types of departments.

_____ 6-2. Scholars argue that American policing has just started the political era of policing.

_____ 6-3. Span of control refers to the crime priorities of a police department.

_____ 6-4. A watchman style of policing is characteristic of lower-class communities where informal police intervention into the lives of residents is used to help keep the peace.

_____ 6-5. The idea of team policing is thought to have originated in Aberdeen, Scotland.

_____ 6-6. Police subculture generally refers to a group of corrupt officers working to undermine the goals of a police organization.

_____ 6-7. Quality-of-life offenses are generally minor law violations that demoralize citizens by creating disorder.

_____ 6-8. The policing reform era that lasted from the 1930s until the 1970s was characterized by pride in professional crime fighting.

_____ 6-9. Although many police departments have dramatically increased recruitment of ethnic minorities, females are still substantially underrepresented.

_____ 6-10. CompStat is a process that originally was developed by the New York City Police Department.

Multiple Choice

6-11. Which of the following aspects of the police mission focuses on responding to quality-of-life offenses?
   a. providing services
   b. apprehending offenders
   c. preventing crime
   d. preserving the peace

6-12. Which historical era of policing is characterized by close ties between police and public officials?
   a. community problem-solving era
   b. renaissance era
   c. political era
   d. reform era

6-13. Which of the following is not a criticism of community policing strategies?
   a. Efforts to promote community policing can demoralize a department.
   b. Not all public officials are ready to accept community policing.
   c. Not all police officers accept this new image of police work.
   d. Goals of community policing are too narrowly defined.

6-14. Which of Wilson's policing styles is becoming increasingly popular today?
   a. service
   b. paternalistic
   c. watchman
   d. legalistic

6-15. Of the three corporate strategies that guide American policing, which one emphasizes an increased capacity to deal with crimes that are not well controlled by traditional methods?
    a. community policing
    b. corporation policing
    c. strategic policing
    d. problem-solving policing

6-16. Which factor does not influence the discretionary decisions of individual officers?
    a. background of the officer
    b. pressures from crime victims
    c. departmental policy
    d. All are factors that might influence police discretion.

6-17. Officer Sally Kainer works in a department she describes as being concerned with community problems. She has been encouraged by the department to develop ties with other community agencies, such as the local chapter of Big Brothers/Big Sisters, and to rely on them for assistance. Which of Wilson's policing styles does Sally's department represent?
    a. service style
    b. paternalistic style
    c. watchman style
    d. legalistic style

6-18. What two factors determine the extent that a police department will be engaged in terrorism prevention activities?
    a. media pressure; number of officers
    b. budget; assessed likelihood of attack
    c. community pressure; legislative policy
    d. size of the police department; public concern about terrorism

6-19. Neighborhood Watch and drug awareness workshops are examples of
    a. police-community relations programs.
    b. team policing programs.
    c. police crime-fighting activities.
    d. innovative police strategies.

6-20. Enforcing the strict letter of the law characterizes the _____ style of policing.
    a. service
    b. paternalistic
    c. legalistic
    d. watchman

Fill-In

6-21. The _____ style of policing is marked by a concern for order maintenance.

6-22. The _____ era of policing is characterized by pride in professional crime fighting.

6-23. _____ retains the traditional police goal of professional crime fighting but enlarges the enforcement target to include nontraditional types of criminals.

6-24. A department using the _____ style of policing may take a hands-off approach to otherwise disruptive or problematic forms of behavior that are not violations of the criminal law.

6-25. _____ is the number of police personnel or the number of units supervised by a particular commander.

6-26. _____ assumes that many crimes are caused by existing social conditions and that crimes can be controlled by uncovering and effectively addressing underlying social problems.

6-27. _____ are activities (such as administration and training) that provide support for line operations.

6-28. _____ is a collaborative effort between the police and the community that identifies problems of crime and disorder and involves all elements of the community in the search for solutions to these problems.

6-29. The _____ style of policing is marked by a concern with helping rather than strict enforcement.

6-30. _____ is the increasing formalization of police work and the rise in public acceptance of the police that accompanies it.

Crossword Puzzle

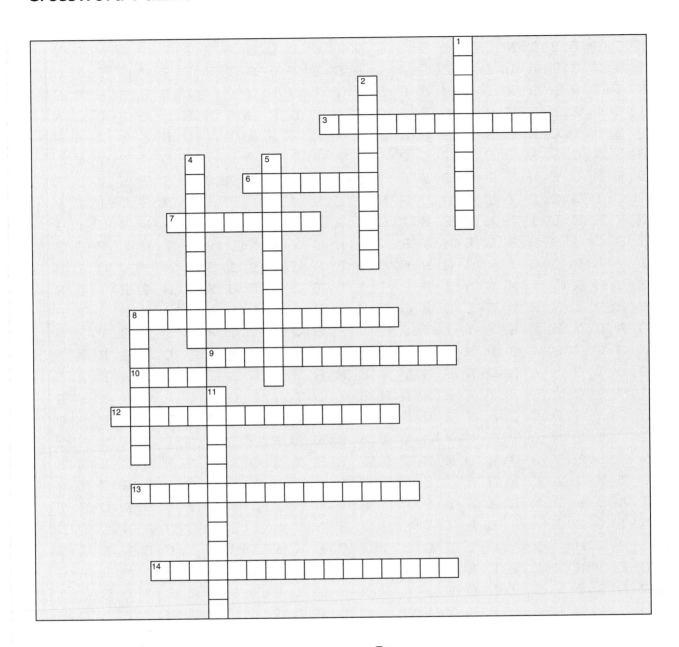

Across

3. The time it takes to respond to a call for service.
6. Style of police department likely to use community policing.
7. Departments in Wilson's typology concerned with order maintenance.
8. The unbroken line of authority.
9. Number of units supervised by a particular commander.
10. Official program of some states to set training standards for law enforcement agencies.
12. Police line operations support.
13. The increasing formalization of police work.
14. Also called police culture.

Down

1. The physical are in which police collect evidence after a crime.
2. An exercise in choice.
4. Departments in Wilson's typology concerned with strict enforcement of the law.
5. Versatile police team assigned to a fixed district.
8. A crime analysis process developed by the NYPD in the 1990s.
11. The special responsibility to adhere to moral duty and obligation that is inherent in police work.

Word Search Puzzle

```
F I R I U I E T N I F I S C G N I C I L O P M A E T O M O Y
M T I N Y C T A L I L E G A L I S T I C S T Y L E C R I I N
E O N I T P H R R T L M G S E I T T O F N O M A D R S R E S
P I I L C S I T V S A O P I S N C U L N S I N M S O S O C A
C P P O L I C E C O M M U N I T Y R E L A T I O N S L I E E
O E S L A C S E I E C T I O I E N I A Y T S I N O O E Y Y L
N G P E M U E N O I E C F R G O P I R F N E O E S E S V D S
G N I C I L O P Y T I N U M M O C S N O P I I O A S T I T R
T C N V N E L I A L M E E A C R R A I E T E C S P N E N I I
A C R S C S S N E L E M V R V L H T N A N D P O I R L P E R
T N I I L R O O I V S M N N C O A S G L S I S M M Y V C I S
I V E C M R I T M E N I P H T R O I O U N O N S M P R T P R
E T G R O I Y M O N L O A L E M T E R I L L A I F E S N T H
C T O A U Y N E E T I I Y P S S R S G V T I F L Y A S T R N
L I I C S T S A G P N I O O E M S T A G N N V A C L A N A A
E E O O T O L A L O R F N V M S M B N O U E D N O M S E R T
E E I G S C E U F I F E N L N D I L I Y U O L O E O R N Y N
E T F O N N D C C A N I V N F L T T Z N I P E I L R E U R U
V L I T U T O L T B Y V G E I S E R A E I E M S I P R S M Y
R C Y I L M V S G R U M E T N R L E T I I R I S N N S H E E
R B F T M I A O A N A S Y S C T N R I E O A T E I R R T T N
A I I A S F R N L Z S F E S T E I S O E S T E F P N A O G T
B I N I I E I R S L A T I C G I E O N N I I S O U A N T P N
N D I R N M C F A C L D C S I I G L N N E O N R C E N N I S
O I O P I N N I T C E G I T O L C A A E R N O P O A M E E O
I L D L S O T O V L O E S R P N O T T F I S P T E T O E I Y
A M E Y A O R O U R H Y A N I A O P L I T N S P N T R L O N
I R I T M M N L N R E I N I M O G C O S O C E R C O O T I Y
P E N L C C E P I O A S L S T I C I E R I N R A O V O I E O
A G Y I N E O N F I C R I M E S C E N E Z S S H T E S R T O
```

Chain of Command
Community Policing
CompStat
Crime Prevention
Crime Scene
Criminal Investigation
Descretion
Ethics
Learning Organization
Legalistic Style

Line Operations
Police-Community Relations
Police Subculture
Preliminary Investigation
Professionalism
Response Time
Service Style
Solvability Factor
Staff Operations
Team Policing

chapter 7

Policing:
Legal Aspects

OUTLINE

Introduction
The Abuse of Police Power
Individual Rights
Search and Seizure
Arrest
The Intelligence Function

LEARNING OBJECTIVES

After reading this chapter, you should be able to:

- Explain how the Bill of Rights and democratically inspired legal restraints on the police help ensure personal freedoms in our society

- Describe the nature of due process and the specific constitutional amendments on which due process guarantees are based

- Explain the importance of the exclusionary rule and the fruit of the poisoned tree doctrine

- Define *arrest*, and describe how popular depictions of the arrest process by the police may not be consistent with legal understandings of the term

- Describe the circumstances under which police officers may search vehicles and the extent to which such searches are permissible

- Explain how the need to ensure public safety justifies certain suspicionless searches

- Recite the *Miranda* warnings, and describe in detail recent U.S. Supreme Court cases that have affected *Miranda* warning requirements

- Describe the nature of electronic evidence, and explain how first-on-the-scene law enforcement personnel should handle it

[73]

Chapter Summary

Chapter 7 examines the legal constraints on police behavior. It discusses how law enforcement agents are constrained by procedural law, highlighting the legal rules that affect the **search and seizure** of evidence, **arrest**, and **interrogation**.

When conducting investigations, law enforcement officers rely heavily on physical evidence to substantiate criminal charges. The legal constraints on evidence collection are found in the **Fourth Amendment**. In general, law enforcement agents get a **warrant** to search for and seize evidence when they can demonstrate **probable cause** to a neutral magistrate (a judge). If probable cause were later found to have been lacking, any items seized would be excluded as evidence. *Weeks* v. *United States* established the **exclusionary rule** for federal cases; *Mapp* v. *Ohio* made this rule applicable to the states.

There are many exceptions to the requirement that law enforcement agents obtain a warrant before collecting evidence, although most of them require that the agents establish probable cause. For example, if a police officer is in a place where he or she is legally allowed to be, then that officer can seize as evidence any contraband *in plain view* (*Harris* v. *United States*), although he or she could not move an object to put it into plain view (*U.S.* v. *Irizarry*, *Arizona* v. *Hicks*). Another exception is a search incident to an arrest. When arresting a suspect, law enforcement agents can search the person and the area in the immediate control of that person (*Chimel* v. *California*, *U.S.* v. *Rabinowitz*) without a warrant. Other exceptions include emergencies, stop-and-frisk situations, concern for public safety, vehicle searches, and consent searches (see Table 7–3 for a complete list of established exceptions to the exclusionary rule).

The probable cause standard also applies to the law of **arrest**. Law enforcement agents arrest, or obtain a warrant to arrest, a suspect when the facts cause a reasonable person to believe that a specific individual has committed a crime. There are, however, instances in which police officers might question someone they suspect of committing a crime but may not make an arrest. For example, a police officer might stop to question a suspicious-looking individual and do a quick pat-down search for weapons (*Terry* v. *Ohio*). If the citizen is able to dispel the concerns of the officer, then that person is free to leave.

Chapter 7 concludes with a discussion of **interrogation**. Law enforcement agents can, and do, question citizens suspected of committing crime, but they cannot conduct an interrogation before ensuring that the suspect is protected against self-incrimination. Courts have prohibited physically coercive techniques when questioning suspects (*Brown* v. *Mississippi*). The privilege against self-incrimination does not prevent officers from using psychologically coercive techniques to elicit confessions as long as the suspect is informed of his or her rights prior to custodial interrogation (*Miranda* v. *Arizona*).

The Fourth and Fifth Amendments mandate the two most significant and controversial procedural constraints on police behavior. These constraints have evolved considerably over the last 40 years because of changes in the ideological makeup of the Supreme Court. For example, evidence obtained based on an invalid warrant can still be used when the officer was acting in "**good faith**" (*United States* v. *Leon*). Law enforcement agents can question suspects without reading them their *Miranda* rights when public safety is at risk (*New York* v. *Quarles*).

Key Concepts

Arrest: The act of taking an adult or juvenile into physical custody by authority of law for the purpose of charging the person with a criminal offense, a delinquent act, or a status offense, terminating with the recording of a specific offense. Technically, an arrest occurs whenever a law enforcement officer curtails a person's freedom to leave.

Bill of Rights: The popular name given to the first ten amendments to the U.S. Constitution, which are considered especially important in the processing of criminal defendants.

Compelling Interest: A legal concept that provides a basis for suspicionless searches when public safety is at issue. (Urinalysis tests of train engineers are an example.) It is the concept upon which the Supreme Court cases of *Skinner* v. *Railway Labor*

TEST

Executives' Association (1989) and *National Treasury Employees Union* v. *Von Raab* (1989) turned. In those cases, the Court held that public safety may sometimes provide a sufficiently compelling interest to justify limiting an individual's right to privacy.

Electronic Communications Privacy Act (ECPA): A law passed by Congress in 1986 establishing the due process requirements that law enforcement officers must meet in order to legally intercept wire communications.

Electronic Evidence: Information and data of investigative value that is stored in or transmitted by an electronic device. *Source*: Adapted from: Technical Working Group for Electronic Crime Scene Investigation, *Electronic Crime Scene Investigation: A Guide for First Responders* (Washington, D.C.: National Institute of Justice, 2001), p. 2.

Emergency Search: A search conducted by the police without a warrant, that is justified on the basis of some immediate and overriding need, such as public safety, the likely escape of a dangerous suspect, or the removal or destruction of evidence.

Exclusionary Rule: The understanding, based on Supreme Court precedent, that incriminating information must be seized according to constitutional specifications of due process, or it will not be allowed as evidence in a criminal trial.

Fleeting Targets Exception: An exception to the exclusionary rule that permits law enforcement officers to search a motor vehicle based upon probable cause but without a warrant. The fleeting-targets exception is predicated upon the fact that vehicles can quickly leave the jurisdiction of a law enforcement agency.

Fruit of the Poisoned Tree Doctrine: A legal principle that excludes from introduction at trial any evidence later developed as a result of an illegal search or seizure.

Good-Faith Exception: An exception to the exclusionary rule. Law enforcement officers who conduct a search, or seize evidence, on the basis of good faith (that is, where they believe they are operating according to the dictates of the law) and who later discover that a mistake was made (perhaps in the format of the application for a search warrant) may still use the seized evidence in court.

Illegally Seized Evidence: Evidence seized without regard to the principles of due process as described by the Bill of Rights. Most illegally seized evidence is the result of police searches conducted without a proper warrant or of improperly conducted interrogations.

Inherent Coercion: The tactics used by police interviewers that fall short of physical abuse but that nonetheless pressure suspects to divulge information.

Interrogation: The information-gathering activities of police officers that involve the direct questioning of suspects.

Landmark Case: A precedent-setting court decision that produces substantial changes in both the understanding of the requirements of due process and in the practical day-to-day operations of the justice system.

Latent Evidence: Evidence of relevance to a criminal investigation that is not readily seen by the   unaided eye.

***Miranda* Triggers:** The dual principles of custody and interrogation, both of which are necessary before an advisement of rights is required.

***Miranda* Warnings:** The advisement of rights due criminal suspects by the police before questioning begins. *Miranda* warnings were first set forth by the Supreme Court in the 1966 case of *Miranda* v. *Arizona.*

Plain View: A legal term describing the ready visibility of objects that might be seized as evidence during a search by police in the absence of a search warrant specifying the seizure of those objects. To lawfully seize evidence in plain view, officers must have a legal right to be in the viewing area and must have cause to believe that the evidence is somehow associated with criminal activity.

Probable Cause: A set of facts and circumstances that would induce a reasonably intelligent and prudent person to believe that a particular other person has committed a specific crime. Also, reasonable grounds to make or believe an accusation. Probable cause refers to the necessary level of belief that would allow for police seizures (arrests) of individuals and full searches of dwellings, vehicles, and possessions.

Psychological Manipulation: Manipulative actions by police interviewers, designed to pressure suspects to divulge information, that are based upon subtle forms of intimidation and control.

Reasonable Suspicion: The level of suspicion that would justify an officer in making further inquiry or in conducting further investigation. Reasonable suspicion may permit stopping a person for questioning or for a simple pat-down search. Also, a belief, based on a consideration of the facts at hand and on reasonable inferences drawn from those facts, that would induce an ordinarily prudent and cautious person under the same circumstances to conclude that criminal activity is taking place or that criminal activity has recently occurred. Reasonable suspicion is a *general* and reasonable belief that a crime is in progress or has occurred, whereas probable cause is a reasonable belief that a *particular* person has committed a *specific* crime. See also **probable cause**.

Search Incident to an Arrest: A warrantless search of an arrested individual conducted to ensure the safety of the arresting officers. Because individuals placed under arrest may be in possession of weapons, courts have recognized the need for arresting officers to protect themselves by conducting an immediate search of arrestees without obtaining a warrant.

"Sneak and Peek" Search: A search that occurs in the suspect's absence and without his or her prior knowledge.

Suspicionless Search: A search conducted by law enforcement personnel without a warrant and without suspicion. Suspicionless searches are only permissible if based upon an overriding concern for public safety.

Writ of *Certiorari*: A writ issued from an appellate court for the purpose of obtaining from a lower court the record of its proceedings in a particular case. In some states, this writ is the mechanism for discretionary review. A request for review is made by petitioning for a writ of *certiorari*, and the granting of review is indicated by the issuance of the writ.

Key Cases

Alabama v. *White*: The Court ruled that an anonymous tip could form the basis for a stop when the informant accurately predicts the behavior of the suspect (*Alabama* v. *White*, 110 S.Ct. 2412 [1990]).

Arizona v. *Fulminante*: The Court ruled that a confession was coerced in this specific case but also found that a coerced confession can be a harmless trial error if other evidence still proves guilt (*Arizona* v. *Fulminante*, 111 S.Ct. 1246 [1991]).

Brecht v. *Abrahamson*: The Court held that prosecutorial efforts to use a defendant's silence against him or her will not invalidate a finding of guilt by a jury unless the "error had substantial and injurious effect or influence in determining the jury's verdict" (*Brecht* v. *Abrahamson*, 113 S.Ct. 1710, 123 L.Ed.2d 353 [1993]).

Brown v. *Mississippi*: Law enforcement agents cannot use physically coercive interrogation techniques to elicit confessions (*Brown* v. *Mississippi*, 297 U.S. 278 [1936]).

California v. *Hodari D.*: The Court held that if a suspect runs from the police and discards incriminating evidence, the suspect can be arrested based on that evidence (*California* v. *Hodari D.*, 111 S.Ct. 1547 [1991]).

Carroll v. *United States*: A warrantless search of an automobile or other vehicle is valid if based on probable cause that contraband is present (*Carroll* v. *U.S.*, 267 U.S. 132 [1925]).

Chimel v. *California*: A search, incident to a lawful arrest, is limited to the area in the immediate control or grabbing area of the suspect (*Chimel* v. *California*, 395 U.S. 752 [1969]).

Dickerson v. *U.S.*: Upheld the 1966 U.S. Supreme Court decision of *Miranda* v. *Arizona*. (*Dickerson* v. *U.S.*, 530 U.S. 428 [2000]).

Escobedo v. *Illinois*: The case that recognized the right to have legal counsel present during police interrogation (*Escobedo* v. *Illinois*, 378 U.S. 478 [1964]).

Florida v. *Bostick*: The case that permits warrantless "sweeps" of intercity buses (*Florida* v. *Bostick*, 111 S.Ct. 2382 [1991]).

Horton v. *California*: The courts declared that inadvertence is not a necessary condition to justify a plain-view search (*Horton* v. *California*, 110 S.Ct. 2301, 47 CrL. 2135 [1990]).

Illinois v. *Perkins*: Miranda warnings are not required when a suspect does not believe that he or she is speaking to a law enforcement officer (*Illinois* v. *Perkins*, 495 U.S. 292 [1990]).

Indianapolis v. *Edmond*: In this case, the Supreme Court decided to strike down a narcotics checkpoint, stating that the Fourth Amendment prohibits even a brief "seizure" of a motorist under a program whose purpose is indistinguishable from a general interest in crime control (*Indianapolis* v. *Edmond*, 531 U.S. 32 [2000]).

Kyllo v. *U.S.*: The U.S. Supreme Court held that the use of a device not in general public use to explore details of a private home is surveillance, which is a Fourth Amendment search (*Kyllo* v. *U.S.*, 533 U.S. 27 [2001]).

Mapp v. *Ohio*: The Fourth Amendment's exclusionary rule is applicable to the states through the due process clause of the Fourteenth Amendment (*Mapp* v. *Ohio*, 367 U.S. 643 [1961]).

Minnick v. *Mississippi*: The court held that interrogation may not resume after the suspect has had an opportunity to consult his or her lawyer when the lawyer is no longer present (*Minnick* v. *Mississippi*, 498 U.S. 146 [1990]).

Miranda v. *Arizona*: A person in custody must be advised of various warnings and his or her legal rights prior to being subjected to custodial interrogation (*Miranda* v. *Arizona*, 384 U.S. 436 [1966]).

Nix v. *Williams*: This case created the "inevitable discovery exception" to the Miranda requirements (*Nix* v. *Williams*, 104 S.Ct. 2501 [1984]).

Richards v. *Wisconsin*: The U.S. Supreme Court ruled that police can make "no-knock" entries if announcing their presence might inhibit the investigation of the crime (*Richards* v. *Wisconsin*, 117 S.Ct. 1416 [1997]).

Silverthorne Lumber Co. v. *U.S.*: Established the fruit of the poisoned tree doctrine (*Silverthorne Lumber Co.* v. *U.S.*, 251 U.S. 385 [1920]).

Smith v. *Ohio* (1990): The Court held that an individual has the right to protect his or her belongings from unwarranted police inspection (*Smith* v. *Ohio*, 110 S.Ct. 1288 [1990]).

Terry v. *Ohio*: This case established the stop-and-frisk exception. A citizen can be briefly detained by law enforcement agents without probable cause when the agents have reasonable suspicion to believe the person has committed or is about to commit a crime. An agent can conduct a limited pat-down search of the suspect (*Terry* v. *Ohio*, 392 U.S. 1 [1968]).

U.S. v. *Drayton*: The Supreme Court decided that police officers are not required to advise bus passengers of their right to refuse to cooperate with officers conducting searches. (*U.S.* v. *Drayton*, 122 S.Ct. 2105 [2002]).

U.S. v. *Robinson*: Establishes that a search incident to a lawful arrest does not violate Fourth Amendment protections (*Robinson* v. *U.S.*, 414 U.S. 218 [1973]).

U.S. Department of Justice v. *Landano*: The U.S. Supreme Court required that an informant's identity be revealed through a federal Freedom of Information Act request (*U.S. Dept. of Justice* v. *Landano*, 113 S.Ct. 2014, 124 L.Ed. 2d 84 [1993]).

Weeks v. *United States*: Evidence obtained by federal officers in violation of the Fourth Amendment will be excluded from admission in federal prosecutions (see Exclusionary Rule, *Weeks* v. *United States*, 232 U.S. 383 [1914]).

Wilson v. *Arkansas*: The U.S. Supreme Court ruled that police officers must knock and announce their identity before entering a dwelling, even when they have a search warrant (*Wilson* v. *Arkansas*, 115 S.Ct. 1914 [1995]).

Learning Tips

On Exams, Go with Your First Instinct

It is usually best to stick with your first choice on the objective questions (true-or-false and multiple-choice questions). Avoid going against your first instinct unless, through reflection or deduction, you are convinced that your second answer is correct.

Study with a Friend

It is difficult to remember the holdings of the cases cited in Chapter 7 because there are so many of them. Have a friend or classmate "quiz" you on holdings of the various cases. This will help ensure that you can identify the specifics of the cases when taking the examination.

CJ Today on the World Wide Web

Web links to organizations and agencies related to the material in Chapter 7 include:

WEBSITE TITLE	URL
Police Guide	http://www.policeguide.com
Law Enforcement Links	http://www.leolinks.com
American Bar Association	http://www.abanet.org
American Civil Liberties Union (ACLU)	http://www.aclu.org
American Prosecutors Research Institute	http://www.ndaa.org
U.S. Evidence Law	http://www.law.cornell.edu/topics/evidence.html
Justice Denied	http://www.justicedenied.org
Stanford Law and Policy Review	http://www.stanford.edu/group/SLPR
Kuglick's Forensic Resource and Criminal Law	http://www.kruglaw.com

Student Activities

Activity 1

Recall from the discussion in Chapter 1 that justice requires a fair balance between individual and community interests. The Supreme Court's interpretation of the Fourth Amendment provides an effective illustration of the difficulties in finding a fair balance. A public-order advocate might argue that the exclusionary rule has handcuffed the abilities of the police to effectively protect the community. An individual-rights advocate, on the other hand, might argue that such changes have resulted in positive reform of the police and such rights need to be expanded. What is your opinion? If the president appointed you to the Supreme Court, would you be willing to overturn *Mapp* v. *Ohio* and eliminate the exclusionary rule? Why or why not?

_____

_____

_____

_____

_____

_____

Activity 2

In the following search-and-seizure situations, note whether you think the evidence seized would be excluded in a court of law. In addition, try to note cases that apply to each circumstance.

1. Police Officer A observed an automobile driving the wrong way on a one-way street. When the officer tried to stop the automobile, the driver fled, resulting in a high-speed chase. The chase ended when the driver's car crashed into a telephone pole. Concerned that the car might ignite from a gas leak, the officer pulled the unconscious woman from the car. After he had pulled the woman a safe distance from the car, he went back into the car to locate her purse for identification, at which time he found a knife covered in blood on the front seat. It was later discovered that the knife was used in a murder of another police officer. Should the knife be excluded? What court case(s) justify your decision?

2. While off duty and at a party, Police Officer A was asked by the homeowner to get some ice from his basement. Since the ice machine was not immediately apparent, the officer opened two doors. Behind door number two were six marijuana plants. The officer arrested the homeowner. Would you exclude the marijuana plants? What court case(s) justify your decision?

3. Defendant A was suspected of selling stolen property from his dorm room. An undercover campus police officer knocked on Defendant A's door, and when Defendant A answered, the officer asked for an affordable radar detector. In response, Defendant A said that he just got two new ones last night. While in the room, the officer noticed various other items she suspected as being stolen. She bought one of the radar detectors and then used it to convince a judge to issue a search warrant of the room. Among the items confiscated in the search with the warrant were four radar detectors, three television sets, two air-conditioning units, and 1,500 compact discs. Should this evidence be excluded? What court case(s) justify your decision?

4. Police Officer A and Police Officer B were observing a street corner for drug activity and noticed Defendant A selling drugs to Defendant B. These officers quickly arrived at the scene but were only able to arrest Defendant B. Before they could handcuff him, Defendant B swallowed what appeared to them to be one balloon of heroin. Police Officer B forced his finger down Defendant B's throat, causing him to vomit. Among the expelled material was one balloon of heroin. Would this evidence be excluded? What court case(s) justify your decision?

5. When executing a valid arrest warrant for an assault charge in Defendant A's home, Police Officer A seized a handgun in the search incident to the arrest. Alarmed that her life was in danger, Police Officer A made Defendant A lie with his face down on the floor and quickly perused three adjoining rooms. While walking through the kitchen, she noticed a pile of semiautomatic weapons on the table and seized them as evidence. Should these weapons be excluded? What case(s) justify your decision?

_____

_____

_____

_____

_____

_____

Activity 3

One of the important policy issues being debated in courts and among politicians is whether the *Miranda* decision should be overturned. Visit the Cybrary at http://www.cybrary.info. Use the search function to find websites about the application of the *Miranda* rule. After you peruse several sites, answer the following questions in the space provided below. Should police officers be required to read a *Miranda*-type warning prior to custodial interrogation, or should *Miranda* be overturned? Explain your answer.

_____

_____

_____

_____

_____

_____

Activity 4

Chapter 7 provides an analysis of many landmark cases. The full text of several of these Supreme Court decisions is posted as Library Extras. For example, included is the full text of the *Weeks* v. *U.S.*, *Silverthorne Lumber Company* v. *U.S.*, *Mapp* v. *Ohio*, *Harris* v. *U.S.*, *Terry* v. *Ohio*, *Brown* v. *Mississippi*, and *Miranda* v. *Arizona* decisions. Read the full text of one of these cases. Then, in the space provided below, provide a complete summary of the case. Be sure to discuss the facts of the case and the Court's decision, and then provide the reason(s) for the Court's decision in the case.

_____

_____

_____

_____

_____

Internet Activity

Use the Cybrary (http://www.cybrary.info) to find information about legal issues and policing. Use the search function available to locate information about the exclusionary rule. What kinds of information did you find?

_____

_____

_____

_____

_____

Distance Learning Activity

Write a case scenario that raises a Fourth Amendment concern. Submit the case or cases relevant to resolving this concern. Here is an example of what this exercise asks you to do: Defendant Sally Smith was watching television when a police officer knocked at her door. Sally opened the door and said, "What do you want?" The officer responded, "I just wanted to talk to you about a robbery that occurred over on 8th and Vine." Sally responded, "Sure, come on into my home; I don't have anything to hide." While sitting at the kitchen table, the officer noticed a marijuana plant on a window ledge. The officer then placed her in handcuffs, arresting her for possession of a controlled substance. The officer then searched Sally and found a small bag of cocaine in her right front pocket. The relevant cases are tied to consent issues, plain view, and search incident to arrest.

If your instructor asks you to do so, submit your scenario to the other students in your class and see whether they can identify the key procedural issues and cases.

_____

_____

_____

_____

_____

_____

Student Study Guide Questions

True or False

____ 7-1. Most jurisdictions allow arrest for a felony without a warrant as long as probable cause is established.

____ 7-2. Officers may not stop and question an unwilling citizen when they have no reason to suspect him or her of a crime.

____ 7-3. Hidden evidence is considered any evidence not readily seen by the unaided eye.

____ 7-4. Public safety may provide a sufficiently compelling interest such that an individual's right to privacy can be limited under certain circumstances.

____ 7-5. If the police initiate an arrest in a person's home, because of the law regarding search incident to arrest, they could search the entire residence, including opening drawers, closets, and trunks.

____ 7-6. A writ of _certiorari_ is the warrant federal agents need to make an arrest.

____ 7-7. Probable cause must be satisfactorily demonstrated by police officers in a written affidavit to a magistrate before a search warrant can be issued.

____ 7-8. Certain emergencies permit police to search premises without a warrant.

____ 7-9. Nontestimonial evidence, such as blood, cannot be seized as evidence.

____ 7-10. The Electronic Communications Privacy Act prohibits law enforcement officers from seizing electronic communications under any circumstances.

Multiple Choice

7-11. Which of these statements about the search and seizure of evidence is false?
   a. A warrantless search of an automobile is valid if it is based on probable cause that contraband is present.
   b. Evidence viewed by an officer in plain view, when legally in a place where the officer is allowed to be, will not be excluded.
   c. Evidence illegally seized by the police cannot be used in a trial under most circumstances.
   d. In all circumstances, police officers must get a warrant in order to seize evidence.

7-12. Which constitutional amendment establishes legal boundaries for the search and seizure of evidence?
   a. Fourth
   b. Fifth
   c. First
   d. Second

7-13. Which constitutional amendment establishes legal boundaries for the interrogation of suspects?
   a. Fourth
   b. Fifth
   c. First
   d. Second

7-14. Which of the following legal principles excludes from introduction at trial any evidence obtained as a result of an illegal search or seizure?
   a. plain-view doctrine
   b. public-safety exception
   c. good-faith exception
   d. fruit of the poisoned tree doctrine

7-15. Which U.S. Supreme Court case established the public-safety exception to the *Miranda* rule?
   a. *Brown v. Mississippi*
   b. *New York v. Quarles*
   c. *Mapp v. Ohio*
   d. *Weeks v. United States*

7-16. Which of the following U.S. Supreme Court cases does *not* involve police interrogation of suspects?
   a. *Brown v. Mississippi*
   b. *Chimel v. California*
   c. *Miranda v. Arizona*
   d. *Escobedo v. Illinois*

7-17. Which U.S. Supreme Court case made the exclusionary rule applicable to the states?
   a. *Brown v. Mississippi*
   b. *New York v. Quarles*
   c. *Mapp v. Ohio*
   d. *Weeks v. United States*

7-18. Which of the following U.S. Supreme Court cases does *not* involve the search of a vehicle?
   a. *United States v. Ross*
   b. *United States v. Leon*
   c. *Carroll v. United States*
   d. *South Dakota v. Opperman*

7-19. In which of the following situations would a law enforcement agent not be required to read a suspect the *Miranda* warnings?
  a. A suspect makes a spontaneous statement, such as stating "I just killed my wife," to officers when arriving at the scene.
  b. A police officer arrests a person for robbery and assault. When traveling to the police station for booking purposes, she asks the suspect, "What do you know about this robbery?"
  c. An off-duty police officer apprehends a purse snatcher. As the officer waits for a police car to transport the suspect, he asks, "How many purses have you stolen in the last month?"
  d. Jason Melo, convicted of rape and burglary, was serving time in a maximum-security prison. He was also a suspect in a murder investigation. In the visiting room of the prison, the detective asked Jason, "Did you murder your brother-in-law?"

7-20. In which of the following situations would a law enforcement officer be able to conduct a search if he or she did not have probable cause to do so?
  a. vehicle search
  b. search incident to an arrest
  c. suspicionless search
  d. none of the above

Fill-In

7-21. The case that established the good-faith exception to the exclusionary rule is

_____.

7-22. The case that articulated the fruit of the poisoned tree doctrine is

_____.

7-23. The case that established a two-pronged test to the effect that informant information could establish probable cause if both criteria were met is

_____.

7-24. The case that established the famous requirement of police to advise a suspect of his or her rights is _____.

7-25. The case that first recognized the need for emergency searches is

_____.

7-26. The case that held a search incident to an arrest invalid when it goes beyond the person arrested and the area subject to that person's "immediate control" is _____.

7-27. The case that established the stop-and-frisk exception to the exclusionary rule is _____.

7-28. The case that placed limits on an officer's ability to seize evidence discovered during a pat-down search is _____.

7-29. The case that made the exclusionary rule applicable to the states is

_____.

7-30. The case that established the exclusionary rule in federal cases is

_____.

Crossword Puzzle

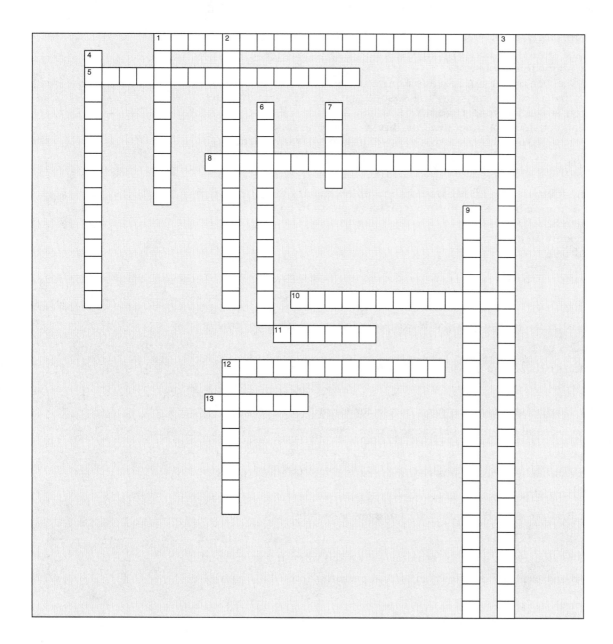

Across

1. The concept central to *National Treasury Employees Union* v. *Von Raab*.
5. The tactics used by police interviewers that fall short of physical abuse but that nonetheless pressure suspects to divulge information.
8. Exception established in *U.S.* v. *Leon*.
10. Police activity regulated by *Brown* v. *Mississippi*.
11. Amendment concerned with unreasonable searches and seizures.
12. The required standard for a search warrant.
13. Evidence of relevance to a criminal investigation that is not readily seen by the unaided eye.

Down

1. Writ of _____.
2. This rule means that evidence illegally seized by the police cannot be used in a trial.
3. ECPA.
4. Case establishing the famous requirement of a rights advisement of suspects by police.
6. Cases that produce substantial changes in the understanding of the requirements of due process.
7. Amendment providing protection against self-incrimination.
9. Exception predicated upon the fact that vehicles can quickly leave the jurisdiction.
12. *Arizona* v. *Hicks* focuses on this exclusionary rule exception.

Word Search Puzzle

```
E K E E P D N A K A E N S E N C C R E N W U N L A D R E N N
L A T E N T E V I D E N C E L C M S N N E E L A N T E N R K
E C C A E I V Y I B W L O C S C R T A E C X I G O D O E D T
L C T P K N E L U R Y R A N O I S U L C X E T V K P E I R L
G A G A U T E Y P N Y M C T T T N C R O E I X O N N E S O O
N N T P L E N I P W S I N P I A O K W F S G V N N I P I D R
U I C E R R N P I C S I O I G G A R E D G N W R G A A F I T
I E N T R R I E I O A E I I A P I O T H N K A T T G I L L K
C I C E T O S O I M A I T I E N I U C C I G E N G V E S P P
C I E E R G S N O P V D P T C Y P R A T N D R A I N C I I M
L C G A A A W T E E K E E A E E A R N N R E M I O X E A O E
E N I T E T E M E L S E C I T E C E O M A M I R A G S H N E
E N R N R I E E S L A R X R S R E E O B W O P I G I E U I N
L L P G N O C G N I E P E S I T C D R N A U M T R C C N E L
A S U B S N R G C N T C S G R E T S E O D B R E P C H O N C
T X N I E S P O S G U E T I G C D I A S N R L E C E C H I B
I V O O D N S K G I L S E R H I R R T D A F R E R I C R L N
N E L I C R N I E N L L G C O G R T N P R E G E C R A A W D
R E P D T S A O T E N R I E N E T N R I P N S A A N C G E
L N N E V N U I I E H I A N N E I M A A M T E E N D U E T O
R F N C E R C R D R E L T D I T E C P D C E S R M M C S T A
R H C N I I S R R E O R G E P A A C E O N Y L A L A N T E A
T X T X P E R A N S E A N O E I E U E V C A R D N R I H A I
E I E S U L L T C T E R I C Y L O R O N I K R I G T V E E S
G S U E M I A S R O S D T E K A C R E D C D O I C E E I T S
I S R N I R R E R E E C E H E I E G O A R I E R M O D T I A
D A E M R A I R D D X T E E O N R E S T A G G N H E N N K T
L A E F N E R R E O A I L N T E I E A D G L C D C L R E C E
O E M O E P I A X M A G F T M R E C A S T O K C I E E G R R
A N S S G O O D F A I T H E X C E P T I O N O E I L N E L N
```

Arrest
Compelling Interest
ECPA
Electronic Evidence
Emergency Search
Exclusionary Rule
Fleeting Targets Exception
Good Faith Exception
Inherent Coercion

Interrogation
Landmark Case
Latent Evidence
Miranda Triggers
Miranda Warnings
Plain View
Probable Cause
Sneak and Peek
Suspicionless Search

Policing: Issues and Challenges

chapter

8

LEARNING OBJECTIVES

After reading this chapter, you should be able to:

- Describe the police working personality, and relate it to police culture

- List and describe different types of police corruption, and discuss possible methods for building police integrity

- Explain the dangers of police work, and discuss what can be done to reduce those dangers

- Describe the situations in which police officers are most likely to use force, and provide some guidelines for determining when too much force has been used

- Describe racial profiling, and explain why it has become a significant issue in policing today

- Describe the civil liability issues associated with policing, and identify common sources of civil suits against the police

Chapter Summary

Chapter 8 discusses several important police issues, including police personality and culture, corruption, police use of force, the dangers of police work, and police civil liability.

One powerful influence on law enforcement officers is the police culture. New recruits are molded by the police culture as supervisors and other officers teach rookie officers the informal policies of the department. Thus, there are two sets of rules that new police officers must learn and follow. The first set of rules includes those formal departmental policies and legal constraints that the officer learns in the training academy. The second set of rules involves the informal socialization that takes place as officers interact with older, experienced officers who teach how formal rules are interpreted. For example, experienced officers might explain to a new recruit that accepting free meals or bribes is expected, despite departmental policy clearly forbidding such behavior. The text discusses such activities in the section on police **corruption**, noting its historical pervasiveness. Chapter 8 also discusses how police departments have attempted to respond to police corruption.

Chapter 8 also discusses the dangers of police work. Police work is dangerous, and officers are killed in the line of duty. For example, more than 150 law enforcement officers were killed in 2002. The rate of violent death of law enforcement officers, however, is relatively small. There are several other dangers discussed in this chapter. Law enforcement officers are exposed to disease and infected evidence and must take necessary precautions or risk being infected with the agents that cause AIDS, hepatitis B, or tuberculosis. Others dangers include the stress and fatigue of police work. Stress is probably the least visible of police dangers, but its impact on officers is enormous.

Police use of force is also examined in Chapter 8. The use of force by police officers is very rare. When used, force is typically used in an arrest situation when the suspect resists or is under the influence of drugs or alcohol. Deadly force is defined as the force likely to cause death or great bodily harm. The use of deadly force is a significant issue for law enforcement because of the potential civil liability, and *Tennessee* v. *Garner* is an important case, as it specifies the conditions under which deadly force can be used in the apprehension of suspected felons.

Another area of civil liability discussed in Chapter 8 is **racial profiling**. Called "driving while black" or "driving while brown," racial profiling comprises those police-initiated actions that are based on race, ethnicity, or national origin rather than the behavior of the individual or crime-specific information.

There are several common sources of civil suits brought against police departments. These sources include failure to protect property, failure to render proper medical assistance, false arrest, false imprisonment, and inappropriate use of deadly force. Important considerations for civil suits are **1983 Lawsuits**, which are civil suits brought under Title 42, Section 1983, of the U.S. Code against anyone who denies others their constitutional rights to life, liberty, or property without due process of law, and **Bivens Actions**, which are civil suits, based on the case of *Bivens* v. *Six Unknown Named Defendants*, brought against federal government officials for denying the constitutional rights of others.

Key Concepts

1983 Lawsuit: A civil suit brought under Title 42, Section 1983, of the U.S. Code against anyone who denies others their constitutional rights to life, liberty, or property without due process of law.

Biological Weapon: A biological agent used to threaten human life (for example, anthrax, smallpox, or any other infectious disease). *Source*: Technical Working Group on Crime Scene Investigation, *Crime Scene Investigation: A Guide for Law Enforcement* (Washington, D.C.: National Institute of Justice, 2000), p. 12.

Bivens Action: A civil suit based upon the case of *Bivens* v. *Six Unknown Federal Agents*, brought against federal government officials for denial of the constitutional rights of others.

Civil Liability: Potential responsibility for payment of damages or other court-ordered enforcement as a result of a ruling in a lawsuit. Civil liability is not the same as criminal liability, which means "open to punishment for a crime." *Source*: Adapted from Gerald and Kathleen Hill, *The Real Life Dictionary of the Law*, Web posted at law.com. Accessed June 11, 2003.

Deadly Force: Force likely to cause death or great bodily harm. Also, "the intentional use of a firearm or other instrument resulting in a high probability of death." *Source*: Sam W. Lathrop, "Reviewing Use of Force: A Systematic Approach," *FBI Law Enforcement Bulletin*, October 2000, p. 18.

Excessive Force: The application of an amount and/or frequency of force greater than that required to compel compliance from a willing or unwilling subject. *Source*: International Association of Chiefs of Police, *Police Use of Force in America 2001* (Alexandria, VA: IACP, 2001), p. 1.

Internal Affairs: The branch of a police organization tasked with investigating charges of wrongdoing against other members of the department.

Knapp Commission: A committee that investigated police corruption in New York City in the early 1970s.

Less-Lethal Weapon: A weapon that is designed to disable, capture, or immobilize-but not kill-a suspect. Occasional deaths do result from the use of such weapons, however.

Police Corruption: The abuse of police authority for personal or organizational gain. *Source*: Carl B. Klockers et al., "The Measurement of Police Integrity," *National Institute of Justice Research in Brief* (Washington, D.C.: NIJ, 2000), p. 1.

Police Use of Force: The use of physical restraint by a police officer when dealing with a member of the public. *Source*: National Institute of Justice, *Use of Force by Police: Overview of National and Local Data* (Washington, D.C.: NIJ, 1999).

Police Working Personality: All aspects of the traditional values and patterns of behavior evidenced by police officers who have been effectively socialized into the police subculture. Characteristics of the police personality often extend to the personal lives of law enforcement personnel.

Problem Police Officer: A law enforcement officer who exhibits problem behavior, as indicated by high rates of citizen complaints and use-of-force incidents and by other evidence. *Source*: Samuel Walker, Geoffrey P. Alpert, and Dennis J. Kenney, *Responding to the Problem Police Officer: A National Study of Early Warning Systems* (Washington, D.C.: NIJ, 2000).

Racial Profiling: "Any police-initiated action that relies on the race, ethnicity, or national origin rather than (1) the behavior of an individual or (2) on information that leads the police to a particular individual who has been identified as being, or having been, engaged in criminal activity." *Source*: Deborah Ramierz, Jack McDevitt, and Amy Farrell, *A Resource Guide on Racial Profiling Data Collection Systems: Promising Practices and Lessons Learned* (Washington, D.C.: USDOJ, 2000), p. 3.

Key Cases

Biscoe v. *Arlington County*: Alvin Biscoe was awarded $5 million after he lost both legs in an accident with a police officer involved in a high-speed chase. This case demonstrates that officers that drive in a way that places others in danger may find themselves the subject of civil suits (*Biscoe* v. *Arlington County*, 238 U.S. App. D.C. 206, 738 F.2d 1352, 1362 [1984]).

Bivens v. *Six Unknown Federal Agents*: This case established a path for legal action against agents enforcing federal laws. (*Bivens* v. *Six Unknown Federal Agents*, 403 U.S. 388 [1971]).

City of Canton, Ohio v. *Harris*: This case focuses on a department's training regimen. The Supreme Court held that a failure to train, when based on a deliberate indifference to the rights of persons, can lead to civil liability (*City of Canton, Ohio* v. *Harris*, 489 U.S. 378 [1989]).

Graham v. *Connor*: The Court established the standard of "objective reasonableness" by which an officer's use of deadly force could be assessed in terms of "reasonableness at the moment." (*Graham* v. *Connor*, 490 U.S. 386, 396-397 [1989]).

Hunter v. *Bryant*: This case applies to the issue of "qualified immunity" for officers in the line of duty. When making an arrest without a warrant, an officer is given immunity from civil liability when he or she makes a mistake. However, the determination of probable cause to make that arrest must have been reasonable (*Hunter* v. *Bryant*, 112 S.Ct. 534 [1991]).

Idaho v. *Horiuchi*: The holding in this case from the Ninth U.S. Circuit Court of Appeals ruled that federal law enforcement officers are not immune from state prosecution where their actions violate state law with malice or excessive zeal (*State of Idaho* v. *Horiuchi*, No. 98-30149 [9th Cir. 06/05/2001]).

Malley v. *Briggs*: In this case, the court decided that a police officer can be held liable for monetary damages if he or she makes an arrest or search for property based on a bad warrant. An officer is liable if it can be shown that reasonably well-trained officers would have known that the warrant failed to establish probable cause. (*Malley* v. *Biggs*, 475 U.S. 335, 106 sect. 1092 [1986]).

Maurice Turner v. *Fraternal Order of Police*: The court supported drug testing based on a reasonable suspicion of drug abuse (*Maurice Turner* v. *Fraternal Order of Police*, 500 A.2d 1005 [D.C. 1985]).

Tennessee v. *Garner*: This case specified the conditions under which deadly force could be used in the apprehension of suspected felons (*Tennessee* v. *Garner*, 471 U.S. 1 [1985]).

REMEMBER

Chapter 1 reviews the stages of the criminal justice process. Remember the steps that have to occur before pretrial activities can begin. Police officers must be made aware of an offense, conduct an investigation, and make an arrest. Upon arrest, pretrial activities begin. The first appearance through the arraignment is discussed in Chapter 8. The next steps of the court process, examined in Chapters 9 and 10, include the trial and sentencing stages.

Learning Tips

Tests

Managing review time is essential for test preparation. Instant reviews, which should occur either directly after the class meeting or during your assigned readings, start the learning and memorization process. Weekly reviews should be more focused than instant reviews. Final reviews are the most in-depth reviews. They should be conducted within the week prior to the exam. Final reviews help demonstrate the big picture and further understanding of the information provided during the entire class. Used together, instant, weekly, and final reviews provide the foundation for successful test preparation.

Before the Test

Be sure to arrive early for exams. This will allow time for relaxation and general preparation. Avoid talking to other students about their test preparation. This will only cause more anxiety. Listen to all instructions while the exam is being distributed. As redundant as it may seem, read the directions twice. You may lose significant points for not following the simplest instructions. Before beginning, if necessary, take a minute to release all test anxieties and to relax your mind.

CJ Today on the World Wide Web

Web links to organizations and agencies related to the material in Chapter 8 include:

WEBSITE TITLE	URL
Police Stress	http://stressline.com
Abner Louima Torture Case	http://www.thesmokinggun.com/torture/torture.htm

WEBSITE TITLE	URL
AJAX	http://www.sagal.com/ajax.ajax.htm
American Police Hall of Fame and Museum	http://www.aphf.org
Beside the Badge	http://my.dmci.net/~lmcpub/
California Law Enforcement Basic	http://www.clew.org/Tm/TmCtrs/BasicAcad.html
California Law Enforcement Image	http://www.calpoliceimage.com
Campus Law Enforcement	http://dpsw.usc.edu/UnivPDWeb.html
Heavy Badge	http://www.heavybadge.com
Ira Wilsker's Law Enforcement Sites	http://www.ih2000.net/ira

Student Activities

Activity 1

LIBRARY extra

Read **Library Extra 8–1** on promoting police integrity. What does the author suggest are the key principles for promoting police integrity?

_____

_____

_____

_____

_____

_____

Activity 2

LIBRARY extra

For this activity, first read the short research report on police use of deadly force posted at **Library Extra 8–6**. This report presents findings from a study on the use of force by and against Phoenix police officers. After reading the report, summarize the findings in the space provided below. In your synopsis, be sure to answer the following questions: How often do the police use force? How often do suspects use force against the police? What type of force is used in arrest situations? What factors predict police use of force?

_____

_____

_____

_____

_____

Activity 3

Compile a list of the police civil liability cases discussed in this chapter. What are the major findings of each case?

_____

_____

_____

_____

Activity 4

Use the Cybrary (http://www.cybrary.info) to find articles about racial profiling. Describe these studies and their findings.

_____

_____

_____

_____

_____

_____

Internet Activity

Use the Cybrary (http://www.cybrary.info) to find articles about police stress. What kinds of studies did you find? What do they deal with? What were the findings or results of each of these studies?

_____

_____

_____

_____

_____

_____

Distance Learning Activity

Visit a number of police memorial websites. What type of information is included at these websites? Assemble a notebook (or disk) containing the information you have gathered. Your instructor may request that you submit the material.

_____

_____

_____

_____

_____

_____

Student Study Guide Questions

True or False

_____   8-1.   Most large law enforcement agencies have their own internal affairs division.

_____   8-2.   Barker and Carter describe acts of occupational deviance as those that further the goals of law enforcement.

____ 8-3. Meat-eating police corruption is the most common form of police deviance, involving mostly small bribes or relatively small services.

____ 8-4. Police officers who have adopted a "working personality" are primarily concerned with fairness.

____ 8-5. The Knapp Commission investigated police use of deadly force in the late 1990s.

____ 8-6. In *Malley* v. *Briggs*, the Supreme Court banned random drug testing of police officers.

____ 8-7. Formal academy training is far more important in determining how rookies will see police work than is their informal socialization into the police culture.

____ 8-8. Currently, the fleeing felon rule guides police decision making in deadly force situations.

____ 8-9. Less-lethal weapons are designed to disable but not kill a suspect.

____ 8-10. A federal lawsuit against the police is often called a 2003 lawsuit.

Multiple Choice

8-11. Which type of police corruption occurs in order to further the organizational goals of law enforcement?
   a. meat-eating
   b. grass-eating
   c. occupational deviance
   d. abuse of authority

8-12. Which type of police corruption is motivated by the desire for personal benefit?
   a. meat-eating
   b. grass-eating
   c. occupational deviance
   d. abuse of authority

8-13. Which Supreme Court case is not directly relevant to police civil liability issues?
   a. *Malley* v. *Briggs*
   b. *City of Canton, Ohio* v. *Harris*
   c. *Tennessee* v. *Garner*
   d. *Board of County Commission of Bryan County, Oklahoma* v. *Brown*

8-14. What division in a police department investigates charges that officers are guilty of wrongdoing?
   a. strategic investigations
   b. intelligence
   c. internal affairs
   d. officer supervision

8-15. Historically, officers were allowed to use deadly force to prevent the escape of a suspected felon. This was known as the
   a. deadly force statute.
   b. "shoot to kill" policy.
   c. escaping suspect doctrine.
   d. fleeing felon rule.

8-16. A police officer can be sued for
   a. false arrest.
   b. failure to prevent a foreseeable crime.
   c. negligence in the care of persons in police custody.
   d. all of the above.

8-17. Officers who have adopted the police working personality are often
   a. cynical.
   b. authoritarian.
   c. prejudiced.
   d. all of the above.

8-18. What standard for deadly force was established in *Graham* v. *Connor*?
   a. objective reasonableness
   b. probable cause
   c. clear and present danger
   d. best guess

8-19. What commission provided the grass-easting and meat-eating distinctions to describe types of police corruption?
   a. The Johnson Commission
   b. The Nixon Commission
   c. The Knapp Commission
   d. The Burger Commission

8-20. What area of police civil liability received a significant amount of media attention in the late 1990s?
   a. deadly force
   b. drug testing
   c. racial profiling
   d. false arrest

Fill-In

8-21. A _____ is likely to have high rates of citizen complaints.

8-22. The _____ encompasses all aspects of the traditional values and patterns of behavior evidenced by police officers who have been effectively socialized into the police subculture.

8-23. _____ is the use of physical restraint by a police officer.

8-24. Who developed the term "police working personality"? _____

8-25. A _____ is an agent used to threaten human life, such as anthrax.

8-26. _____ is the branch of the police department that investigates wrongdoing among members of the department.

8-27. _____ is the abuse of police authority for personal or organizational gain.

8-28. Civil suits brought under Title 42, Section 1983, of the United States Code are called _____.

8-29. _____ is the name given to civil suits brought against federal government officials for denial of the constitutional rights of others.

8-30. _____ is the increasing formalization of police work and the rise in public acceptance of the police that accompanies it.

Crossword Puzzle

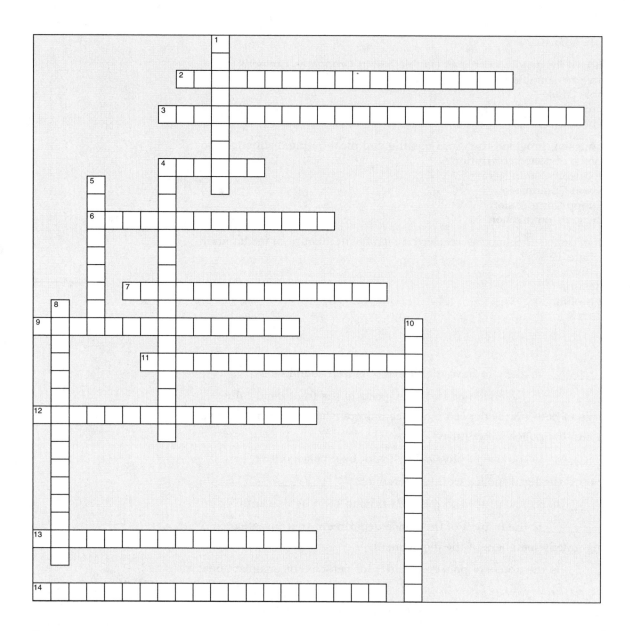

Across

2. When drug testing of police officers can occur.
3. All aspects of the traditional values and patterns of behavior evidenced by police officers who have been effectively socialized into the police subculture.
4. _____ v. *Six Unknown Federal Agents*.
6. Payment for a ruling in a lawsuit.
7. Any police-initiated action that relies on race, ethnicity, or national origin.
9. This unit polices the police.
11. A weapon designed to disable but not kill.
12. The abuse of police authority for personal or organizational gain.
13. The use of physical restraint by a police officer.
14. Police officers with high rates of citizen complaints.

Down

1. Type of immunity given to police officers generally.
4. Anthrax or smallpox.
5. The type of force greater than is required for compliance.
8. Famous police corruption commission.
10. This case specified the conditions under which deadly force could be used in the apprehension of suspected felons.

Word Search Puzzle

```
L S I E P V A C D I P T K N A P P C O M M I S S I O N C C A
R E C I F F O E C I L O P M E L B O R P T E L P N I I L I L
R L S I E I E C F S D E E T R C O R R U P T I O N V I C Y E
E K R N O C E A B L G I P N L A L E M L A E A S I D L L P L
T R P N O M C O C I S I I P I I C B I I I F F L F F P O I E
I I A N O P T E I G O C L M S E A I M N E E L G N A L I P E
C E H R A I A S G R I C A I T I K A A N T I L S L I P R I S
E L M I L L F E N I S O E C R Y F C C L A R R L C U C U U A
N T X E A R V I W R I I C F P O S I L B P P O E N R C R L U
E C M N S R O I P L S N E W N N Y L I T G R W O R C S I N I
T C O L F S R R S D A P S L I E C L S Y I O O E G P W A K R
A L L V T I N A O C E H I O C F I S U I R P I F E O A C O T
N O P I I O O N F T I Y T R I T N U T K A F O S I I P S L E
S O O L Y E N O P A O N O E Y N A E I B E A O S N L S L A S
L D I O U E O R R K L F T T L P O N E S E E W E O E I N Y C
E G G T O R I L E I Y O O E P S G E R O X R I R P O L N G R
U H E P C O N S N L R V R T G P S I L L C I F T A A E R G K
C O N W A A E T D N Y C E O E R A E L P E B I S E P L A P T
N E L C U U S A N L S I P R G F I A L V S I O E W S A N N I
L E N I R O E N R E C O S S F I I T R P S P A C L S A S I R
D M E O C D S E E F S O I A A O T G Y E I N T I A C C A O G
I O I E E G L V E V N I L E P C L L S U V R G L C T A E W V
O S R E R C A E B A I A E E C B O O M F E F E O I I W R I C
C E Y N L O N O L E N B E L O E M R R S F A H P G E O T L R
L E I F E R R I S R T C I P M I O O Y C O S I E O T S R A A
C L R E O Y T R E I T T S R C S A P B E R I I O L N R O E L
H A E I C Y L T V R L C L C O L L P S N C T O V O S S P I T
O I C I N L N C A P I I P R F R G R E P E G E V I R E E S O
S C L I I I L T E R U T L U C E C I L O P T C L B C I P N E
C I A M N W P O O I U S Y O I F O I V T I I I N C I E C L O
```

Biological Weapon
Bivens Action
Civil Liability
Corruption
Deadly Force
Excessive Force
Integrity
Internal Affairs

Knapp Commission
Less-Lethal Weapons
Police Culture
Police Stress
Police Working Personality
Problem Police Officer
Racial Profiling

chapter
9

The Courts:
Structure
and Participants

LEARNING OBJECTIVES

After reading this chapter, you should be able to:

■ Describe the development of the American court system

■ Explain the concept of the dual-court system in America

■ Identify some of the differences between the state and federal court systems

■ Identify and explain the roles of the professional members of the courtroom work group

■ Discuss indigent defense, and know what forms it takes in the United States

■ Identify and explain the roles of the nonprofessional courtroom participants

■ Explain the roles of expert and lay witnesses in a criminal trial, and describe how their testimony might differ

■ Explain how professional and nonprofessional courtroom participants work together to bring most criminal trials to a successful close

Chapter Summary

Chapter 9 provides an introduction to the American court system. It discusses the history of the dual-court structure in America, highlighting the decisions made at the various state and federal court levels. The text also describes the roles and responsibilities of "professional" and "nonprofessional" members of the courtroom work group.

The American court system is unique in many ways. One of its distinctive characteristics is that it is a dual-court system of state and federal courts. The founding fathers thought an essential feature of the new republic would be the power of individual states to retain authority and autonomy separate from federal control. However, the nation's founders also created a federal court system to mediate violations of federal law and resolve violations of due process guarantees.

Most states have a three-level court structure. Trial courts are at the lowest level. Trial courts of limited or special jurisdiction hear only cases involving very minor crimes, such as misdemeanors and traffic violations. A judge, rather than a jury, usually resolves these cases. **Trial courts of general jurisdiction**, however, hear any criminal case and also provide the first level of appeal for cases decided in a court of limited jurisdiction. These decisions can then be appealed to the state **intermediate appellate court**. Appellate courts are concerned with reviewing the case on the record and will not conduct a new trial. Finally, all states have supreme courts, generally referred to as **courts of last resort**. The text provides a discussion of the Florida system to illustrate the various levels of a state court system.

The text also describes the **federal court system**. There are 94 district courts in the federal system. These courts are considered the trial courts of the federal system. The U.S. courts of appeals provide the first level of appeal in the federal system. These courts, often referred to as circuit courts, are responsible for reviewing decisions from the federal district courts. The federal Supreme Court is the most powerful court in the United States. This Court reviews circuit court and state supreme court decisions.

Chapter 9 describes the courtroom work group. The first "professional" courtroom work group member discussed in Chapter 9 is the **judge**. The primary responsibility of the judge is to ensure that justice prevails. The judge is probably the most powerful individual in the courtroom, able to influence the outcome of a case by ruling on matters of law, procedure, and sentence. The text describes the qualifications necessary to be a judge and the selection of judges. Some judges are elected officials, others are appointed, and others are selected by the Missouri Plan. Although judges are generally well respected and highly ethical, the text describes several examples of judicial misconduct.

The prosecuting attorney is responsible for representing the public and thus presents the state's case against the defendant. **Prosecutors**, typically with the help of several assistants, are responsible for deciding the appropriate charges for a defendant, preparing a case for each step of the court process, introducing evidence and witnesses to support the charges at trial, and perhaps advising the police. If the defendant is convicted, prosecutors make sentencing recommendations. The text also describes the significant amount of discretion possessed by prosecutors. Their discretion is limited, however, by a series of court decisions discussed in the text. For example, prosecutors are required to disclose any evidence that the defense requests (*U.S. v. Bagley*).

The prosecutor's main adversary is the **defense attorney**. While the prosecutor is responsible for case and trial preparation on behalf of the state, the defense attorney does the same for the defendant. The text describes the types of attorneys who provide criminal defense in the criminal justice system. In addition, it explains many of the important right-to-counsel cases. According to the Supreme Court's interpretation of the Sixth Amendment, defendants who face imprisonment if convicted and who are too poor to pay for an attorney are appointed counsel. These court decisions have forced states to provide counsel to indigent defendants using an assigned counsel, public defense, or contract arrangement system.

There are various other "professional" members discussed in Chapter 9. The bailiff, for example, keeps order in the courtroom and maintains physical custody of the jury. The local court administrator is responsible for managing the local court. The court reporter creates the record of all that occurs at trial. The clerk of courts maintains court records, swears in witnesses, and marks for identification all physical evidence introduced at trial. Finally, expert witnesses have special knowledge and skills recognized by the court as relevant to the determination of guilt or innocence.

Finally, Chapter 9 discusses the various "nonprofessional courtroom participants." Although not considered members of the courtroom work group, these outsiders can have a significant impact on the trial process. Lay witnesses provide testimony relevant to a specific case. Jurors hear the evidence presented and then make a determination regarding guilt. Crime victims have historically been considered the forgotten members of the criminal justice process, but their standing is changing. The defendant is also considered an outsider, but he or she has to be present at trial and can try to defend himself or herself. Finally, the press is often present in the courtroom, especially in celebrated cases, and may influence trial processes by publicizing facts about the case prior to trial or being present to record and publish trial testimony.

Key Concepts

Appeal: Generally, the request that a court with appellate jurisdiction review the judgment, decision, or order of a lower court and set it aside (reverse it) or modify it.

Appellate Jurisdiction: The lawful authority of a court to review a decision made by a lower court.

Bailiff: The court officer whose duties are to keep order in the courtroom and to maintain physical custody of the jury.

Change of Venue: The movement of a suit or trial from one jurisdiction to another or from one location to another within the same jurisdiction. A change of venue may be made in a criminal case to ensure that the defendant receives a fair trial.

Community Court: A low-level court that focuses on quality-of-life crimes that erode a neighborhood's morale, that emphasizes problem solving rather than punishment, and that builds upon restorative principles like community service and restitution.

Court of Last Resort: The court authorized by law to hear the final appeal on a matter.

Courtroom Work Group: The professional courtroom actors, including judges, prosecuting attorneys, defense attorneys, public defenders, and others who earn a living serving the court.

Defense Counsel: A licensed trial lawyer hired or appointed to conduct the legal defense of an individual accused of a crime and to represent him or her before a court of law. Also called *defense attorney.*

Dispute Resolution Center: An informal hearing place designed to mediate interpersonal disputes without resorting to the more formal arrangements of a criminal trial court.

Expert Witness: A person who has special knowledge and skills recognized by the court as relevant to the determination of guilt or innocence. Unlike lay witnesses, expert witnesses may express opinions or draw conclusions in their testimony.

Federal Court System: The three-tiered structure of federal courts, comprising U.S. district courts, U.S. courts of appeal, and the U.S. Supreme Court.

Judge: An elected or appointed public official who presides over a court of law and who is authorized to hear and sometimes to decide cases and to conduct trials.

Judicial Review: The power of a court to review actions and decisions made by other agencies of government.

Jurisdiction: The territory, subject matter, or people over which a court or other justice agency may exercise lawful authority, as determined by statute or constitution. See also *Venue.*

Juror: A member of a trial or grand jury who has been selected for jury duty and is required to serve as an arbiter of the facts in a court of law. Jurors are expected to render verdicts of "guilty" or "not guilty" as to the charges brought against the accused, although they may sometimes fail to do so (as in the case of a hung jury).

Lay Witness: An eyewitness, character witness, or any other person called upon to testify who is not considered an expert. Lay witnesses must testify to facts only and may not draw conclusions or express opinions.

Original Jurisdiction: The lawful authority of a court to hear or act upon a case from its beginning and to pass judgment on the law and the facts.

Prosecutor: An attorney whose official duty is to conduct criminal proceedings on behalf of the state or the people against those accused of having committed criminal offenses. Also called *county attorney; district attorney (DA); state's attorney; U.S. attorney.*

Prosecutorial Discretion: The decision-making power of prosecutors, based upon the wide range of choices available to them, in the handling of criminal defendants, the scheduling of cases for trial, the acceptance of negotiated pleas, and so on. The most important form of prosecutorial discretion lies in the power to charge, or not to charge, a person with an offense.

Public Defender: An attorney employed by a government agency or subagency, or by a private organization under contract to a government body, for the purpose of providing defense services to indigents or an attorney who has volunteered such service.

State Court Administrator: A coordinator who assists with case-flow management, operating funds budgeting, and court docket administration.

State Court System: A state judicial structure. Most states have at least three court levels: generally, trial courts, appellate courts, and a state supreme court.

Subpoena: A written order issued by a judicial officer or grand jury requiring an individual to appear in court and to give testimony or to bring material to be used as evidence. Some subpoenas mandate that books, papers, and other items be surrendered to the court.

Trial de Novo: Literally, "new trial." The term is applied to cases that are retried on appeal, as opposed to those that are simply reviewed on the record.

Victim-Assistance Program: An organized program that offers services to victims of crime in the areas of crisis intervention and follow-up counseling and that helps victims secure their rights under the law.

Key Cases

Argersinger v. *Hamlin*: The Court required adequate legal representation for anyone facing a potential sentence of imprisonment (407 U.S. 25 [1972]).

Burns v. *Reed*: "A state prosecuting attorney is absolutely immune from liability for damages...for participating in a probable cause hearing, but not for giving legal advice to the police" (*Burns* v. *Reed*, 500 U.S. 478 [1991]).

Crosby v. *U.S.*: A defendant may not be tried in absentia even if he or she was present at the beginning of a trial and his or her absence is due to escape or failure to appear (*Crosby* v. *U.S.*, 113 S.Ct. 748, 122 L.Ed. 2d 25 [1993]).

Demarest v. *Manspeaker*: Federal prisoners who are subpoenaed to testify are entitled to witness fees just as nonincarcerated witnesses would be (*Demarest* v. *Manspeaker et al.*, 498 U.S. 184, 111 S.Ct. 599, 112 L.Ed. 2d 608 [1991]).

Gideon v. *Wainwright*: This case extended the right to appointed counsel in state courts to all indigent defendants charged with a felony (*Gideon* v. *Wainwright*, 372 U.S. 335 [1963]).

REMEMBER

Chapter 7 discussed several landmark cases. Ask students to walk a case, such as *Mapp* v. *Ohio*, through the various tiers of the dual-court structure.

Herrera v. *Collins*: New evidence of innocence is no reason for a federal court to order a new state trial if constitutional grounds are lacking (*Herrera* v. *Collins*, 113 S.Ct. 853, 122 L.Ed. 2d 203 [1993]).

Imbler v. *Pachtman*: Held that state prosecutors are absolutely immune from liability for their conduct in initiating a prosecution and in presenting the state's case (*Imbler* v. *Pachtman*, 424 U.S. 409 [1976]).

Keeney v. *Tamayo-Reyes* (1992): A defendant is entitled to a federal evidentiary hearing only "if he can show cause for his failure to develop the facts in the state-court proceedings and actual prejudice resulting from that failure, or if he can show that a fundamental miscarriage of justice would result from failure to hold such a hearing." (*Keeney, Superintendent, Oregon State Penitentiary* v. *Tamayo-Reyes*, 113 S.Ct. 853, 122 L.Ed. 2d 203 [1992]).

Marbury v. *Madison*: In this case, the court established its authority as the final interpreter of the U.S. Constitution (*Marbury* v. *Madison*, 1 Cranch 5 U.S. 137).

Zafiro v. *U.S.*: Defendants charged in federal courts with similar or related offenses may be tried together—even when their defenses differ substantially (*Zafiro* v. *U.S.*, 113 S.Ct. 933, 122 L.Ed. 2d 317 [1993]).

Learning Tips

Learning to Write

One of the most important skills you can acquire is the ability to write well. The ability to communicate effectively in writing is essential for professional success. Although learning to write can be a painful learning process, the investment you make in developing your skills now will have long-term benefits. The best way to improve your writing skills is to have others review your work and provide constructive criticism. Thus, be a frequent visitor to your university writing center, ask friends and fellow students to critique your work, and learn from the feedback you receive from your professors.

Essay Questions on Exams

Essay questions cause anxiety for many students. To reduce anxiety, read the entire question first. Then reread the question, underlining key words and noting specific parts and instructions within the question. Write a quick outline. This will keep your answer focused, as well as minimizing your chances of forgetting important parts. Finally, because the grading of essay exams is partly subjective, it is good practice to write legibly, skip lines, keep your answers concise, and use only one side of the paper.

CJ Today on the World Wide Web

Web links to organizations and agencies related to the material in Chapter 9 include:

WEBSITE TITLE	URL
Supreme Court of the United States	http://www.supremecourtus.gov
U.S. Federal Judiciary	http://www.uscourts.gov
Federal Courts	http://www.law.emory.edu/FEDCTS
National Center for State Courts	http://www.ncsconline.org
Professional Bail Agents of the United States	http://www.pbus.com
CourtTV On-Line	http://www.courttv.com
Courts.Net	http://www.courts.net
Florida CyberCourt Home Page	http://www.flcourts.org
International Court of Justice	http://www.icj-cij.org

Student Activities

Activity 1

Chapter 9 describes Florida's court system. Choose a state other than Florida and see if you can determine the court structure and jurisdiction of courts in that state. In the space provided below, compare and contrast what you learn about your chosen state with the Florida system.

_____

_____

_____

_____

_____

_____

Activity 2

Determine whether there is a dispute-resolution center near you. If so, visit that center to learn more about it. Interview professionals and volunteers who work for the center to determine the types of cases handled, the caseload, and how the center supports or replaces traditional court processes. If you are unable to locate a dispute-resolution center, then visit three websites that deal with dispute-resolution and mediation issues. The Web links list several outstanding sites. Discuss what you learned about dispute-resolution centers in the space provided below.

_____

_____

_____

_____

_____

Activity 3

The Supreme Court is one of the most powerful institutions in America. The decisions of this court have had significant impact on both social and criminal justice issues. Some of the greatest legal minds of American history served as justices of the Supreme Court. Through this activity, you will learn more about a justice who served on the Supreme Court. You can choose a current member of the Court or any other historic justice. Use the Web and media databases to identify and gather information about the justice you selected. Use your university library to find additional information. In the space provided below, write a description of the justice you selected, and include a discussion of some of the important cases that he or she helped decide.

_____

_____

_____

_____

_____

Activity 4

Ethical issues for the courtroom work group: Put yourself in the place of each courtroom work group participant listed below and explain how you would handle each dilemma.

THE PROSECUTOR

1. While preparing the case against an accused arson defendant, you discover a witness who provides an alibi for the defendant. Do you tell the defense attorney about your discovery? Would it make any difference if the defendant were involved in organized crime? What if the defendant were charged with murder and arson?

2. After you have successfully prosecuted a rapist, you uncover evidence that indicates that the victim in the case created the story to avenge a love affair that went sour. What do you do? What would you do if you knew that the suspect was charged with rape on two other occasions but was not convicted due to legal technicalities?

THE DEFENSE ATTORNEY

1. You are asked to represent a defendant who cannot afford to pay your full fee at the present time. Should you work out an arrangement so that your client pays you a $1,000 retainer now and pays the rest of the fee if and when she is acquitted (recognizing that conviction would result in incarceration and no real opportunity to earn the money for your fee)?

2. Your client informs you that she did in fact murder her mom. Should you inform the court of this information? Possessing such knowledge, should you allow your client to take the stand and deny her guilt?

THE JUDGE

1. At arraignment, you ask a defendant if he has yet obtained counsel. He replies that he wants to defend himself. He has a fifth-grade education and works as a day laborer for a local construction firm. He is charged with armed robbery and faces ten years in prison. Should you let him defend himself?

2. You are assigned to preside over a jury trial in a gruesome homicide case that has been widely publicized in the area. Although the defense does not request it, should you order a change of venue?

_____

_____

_____

_____

_____

Internet Activity

Use the Cybrary (http://www.cybrary.info) to locate a detailed description of a state court system (perhaps the court system in your home state). Describe the various courts that comprise the system, the staff roles, and the administrative agencies (for example, the administrative office of state courts). Outline the functions of each.

_____

_____

_____

_____

_____

Distance Learning Activity

This distance learning assignment is designed to help you learn more about the United States Supreme Court. Visit the Supreme Court's website at http://www.supremecourt us.gov. Explore the various links from this page. List ten facts that you learned about the Supreme Court from this exercise. Submit these facts if your instructor asks you to do so.

_____

_____

_____

_____

_____

_____

Student Study Guide Questions

True or False

____ 9-1. The prosecution must disclose any evidence related to a case that the defense requests.

____ 9-2. The federal court system consists of three tiers, including the U.S. district courts, U.S. courts of appeal, and the U.S. Supreme Court.

____ 9-3. Federal judges are usually elected officials who then serve life terms on the bench.

____ 9-4. The case of *Marbury* v. *Madison*, decided in 1803, was the first instance in which the U.S. Supreme Court declared its authority to review the actions of Congress to determine whether they comply or conflict with the Constitution.

____ 9-5. In the 1993 case of *Herrera* v. *Collins*, the U.S. Supreme Court ruled that new evidence of innocence is not a sufficient reason for a federal court to order a new state trial if there are no constitutional grounds for appeal.

____ 9-6. The phrase "courtroom work group" refers to all persons who are licensed to practice law and who earn their living primarily in the courtroom.

____ 9-7. The jurisdiction of a court can refer to the territory, subject matter, or persons over which a court may lawfully exercise its authority.

____ 9-8. A defense attorney who is aware that her client is about to commit perjury on the stand is obligated to inform the court of this fact, even if it violates the attorney-client privilege.

____ 9-9. The Missouri Plan is a method typically used to select state prosecutors.

____ 9-10. Dispute-resolution centers are generally not allowed to mediate disputes when criminal charges are pending against either of the disputants.

Multiple Choice

9-11. *Indigency* refers to criteria used by
a. the courts to establish the amount of bail.
b. judges to determine eligibility of defendants for court-appointed counsel.
c. the state police in establishing crime enforcement levels.
d. the prosecutor's office to determine a witness's reliability.

9-12. State courts are generally divided into three levels, with _____ at the top of the hierarchy.
   a. courts of limited jurisdiction
   b. intermediate appellate courts
   c. courts of last resort
   d. trial courts

9-13. When the U.S. Supreme Court orders the lower court to "forward up the record" of a case that has been tried so the high court can review it, it issues a
   a. writ of trial *de novo*.
   b. *nolo contendere*.
   c. writ of *mandamus*.
   d. writ of *certiorari*.

9-14. The Missouri Plan is a mechanism suggested by the American Bar Association for
   a. limiting judicial discretion during sentencing.
   b. the merit plan selection of judges.
   c. reducing endless appeals by defendants.
   d. speeding the flow of cases through the courts.

9-15. The *jurisdiction* of a court is
   a. the geographic area it covers.
   b. the subject matter it deals with.
   c. its place in the hierarchy of the court system.
   d. all of the above.

9-16. State court administrators are responsible for all of the following except
   a. training support personnel.
   b. ruling on issues of law.
   c. managing court case flow.
   d. coordinating between state court levels and jurisdiction.

9-17. As discussed in the text, criminal law is a field that
   a. attracts many prestigious lawyers.
   b. is a high-status segment of the legal profession.
   c. few law students actively choose to pursue.
   d. has high financial rewards for most practitioners.

9-18. Under the _____ system, legal services for defendants are provided by private practice attorneys paid for by the court and selected from a roster of all practicing criminal attorneys within the jurisdiction of the court.
   a. retained counsel
   b. contract
   c. public defender
   d. court-appointed counsel

9-19. In *Gideon* v. *Wainwright* (1963), the U.S. Supreme Court held that
   a. in federal cases, the right to counsel becomes applicable as soon as a defendant is arrested.
   b. the right to counsel applies not only to state trials of defendants charged with felonies but in all trials of defendants that might result in a jail sentence.
   c. a defendant has a right to counsel when submitting a guilty plea to the court for any offense.
   d. the right to appointed counsel applies to all indigent defendants in state court who are charged with a felony.

9-20. The 1803 case of _____ established the U.S. Supreme Court's authority as final interpreter of the U.S. Constitution.
   a. *Marbury* v. *Madison*
   b. *Herrera* v. *Collins*
   c. *McNabb* v. *U.S.*
   d. *Brady* v. *U.S.*

Fill-In

9-21. The court officer who keeps order in the courtroom and maintains custody of the jury is the _____.

9-22. _____ of general jurisdiction are the first level of appeal from trial courts of limited jurisdiction.

9-23. _____ involves moving a trial from one jurisdiction to another.

9-24. The _____ assists with the management of cases, budgeting, and docket administration.

9-25. _____ means, literally, "new trial."

9-26. The highest level appellate court in a state system is often referred to as the _____ because no legal recourse remains available to the defendant within the state system.

9-27. The lawful authority of a court to review a decision made by a lower court is called _____.

9-28. A _____ is issued when an appellate court agrees to hear a case. It orders the lower court to forward up the records of the case.

9-29. A(n) _____ is a person who has special knowledge recognized by the court as relevant to the determination of the guilt or innocence of the accused.

9-30. A(n) _____ is a written order requiring someone to appear in court to testify.

Crossword Puzzle

Across

2. All who earn a living serving the court.
3. To review the judgment, decision, or order of a lower court.
5. The person who tries to maintain order in the court.
7. An elected or appointed public official who presides over a court of law and who is authorized to hear and sometimes to decide cases and to conduct trials.
8. An eyewitness is this type of witness.
9. A new trial.
10. A court that focuses on quality-of-life crimes.
11. Authority of a court to hear a case from its beginning and to pass judgment.
12. A written order that requires a person to appear at a designated court.

Down

1. The U.S. district courts, U.S. courts of appeal, and the U.S. Supreme Court.
2. The court authorized by law to hear the final appeal on a matter.
3. Authority of a court to review a decision made by a lower court.
4. The motion sometimes used in a high-profile case.
6. The power of a court to review actions and decisions made by other agencies of government.
7. Six or 12 persons make up this.

Word Search Puzzle

```
U O R S T P I B M O I U S N I E S S E N T I W T R E P X E O
F A A R U F D P R O S E C U T O R U H E E R R U U S P R E U
U A E T I N T W M J O T U D I O A O O O R Y O F E D I O E E
A E Y A D O A O E P R J M F L R U D L I O M T E P W Y V O T
N F A S R I R I T D L S N O P J T U A E R D O O E S I U O I
T B W E C T T O S U N T A T R Y R V E S U T R O J C P F C S
R D S X U C E S Y C O E C W C V G N N U J I F U T I J S I E
S I O M T I D L S O L A E P P A A F C I D U E I P R I R B A
P A S C F D R L T R M J T M A D U E P J E O M T U S I A N O
U S S P N S P R R E T P U N I I C D P E I A E N B A I C E L
O T E L I I I U U C C N M D A T R U C P S N A Y L L I S C O
I O E N S R C A O C M E A T I I O O U S O E X A I F O D E O
O U R E N U E C C R U O I S O C M U I G W R Y F C I A R C T
R S I T P J E I L O G R E A I M I S P I V O F A D N S E A G
J E S L P T S E A U F K E R U S T A E E M I E M E S T D O L
J C D E I R L A R T O D R N B A C O L E I Y D U F U N M D E
E C E L E E E T E O E F I O N T V E T R G I E U E B T U O R
S S N I A C R P D K N T V C W O A S U O E D E A N P C A T C
W E D S P Y V M E E Y B E U N M Y P S N M V U M D O A M C R
U A T U A T W A F C O P R E R S O E S A E R I J E E R A O S
T S L S U E C I O T R U D R T O L O I G G V G E R N U R W E
G R R I S N N U T O N L A R O E R M R T D I F R W A E I E F
L O R R A I R A G N A W U A U V C R A T E P L O R Y V R O W
T S L S R T A R U I E O C S O E E E V U R R E C E P I U T U
P T D R S O A T R U C S C O P R Y V Y A E U I L K G N M T N
N T R T N M T T E E E S S I P A U B S G R W O R J O N N L U
T J A U F O R S T E T R P T M T U L N E S C O C R R Y A E J
S U C R O A R A N N E T D E F E N S E A T T O R N E Y P H O
O U F L E I T G N O I T C I D S I R U J E T A L L E P P A C
A C M T A S J R E A O I L S N B O C W G D C O Y P U S O B O
```

Appeal
Appellate Jurisdiction
Bailiff
Change of Venue
Community Court
Courtroom Word Group
Defense Attorney
Expert Witness
Federal Court System
Judge

Judicial Review
Jurisdiction
Juror
Lay Witness
Prosecutor
Public Defender
State Court System
Supoena
Trial *de Novo*
Victim-Assistance Program

Pretrial Activities and the Criminal Trial

OUTLINE

LEARNING OBJECTIVES

After reading this chapter, you should be able to:

- List and explain the steps typically taken during pretrial activities

- Explain plea-bargaining, and discuss its impact on the criminal justice system

- Describe the various stages of a criminal trial

- Explain the hearsay rule, and identify recognized exceptions to it

- Explain the possible benefits of a professional jury system

- Describe methods that have been suggested for improving the adjudication process

Chapter Summary

A fundamental concept of criminal justice in the United States is that the criminal justice system is an adversarial system. Justice is achieved when a talented adversary is able to convince a judge or jury that his or her perspective is the correct one. Chapter 10 focuses on two issues central to understanding this adversarial system. First, the text describes the pretrial activities. Second, the text describes the trial process.

Chapter 10 describes the early steps of the long and arduous court process. Usually within 48 hours after arrest, a suspect appears before a judge for his or her **first appearance**. During this stage, the legality of the arrest is assessed, the defendant is informed of the charges, and the decision on whether to release or detain pending trial is made. Judges have several bail options as well as a number of alternatives. Some alternative bail programs include: **release on recognizance (ROR)**; **property bonds**; **deposit bail**; **conditional release**; **third-party custody**; **unsecured bond**; and **signature bond**. Suspects then experience either a **grand jury hearing** or a **preliminary hearing**. There are significant differences between these two types of hearings, but the purpose of both is to filter cases out of the system if there is insufficient evidence to pursue the charges. Finally, the defendant is again informed of the charges and asked to make a plea at the **arraignment** stage. Defendants will plead either guilty, not guilty, or *nolo contendere* (no contest).

This chapter also provides a discussion of **plea-bargaining**. Think of plea-bargaining as a negotiation process that involves the defendant, defense counsel, and the prosecutor. Defendants frequently waive their right to a trial and plead guilty, hoping to get something in return, such as a reduced sentence. Prosecutors and defense attorneys also benefit from the plea-bargaining process because it helps keep cases moving through the court system.

Chapter 10 concludes with a discussion of the trial process. Once initiated, the first step in the trial process is **jury selection**. Attorneys, and in some jurisdictions the judge, select members of the jury through the *voir dire* process. Potential jurors can be dismissed by using **challenges for cause** and **peremptory challenges**. After the jury is selected, the prosecution and defense will make **opening statements**. After these statements are completed, then the prosecution and the defense present various types of evidence, such as **real**, **circumstantial**, and **direct**. **Closing arguments** provide a review and a summation of the evidence. The judge then charges the jury and provides instructions on deliberation. Finally, the jury deliberates on the evidence presented during the trial and returns to the court with a verdict.

Key Concepts

Adversarial System: The two-sided structure under which American criminal trial courts operate that pits the prosecution against the defense. In theory, justice is done when the most effective adversary is able to convince the judge or jury that his or her perspective on the case is the correct one.

Bail Bond: A document guaranteeing the appearance of the defendant in court as required and recording the pledge of money or property to be paid to the court if he or she does not appear, which is signed by the person to be released and anyone else acting in his or her behalf.

Circumstantial Evidence: Evidence that requires interpretation or that requires a judge or jury to reach a conclusion based upon what the evidence indicates. From the close proximity of a smoking gun to the defendant, for example, the jury might conclude that she pulled the trigger.

Closing Argument: An oral summation of a case presented to a judge, or to a judge and jury, by the prosecution or by the defense in a criminal trial.

Competent to Stand Trial: A finding by a court, when the defendant's sanity at the time of trial is at issue, that the defendant has sufficient present ability to consult with his or her attorney with a reasonable degree of rational understanding and that the defendant has a rational as well as factual understanding of the proceedings against him or her.

Conditional Release: The release by executive decision of a prisoner from a federal or state correctional facility who has not served his or her full sentence and whose freedom is contingent on obeying specified rules of behavior.

Danger Law: A law intended to prevent the pretrial release of criminal defendants judged to represent a danger to others in the community.

Direct Evidence: Evidence that, if believed, directly proves a fact. Eyewitness testimony and videotaped documentation account for the majority of all direct evidence heard in the criminal courtroom.

Evidence: Anything useful to a judge or jury in deciding the facts of a case. Evidence may take the form of witness testimony, written documents, videotapes, magnetic media, photographs, physical objects, and so on.

First Appearance: An appearance before a magistrate during which the legality of a defendant's arrest is initially assessed and the defendant informed of the charges on which he or she is being held. At this stage in the criminal justice process, bail may be set or pretrial release arranged. Also called *initial appearance.*

Hearsay: Something that is not based upon the personal knowledge of a witness. Witnesses who testify about something they have heard, for example, are offering hearsay by repeating information about a matter of which they have no direct knowledge.

Hearsay Rule: The long-standing precedent that hearsay cannot be used in American courtrooms. Rather than accepting testimony based upon hearsay, the court will ask that the person who was the original source of the hearsay information be brought into court to be questioned and cross-examined. Exceptions to the hearsay rule may occur when the person with direct knowledge is dead or is otherwise unable to testify.

Jury Selection: The process whereby, according to law and precedent, members of a particular trial jury are chosen.

Nolo Contendere: A plea of "no contest." A no-contest plea may be used when the defendant does not wish to contest conviction. Because the plea does not admit guilt, however, it cannot provide the basis for later civil suits that might follow upon the heels of a criminal conviction.

Opening Statement: The initial statement of an attorney or the defense, made in a court of law to a judge, or to a judge and jury, describing the facts that he or she intends to present during trial to prove the case.

Peremptory Challenge: The right to challenge a potential juror without disclosing the reason for the challenge. Prosecutors and defense attorneys routinely use peremptory challenges to eliminate from juries individuals who, although they express no obvious bias, are thought to be capable of swaying the jury in an undesirable direction.

Perjury: The intentional making of a false statement as part of the testimony by a sworn witness in a judicial proceeding on a matter relevant to the case at hand.

Plea: In criminal proceedings, a defendant's formal answer in court to the charge contained in a complaint, information, or indictment that he or she is guilty or is not guilty of the offense charged or does not contest the charge.

Plea-Bargaining: The process of negotiating an agreement among the defendant, the prosecutor, and the court as to an appropriate plea and associated sentence in a given case. Plea-bargaining circumvents the trial process and dramatically reduces the time required for the resolution of a criminal case.

Pretrial Release: The release of an accused person from custody, for all or part of the time before or during prosecution, upon his or her promise to appear in court when required.

Property Bond: The setting of bail in the form of land, houses, stocks, or other tangible property. In the event that the defendant absconds prior to trial, the bond becomes the property of the court.

Real Evidence: Evidence consisting of physical material or traces of physical activity.

Release on Recognizance (ROR): The pretrial release of a criminal defendant on his or her written promise to appear in court as required. No cash or property bond is required.

Rules of Evidence: Rules of court that govern the admissibility of evidence at a criminal hearing and trial.

Scientific Jury Selection: The use of correlational techniques from the social sciences to gauge the likelihood that potential jurors will vote for conviction or acquittal.

Sequestered Jury: A jury that is isolated from the public during the course of a trial and throughout the deliberation process.

Speedy Trial Act: A 1974 federal law requiring that proceedings against a defendant in a criminal case begin within a specified period of time, such as 70 working days after indictment. Some states also have speedy trial requirements.

Testimony: Oral evidence offered by a sworn witness on the witness stand during a criminal trial.

Verdict: The decision of the jury in a jury trial or of a judicial officer in a nonjury trial.

Key Cases

County of Riverside (CA) v. *McLaughlin:* "A jurisdiction that provides judicial determinations of probable cause within 48 hours of arrest will, as a general matter, comply with the promptness requirement." Weekends and holidays are not excluded from this 48-hour provision, and in some cases, an even quicker arraignment may be appropriate (*County of Riverside* v. *McLaughlin*, 111 S.Ct. 1661 [1991]).

Coy v. *Iowa:* The Supreme Court ruled that a courtroom screen used to shield child witnesses from visual confrontation violated the Sixth Amendment's confrontation clause (*Coy* v. *Iowa*, 487 U.S. 1012, 108 S.Ct. 2798 [1988]).

Doggett v. *U.S.:* A delay of 8 1/2 years violated the speedy trial provisions because it resulted from government negligence (*Doggett* v. *U.S.*, 112 S.Ct. 2686 [1992]).

Edmonson v. *Leesville Concrete Co., Inc.:* Peremptory challenges based on race are not acceptable in civil lawsuits (*Edmonson* v. *Leesville Concrete Co., Inc.*, 500 U.S. 614, 111 S.Ct. 2077, 114 L.Ed. 2d 660 [1991]).

Fex v. *Michigan:* Ruled that the 180-day speedy trial provision does not commence until the prisoner's disposition request has actually been delivered to the court and to the prosecutor of the jurisdiction that lodged the detainer against him (*Fex* v. *Michigan*, 113 S.Ct. 1085, 122 L.Ed. 2d 406 [1993]).

Georgia v. *McCollum:* Defendants (and their attorneys) cannot use peremptory challenges to exclude potential jurors on the basis of race (*Georgia* v. *McCollum*, 505 U.S. 42 [1992]).

Idaho v. *Wright:* The Court stated that statements by children are fraught with unreliability, which the confrontation clause is designed to highlight and obviate (*Idaho* v. *Wright*, 497 U.S. 805 [1990]).

Maryland v. *Craig*: Closed-circuit television can be used to shield children who testify in criminal courts (*Maryland* v. *Craig*, 497 U.S. 836, 845–847 [1990]).

McNabb v. *U.S.*: Established that any unreasonable delay in an initial court appearance would make confessions inadmissible if interrogating officers obtained them during the delay (*McNabb.* v. *U.S.*, 318 U.S. 332 [1943]).

Michigan v. *Lucas*: Sixth Amendment guarantee of the right to confront witnesses does not necessarily extend to evidence of a prior sexual relationship between a rape victim and a criminal defendant, and thus rape shield statutes are acceptable (*Michigan* v. *Lucas*, 500 U.S. 145 [1992]).

Miller-El v. *Cockrell*: The Supreme Court found that the prosecutor engaged an intentional effort to remove eligible African-Americans from the jury pool (*Miller-El* v. *Cockrell*, No. 01-7662 [U.S. Supreme Court, decided 2003]).

Mu'Min v. *Virginia*: Being aware of a case through pretrial publicity alone is not enough to disqualify a juror. If a prospective juror can be shown to be unbiased by the publicity, he or she can serve (*Mu'Min* v. *Virginia*, 500 U.S. 415 [1991]).

Powers v. *Ohio*: Prosecution cannot systematically exclude jurors on the basis of race through the use of peremptory challenges (*Powers* v. *Ohio*, 499 U.S. 400 [1991]).

Santobello v. *New York*: Plea-bargaining is an important and necessary component of the American system of justice (*Santobello* v. *New York*, 404 U.S. 257 [1971]).

U.S. v. *Montalvo-Murillo*: A defendant has no right to freedom simply because of a "minor" violation of the provisions of the federal Bail Reform Act of 1984 (*U.S.* v. *Montalvo-Murillo*, 495 U.S. 711 [1990]).

White v. *Illinois*: In-court testimony given by a medical provider and the child's babysitter, who repeated what the child had said to them concerning the defendant's sexually abusive behavior, was not subject to hearsay restrictions and was permissible (*White* v. *Illinois*, 112 S.Ct. 736 [1992]).

Zafiro v. *U.S.*: Defendants charged in federal courts with similar or related offenses may be tried together—even when their defenses differ substantially (*Zafiro* v. *U.S.*, 113 S.Ct. 933, 122 L.Ed. 2d 317 [1993]).

Learning Tips

Study Groups I

Group study can be very beneficial. However, make sure to select individuals who are attentive in class, who ask questions, and who participate and take notes. While it is good to join people who have similar academic standards, it is also useful to form groups of individuals from diverse backgrounds. The difference in backgrounds may offer a variety of perspectives and better insight to the course material. Last, keep the size to fewer than six people. Large groups are often counterproductive to effective studying.

Study Groups II

A variety of purposes can be accomplished with study groups. Reviewing class lectures could help answer questions or clarify uncertainties in your notes. Groups can practice quizzing one another. Closer to test time, study groups are a great source for compiling potential test questions. Also, general discussions within the group are a great way to learn the material and reinforce your memory.

CJ Today on the World Wide Web

Web links to organizations and agencies related to the material in Chapter 10 include:

WEBSITE TITLE	URL
Office of the U.S. Attorney General	http://www.usdoj.gov/ag
American Bar Foundation	http://www.abf-sociolegal.org
Prosecuting Attorneys, District Attorneys, Attorneys General and U.S. Attorneys	http://www.co.eaton.mi.us/ecpa/proslist.htm
Delaware Public Defender Home Page	http://www.state.de.us/govern/agencies/pubdefen/indexpd.htm
Federal Magistrate Judges' Association	http://www.fedjudge.org
Illinois Office of the State Appellate Defender	http://www.state.il.us/defender
National Jurist Online For Future Lawyers	http://www.natjurist.com
New York State Defenders Association	http://www.nysda.org
Citizens for Effective Justice	http://www.reducecrime.org
Trial Lawyers for Public Justice	http://www.tlpj.org

Student Activities

Activity 1

BAIL OR NO BAIL?

1. Salvadore Lopez is a 52-year-old farm worker who cannot read. He has a wife and two children. Lopez was charged with smuggling guns, marijuana, and other narcotics across the Mexican border. The prosecutor, when discussing the case with the news media, says that he suspects Mr. Lopez was involved with guns and drugs for years but, until now, has avoided being arrested by authorities. Mr. Lopez claims that he is completely innocent and wouldn't know what marijuana looked like if he saw it. Should he be detained or released? How much bail would you set in order to release? What other information would you need to know?

2. Roger A. Kooney is a 27-year-old electrical engineer. Kooney is charged with vehicular homicide stemming from the death of Chris Pariano. Pariano was stepping out of his pickup truck when Kooney sped down the wrong side of the street. Kooney was drunk at the time, according to police. The police also learned that he had eight previous convictions for drunken driving and 19 other serious vehicular offenses. Should he be detained or released? How much bail would you set in order to release? What other information would you need to know?

3. Edward Savitz is a 50-year-old single man who has a good-paying full-time job and lives in an expensive high-rise apartment. He is charged with the statutory rape of a 16-year-old, sexual abuse of two others, and corrupting the morals of a minor. It is alleged that he paid to have sex with hundreds of boys, but on all occasions the young men agreed to participate. The maximum sentence that he can receive for his crimes is five to ten years. Mr. Savitz has tested positive for HIV, the virus that causes AIDS. Should he be detained or released? How much bail would you set in order to release? What other information would you need to know?

4. At the age of 19 Frank Anderson was convicted of rape and sentenced to prison for three years. Approximately one year after his release, he became a suspect in a number of robberies of women. He threatened a number of the victims with bodily harm if they filed complaints. One 21-year-old victim nevertheless agreed to cooperate with the authorities, and Anderson was arrested and charged with robbery. Shortly after his initial appearance, he was released on bail. Anderson then broke into the 21-year-old woman's house, beat her, kicked her numerous times, and stole $3,000 and a gun. The victim suffered a concussion and needed seven stitch-

es. Anderson was identified and again apprehended and was charged with an additional count of robbery. Should he be detained or released? How much bail would you set in order to release? What other factors would you need to know?

5. An 18-year-old girl, Kim Walak, was arrested for shoplifting. She claimed to be indigent (poor), with no steady source of income; she lived with an unemployed boyfriend; and she had dropped out of school in the eleventh grade. She had one prior arrest for shoplifting, but those charges were dismissed for unknown reasons. Should she be detained or released? How much bail would you set in order to release? What other factors would you need to know?

_____

_____

_____

_____

_____

Activity 2

Historically, courts have resisted allowing cameras in our nation's courtrooms out of a fear that it would adversely impact a defendant's right to fair trial. Courts were concerned that the media's search for the sensational would turn our courtrooms into sideshows. For example, when Bruno Hauptmann was accused of kidnapping the Lindbergh baby, he was convicted in an atmosphere of circus sensationalism that degraded the entire judicial process. Among other things, the prosecutor gave newspaper interviews constantly; although the judge prohibited cameras from taking pictures, a reporter brought a camera into the courtroom and took pictures; and, during the trial, the public applauded state witnesses. Hauptmann was convicted, and appellate courts ruled that the publicity did not bias the final decision. Recently the U.S. Supreme Court decided that it was not unconstitutional for cameras to be in our nation's courtrooms. As discussed in the text, the majority of states now permit such coverage.

Do you think cameras should be allowed in trial courts of general jurisdiction? Be sure to discuss the pros and cons of having cameras in the courtroom. Do you think cameras influence jury verdicts? Why or why not?

_____

_____

_____

_____

_____

Activity 3

Go to the CourtTV website at http://www.courttv.com. This website provides a discussion of many current and famous cases that have received publicity across the country. Choose one of the cases presented on the website and read the facts of the case. In the space provided below, write an opening statement for the prosecutor and an opening statement for the defense attorney. Be sure to use the facts of the case in your statement.

_____

_____

_____

_____

_____

_____

Activity 4

Attend a trial at a local courthouse. In the space provided below, describe the case and the steps of the trial you saw. Were you able to see the complete trial? What was the verdict? Was a jury present? What trial stages did you see? What types of witnesses were called to present evidence? What types of evidence were presented? Was the victim present? What was the defendant's demeanor during testimony? Did the jury appear to be attentive?

_____

_____

_____

_____

_____

_____

Internet Activity

Visit Cornell University Law School's Legal Information Institute at http://www.law.cornell.edu. Describe each of the site's features, paying special attention to the resources available in the sections entitled "Court Opinions," "Law by Source or Jurisdiction," and "Constitutions and Codes." After exploring each feature, describe in detail those that you find most useful. Why do you especially like those features?

_____

_____

_____

_____

_____

_____

Distance Learning Activity

This distance learning exercise will be challenging and time-consuming, but it is an effective way to highlight the stages of the criminal trial. Search the World Wide Web for information about a specific criminal trial. In the space below, highlight the key facts of the case. What facts do you think the prosecutor will emphasize? What facts will the defense attorney emphasize?

_____

_____

_____

_____

_____

Student Study Guide Questions

True or False

_____ 10-1. The process by which a potential juror is interviewed by the prosecutor and defense counsel is *voir dire*.

_____ 10-2. If a defendant chooses not to testify at his or her trial, the prosecutor is allowed to point out to the jury that an innocent person would want to take the stand in an effort to clear his or her name.

_____ 10-3. When using a challenge for cause, a juror can be excused by either the defense or prosecution and no reason for doing so needs to be stated.

_____ 10-4. Grand juries meet in secret, and a person under investigation has no legal right to be present or even notified of a grand jury investigation.

_____ 10-5. The U.S. Supreme Court has ruled that plea-bargaining is an important and necessary component of the American system of justice.

_____ 10-6. A witness's statement that she didn't see the defendant commit the crime but did see him arguing with and threatening the victim shortly before the crime occurred is an example of circumstantial evidence.

_____ 10-7. A sequestered jury is isolated from the public during the course of a trial and throughout the deliberation process.

_____ 10-8. A challenge to the array indicates that the defense attorney does not believe that the pool from which the jury is being selected is representative of the community at large.

_____ 10-9. According to the decision in *McNabb* v. *United States*, a person in custody must have an appearance in court within 48 hours of his or her arrest.

_____ 10-10. Hearsay evidence is automatically excluded from the courtroom, regardless of the circumstances.

Multiple Choice

10-11. The _____ is a sort of "mini-trial" that allows the defendant to challenge the legal basis for his or her detention by examining the evidence in the case and attempting to have it disallowed or refuted.
  a. grand jury
  b. arraignment
  c. preliminary hearing
  d. first appearance

10-12. A purpose of bail is to
  a. examine the sufficiency of the evidence against the accused.
  b. ensure the appearance of the accused individual at trial.
  c. deter future offenses.
  d. protect the community from criminals.

10-13. _____ programs release defendants on their own after a promise to appear at court, with no requirement for posting a cash or property bond.
  a. Voluntary community release
  b. Signature bond
  c. Preventive detention
  d. Release on recognizance

10-14. A grand jury has all of the following characteristics and duties except that it does not
  a. determine if an accused individual should be held over for an actual trial.
  b. meet in secret, with no opportunity for the accused to cross-examine witnesses.

   c. have the option to initiate prosecution independent of the prosecutor.
   d. deliver a verdict of guilty or not guilty in criminal trials.

10-15. The advantage of a plea of *nolo contendere* over a guilty plea is that it
   a. usually results in a lighter sentence for the offender.
   b. protects the accused in the event of a subsequent civil suit.
   c. limits the judge's sentencing alternatives.
   d. allows the defendant to use a legal loophole to avoid responsibility.

10-16. In what year did Congress pass the federal Speedy Trial Act?
   a. 2000
   b. 1985
   c. 1980
   d. 1974

10-17. In jury selection, challenges for cause
   a. are only made by the defense.
   b. are not required to be justified by the attorney requesting the challenge.
   c. deal with sound legal reasons for removing potential jurors.
   d. are ruled upon by the prosecuting attorney.

10-18. Which Constitutional Amendment guarantees a right to an impartial jury?
   a. Fourth
   b. Sixth
   c. Fifth
   d. Eighth

10-19. *Voir dire* is used to determine
   a. judicial bias.
   b. if prospective jurors are biased or hold preconceived notions of guilt or innocence.
   c. the validity of a claim of prosecutorial misconduct.
   d. whether the racial makeup of an impaneled jury violates Supreme Court guidelines.

10-20. The murder weapon would primarily be considered _____ evidence.
   a. direct
   b. real
   c. testimonial
   d. damning

Fill-In

10-21. _____ is that which requires interpretation or that which requires the judge or jury to reach a conclusion based upon what the evidence indicates.

10-22. _____ consists of physical material or traces of physical activity such as tire tracks.

10-23. Removing an unwanted potential juror without the need to disclose a reason for their removal is accomplished by means of a _____.

10-24. _____ is the pretrial release of a defendant based on a written promise to appear at future hearings.

10-25. An appearance before a magistrate at which the legality of the defendant's arrest is reviewed and the defendant is informed of the charges is called the _____.

10-26. A _____ is a sort of "mini-trial" in which the defendant has the opportunity to challenge the legal basis for his or her detention by examining the evidence in the case and attempting to refute it.

10-27. _____ is a false statement made by a sworn witness during a judicial proceeding.

10-28. _____ is a plea of "no contest."

10-29. Court rules that govern the admissibility of evidence at criminal hearings and trials are called _____.

10-30. _____ is a statement that is not based upon the personal knowledge of a witness.

Crossword Puzzle

Across

1. The decision of the jury.
4. The two-sided structure under which American criminal trial courts operate that pits the prosecution against the defense.
6. There is a limited number of this type of challenge.
7. A jury isolated from the public.
9. No contest.
10. The initial statement of an attorney.
12. Release by promise.
13. Oral evidence offered by a sworn witness.

Down

2. Evidence that requires interpretation.
3. The process of negotiating an agreement among the defendant, the prosecutor, and the court as to an appropriate plea and associated sentence in a given case.
5. This law establishes the time periods required for a case to be processed by the court system.
6. What one commits when they lie on the witness stand.
8. An oral summation of a case.
11. Court stage at which bail is typically set.

Word Search Puzzle

```
V I E E N C C P D E D L E T L E R O I P C E P I A N J S N N
P M O C D L E R I C R R E R L E I S E O S V E S D I S O E S
E I Q E N T L E E A T U G E R T E C S I N G T A A O R L J Y
A T E R U A V T E G N M T D A V A I I S I C L E N Y N N R S
E A E E R Z Z R C V U E E D A E T E R R Y I I D G E I U E E
I N E A R E C I Z E O P L E A P C N S S T Y N S E O F P P G
E N E N E Y A A N G E L I O I N T T E S T M L J R R E E T N
C F N C C A P L A G A T D R C V I I E S C E R A L N J E E E
E E H R S S R E R O H N R E A L F U N T C R R A R E E A L
M C T F S R L E P V E C S E E O A I E R I T T I W F C E G L
I N O L S A N L E R I C E F M L I C D R N N T E M N N T L A
N A S P C E N E I R O D E R S U N J C N T I E N E E T R E H
O R P C E H I A D B G D E T N S G U E A O S M D C E T I S C
O A I A E N B S R N S L C N E O M R A E A B I T A C T E C Y
S E O E R N I E A P A R C Q C S E Y A E O V L R Y I T O E R
T P R A N L T N Y J E R U V T E N S L G E E R I O H D M P O
E P E R V Y I R G S R E A A E P H E A T N G R A A O E D R T
V A T S E E U N R S S J N C S E R L C E C I R L N B I S L P
F T L U E J D T F T T E I T L G E O C L M S S T O R V I M
S S P I R E U I E O I A N R A L R C U S I E S O Y S L C J E
R R E E N R E R E A I A T N I I O T E T P N R E L A N Q M R
E I P C E I E J L T R P O E D E S I J O R I E N T C D G A E
P F A E T D E E E T U I L I M L T O E E L I C E T C P E A P
G T E N J G V S Y I T G D E C E E N C O O T L P S C F Y D R
A R T U E I T V T I D G G I D V N T E C N E D I V E B D E E
A O R E D I S L D L A I R T D N A T S O T T N E T E P M O C
P Y E E M O C N E E B R F C R O N R E I I A V E L I E N T R
L T N O S A O A D V E R S A R I A L S Y S T E M E E E I D L
E C N I R C E E C N E D I V E F O S E L U R C R O A O O A R
E Y C E D A T F N O L O C O N T E N D E R E I S J Y S E N O
```

Adversarial System	Opening Statement
Bail Bond	Peremptory Challenge
Circumstantial Evidence	Perjury
Closing Argument	Plea
Competent to Stand Trial	Pretrial Release
Conditional Release	Real Evidence
Danger Law	Release on Recognizance
Direct Evidence	Rules of Evidence
Evidence	Scientific Jury Selection
First Appearance	Sequestered Jury
Hearsay	Testimony
Nolo Contendere	

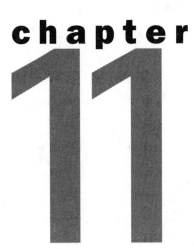

chapter 11

Sentencing

LEARNING OBJECTIVES

After reading this chapter, you should be able to:

- Describe the five goals of contemporary criminal sentencing

- Illustrate the difference between indeterminate and structured sentencing

- Describe the different types of structured sentencing models in use today

- Define mandatory sentencing, and explain how it came about

- Describe truth in sentencing

- Explain the importance of federal sentencing guidelines

- Describe the nature and importance of the presentence investigation report

- Describe the history of victims' rights and services, and discuss the growing role of the victim in criminal justice proceedings today

- List the four traditional sentencing options

- Outline the arguments for and against capital punishment

[121]

Chapter Summary

Duane Harris, having recently pleaded guilty to one count of armed robbery, stood before Judge Joe Marist waiting to hear his sentence. The judge, known by his peers as "Hanging Joe," sentenced Duane to the maximum possible sentence under the law: ten to 25 years in a maximum-security prison. Why did the judge decide to sentence Mr. Harris to the longest prison term possible? What factors did he consider to arrive at his sentence? What other options did he have? Could he have sentenced him to a longer term? Could he have sentenced him to death for the crime?

The text discusses several important aspects of sentencing in Chapter 11. The text describes five goals of contemporary sentencing: retribution, incapacitation, deterrence, rehabilitation, and restoration. **Retribution** corresponds to the just deserts model of sentencing and is best understood from the biblical reference to "eye for an eye, tooth for a tooth." **Incapacitation** seeks to isolate offenders from society. **Deterrence**, both **specific** and **general**, focuses on preventing crimes. **Rehabilitation** seeks to change the offender, and **restoration** seeks to make the victim "whole again."

Chapter 11 also describes types of sentencing practices. Mr. Harris was convicted in a state that uses an **indeterminate sentencing** model. Judges have the most discretion in states adhering to this model. A judge is expected to assess the differences among cases, situations, and offenders in an attempt to tailor the sentence to be appropriate and proportionate. It is also believed that offenders will be more likely to participate in rehabilitation programs if they can reduce the amount of time served.

The text highlights several problems with the indeterminate sentencing model. The most significant criticism is the inequality of sentences. Mr. Harris received the maximum possible sentence under the law. It is possible that another offender, sentenced by another judge in an adjacent courtroom, could receive a probation sentence or significantly fewer years in prison. The personalities of different judges, race of the offender, race of the victim, and social class have all been shown to be factors contributing to disparities in sentence.

In response to the various problems of indeterminate sentencing systems, states and the federal government have revised sentencing practices in order to structure sentencing more precisely. For example, some states have adopted a **determinate sentencing model** that requires offenders to be sentenced to a fixed term. Other states have developed **voluntary/advisory sentencing guidelines**, and some have adopted **presumptive sentencing guidelines**. Guideline jurisdictions specify a presumptive sentence for an offense but also allow the judge to consider **aggravating** and **mitigating** factors. Another type of structured sentencing discussed in the text is **mandatory sentencing**.

In general, judges try to make informed and fair sentencing decisions. The **presentence investigation report** assists judges with their decisions. Provided as a detailed report, as an abbreviated report, or as an oral report to the court, the presentence investigation report provides information about the defendant and the offense. It may also include a recommendation from the probation officer. Another factor that judges may consider when deciding the sentence is the impact of the crime on the victim. **Victim-impact statements** provide an opportunity for crime victims, or surviving family members of a victim, to describe the suffering caused by the crime.

Finally, the text discusses the typical sentencing options available to the judge. Imprisonment and probation are mentioned but are discussed in more detail in later chapters of the text. The frequent use of fines as a criminal sanction is also discussed. Chapter 11 concludes with a discussion of capital punishment.

There are currently nearly 3,800 offenders on death row. The number of offenders executed in a year is relatively small, but those numbers will probably increase because of Supreme Court rulings on *habeas corpus* review. **Capital punishment** is one issue that generates considerable debate. Many people oppose the death penalty because they believe it is not an effective deterrent to crime, is not applied fairly, or is costly, and because there is always a risk of killing an innocent person. However, most of the public supports capital punishment. Revenge, just deserts, and protection are the key supporting arguments of retentionists.

Key Concepts

Aggravating Circumstances: Circumstances relating to the commission of a crime that make it more grave than the average instance of the given type of offense.

Capital Offense: A criminal offense punishable by death.

Capital Punishment: The death penalty. Capital punishment is the most extreme of all sentencing options.

Determinate Sentencing: A model of criminal punishment in which an offender is given a fixed term that may be reduced by good time or gain time. Under the model, for example, all offenders convicted of the same degree of burglary would be sentenced to the same length of time behind bars. Also called *fixed sentencing*.

Deterrence: A goal of criminal sentencing that seeks to inhibit criminal behavior through the fear of punishment.

Equity: A sentencing principle, based upon concerns with social equality, that holds that similar crimes should be punished with the same degree of severity, regardless of the social or personal characteristics of the offenders.

Gain Time: The amount of time deducted from time to be served in prison on a given sentence for participation in special projects or programs.

General Deterrence: A goal of criminal sentencing that seeks to prevent others from committing crimes similar to the one for which a particular offender is being sentenced by making an example of the person sentenced.

Good Time: The amount of time deducted from time to be served in prison on a given sentence as a consequence of good behavior.

Incapacitation: The use of imprisonment or other means to reduce the likelihood that an offender will be capable of committing future offenses.

Indeterminate Sentencing: A model of criminal punishment that encourages rehabilitation via the use of general and relatively unspecified sentences (such as a term of imprisonment of from one to ten years).

Just Deserts: A model of criminal sentencing that holds that criminal offenders deserve the punishment they receive at the hands of the law and that punishments should be appropriate to the type and severity of the crime committed.

Mandatory Sentencing: A structured sentencing scheme that allows no leeway in the nature of the sentence required and under which clearly enumerated punishments are mandated for specific offenses or for habitual offenders convicted of a series of crimes.

Mitigating Circumstances: Circumstances relating to the commission of a crime that may be considered to reduce the blameworthiness of the defendant. See also *Aggravating Circumstances*.

Presentence Investigation: The examination of a convicted offender's background prior to sentencing. Presentence examinations are generally conducted by probation or parole officers and are submitted to sentencing authorities.

Presumptive Sentencing: A model of criminal punishment that meets the following conditions: (1) The appropriate sentence for an offender convicted of a specific charge is presumed to fall within a range of sentences authorized by sentencing guidelines that are adopted by a legislatively created sentencing body, usually a sentencing commission; (2) sentencing judges are expected to sentence within the range or to provide written justification for departure; (3) the guidelines provide for some review, usually appellate, of any departure from the guidelines.

Proportionality: A sentencing principle that holds that the severity of sanctions should bear a direct relationship to the seriousness of the crime committed.

Rehabilitation: The attempt to reform a criminal offender. Also, the state in which a reformed offender is said to be.

Restoration: A goal of criminal sentencing that attempts to make the victim "whole again."

Restorative Justice: A sentencing model that builds upon restitution and community participation in an attempt to make the victim "whole again."

Retribution: The act of taking revenge upon a criminal perpetrator.

Sentencing: The imposition of a criminal sanction by a judicial authority.

Social Debt: A sentencing principle that holds that an offender's criminal history should objectively be taken into account in sentencing decisions.

Specific Deterrence: A goal of criminal sentencing that seeks to prevent a particular offender from engaging in repeat criminality.

Structured Sentencing: A model of criminal punishment that includes determinate and commission-created presumptive sentencing schemes, as well as voluntary/advisory sentencing guidelines.

Truth in Sentencing: A close correspondence between the sentence imposed upon an offender and the time actually served prior to release from prison. *Source*: Lawrence A. Greenfeld, "*Prison Sentences and Time Served for Violence*," Bureau of Justice Statistics Selected Findings, No. 4, April 1995.

Victim–Impact Statement: The in-court use of victim- or survivor-supplied information by sentencing authorities wishing to make an informed sentencing decision.

Voluntary/Advisory Sentencing Guidelines: Recommended sentencing policies that are not required by law.

Writ of *Habeas Corpus*: A writ that directs the person detaining a prisoner to bring him or her before a judicial officer to determine the lawfulness of the imprisonment.

Key Cases

Apprendi v. *New Jersey*: In this Supreme Court case, the Court ruled that other than prior conviction, any fact that enhances the sentence must be submitted to a jury and proved beyond a reasonable doubt. (*Apprendi* v. *New Jersey*, 120 S.Ct. 2348 [2000]).

Atkins v. *Virginia*: The Supreme Court ruled that executing mentally retarded people violates the Constitution's ban on cruel and unusual punishment. (*Atkins* v. *Virginia*, No. 00-8452 [U.S. Supreme Court, decided June 20, 2002]).

Booth v. *Maryland*: Using victim-impact statements in a capital case violated the Eighth Amendment ban on cruel and unusual punishment and could result in the death penalty being imposed in an arbitrary and capricious manner (*Booth* v. *Maryland*, 107 S.Ct. 2529 [1987]).

Coker v. *Georgia*: The Supreme Court concluded that the death penalty is not an acceptable punishment for the crime of rape, concluding that execution would be "grossly disproportionate" to the crime (*Coker* v. *Georgia*, 433 U.S. 584 [1977]).

Coleman v. *Thompson*: State prisoners condemned to die cannot cite "procedural default" (such as a defense attorney's failure to meet a filing deadline for appeals in state court) as the sole reason for an appeal to federal court (*Coleman* v. *Thompson*, 501 U.S. 722 [1991]).

Deal v. *U.S.*: It is possible to try and to convict a defendant for six separate offenses in a single proceeding and use the federal sentencing guidelines to convict and sentence the defendant as a career offender as a consequence (*Deal* v. *U.S.*, 113 S.Ct. 1993, 124 L.Ed. 2d 44 [1993]).

Furman v. *Georgia*: "Evolving standards of decency" might necessitate a reconsideration of the constitutionality of capital punishment. Allowing the jury to decide guilt and the punishment of death at the same time allowed for an arbitrary and capricious application of the death penalty (*Furman* v. *Georgia*, 408 U.S. 238 [1972]).

Gregg v. *Georgia*: The two-step process of a judge or jury deciding guilt and then undertaking a separate sentencing phase was specifically upheld by the Supreme Court (*Gregg* v. *Georgia*, 428 U.S. 153 [1976]).

In re Kemmler: Punishments are cruel when they involve torture or a lingering death; but the punishment of death is not cruel, within the meaning of that word as used in the Constitution (*In re Kemmler*, 136 U.S. 436 [1890]).

McClesky v. *Zandt*: Limits the number of appeals available to a condemned person. After the first appeal, the defendant must show (1) why the subsequent appeal wasn't included in the first appeal and (2) how the defendant was harmed by the absence of the claim (*McCleskey* v. *Zandt*, 499 U.S. 467, 493–494 [1991]).

Mistretta v. *U.S.*: Congress acted appropriately in the creation of the federal sentencing guidelines, and the guidelines could be applied in federal cases nationwide (*Mistretta* v. *U.S.*, 488 U.S. 361, 371 [1989]).

Payne v. *Tennessee*: Reversed the *Booth* decision made four years earlier and held that "victim impact evidence is simply another form or method of informing the sentencing authority about the specific harm caused by the crime in question, evidence of a general type long considered by sentencing authorities" (*Payne* v. *Tennessee*, 501 U.S. 808 [1991]).

Ring v. *Arizona*: The Supreme Court found that "Arizona's enumerated aggravating factors operate as the functional equivalent of an element of a greater offense" (*Ring* v. *Arizona*, No. 01-488 [U.S. Supreme Court, decided June 24, 2002]).

Schlup v. *Delo*: The court ruled that before appeals based upon claims of new evidence can be heard, a petitioner must show that "it is more likely than not that no reasonable juror would have found him guilty beyond a reasonable doubt" (*Schlup* v. *Delo*, 115 S.Ct. 851, 130 L.Ed. 2d 1123 [1995]).

Wilkerson v. *Utah*: Upheld the use of the firing squad as a method of execution (*Wilkerson* v. *Utah*, 99 U.S. 130 [1878]).

Woodson v. *North Carolina*: Laws requiring the mandatory application of the death penalty for specific crimes are prohibited (*Woodson* v. *North Carolina*, 428 U.S. 280 [1976]).

Learning Tips

Reading and Outlining

When reading material, use the textbook's chapter outline, the student study guide's chapter outline, or create an outline yourself to guide your way through the information as you progress through the reading. Make the outlines more comprehensive by adding headings, notes, and thoughts. Whether using the provided outlines or your own method, outlining makes difficult material more understandable and allows you to see the larger picture rather than getting caught up in insignificant details or trivia.

Study Sessions

Avoid scheduling long study sessions. Four two-hour study sessions are far more productive than one eight-hour session. The amount of time actually spent productively in excessively long study sessions is very small. However, if long study sessions are

REMEMBER

The judge is one of the most important members of the courtroom work group. Remember that the courtroom work group can be defined as the professional courtroom actors, including judges, prosecuting attorneys, defense attorneys, public defenders, and others who earn a living serving the court. Judges are concerned with justice, applying the law, and ensuring that the defendant receives a fair trial. In addition, one of the most important decisions the judge is required to make is the sentencing decision.

inevitable, be sure to give your mind and body a break for a few minutes each hour. Also, be sure to study a variety of subjects. Studying similar subjects back to back is usually unproductive.

CJ Today on the World Wide Web

Web links to organizations and agencies related to the material in Chapter 11 include:

WEBSITE TITLE	URL
National Association of Sentencing Advocates (NASA)	http://www.sentencingproject.org/nasa
State Sentencing Commissions	http://www.ussc.gov/states/nascaddr.htm
The Coalition for Federal Sentencing Reform	http://www.sentencing.org
United States Sentencing Commission	http://www.ussc.gov
ACLU's Death Penalty Page	http://www.aclu.org/death-penalty
Amnesty International Death Penalty Campaign	http://www.web.amnesty.org/rmp/ dplibrary.nsf/index?openview
Death Penalty Focus	http://www.deathpenalty.org
Death Penalty Information Center (DPIC)	http://www.deathpenaltyinfo.org
Death Penalty Resources	http://sun.soci.niu.edu/~critcrim/dp/ dp.html

Student Activities

Activity 1

In the space provided, answer the questions at the end of each scenario.

1. Darryl Jackson is a 20-year-old unemployed male. He is addicted to cocaine, has no family, and is homeless. He has three prior felony convictions (all drug possession). He has recently been convicted of his fourth felony (a burglary), and you are the judge deciding his fate. The sentencing statute allows you to sentence Darryl with anywhere from a minor fine to life imprisonment (or any combination of punishments). The specific facts of the case:

   On October 18, Darryl Jackson entered the apartment of Angela Starter. He entered by picking the lock on her back door. He stole her stereo ($1,500), jewelry ($3,500), and Matchbox car collection ($800). When Darryl was leaving her apartment, a security officer stopped and apprehended him for the Starter burglary. Darryl claimed he needed to sell the goods so that he would have money for food.

   What sentence would you give Darryl?

2. Ron Kuzak is a 20-year-old male. He is a college student with a 3.6 grade point average, works part-time at McDonald's, and goes to church on Sunday (he sings in the choir). He is also addicted to cocaine. He has three prior felony convictions (all drug possession). He has recently been convicted of his fourth felony (a burglary), and you are the judge deciding his fate. The sentencing statute allows you to sentence Ron with anywhere from a minor fine to life imprisonment (or any combination of punishments). The specific facts of the case:

   On October 18, Ron Kuzak entered the apartment of Joni McDougal. He entered by picking the lock on her back door. He stole her watch ($1,500), diamond ring ($3,500), and Beanie Baby collection ($800). When Ron was leaving her apartment, a security officer stopped and apprehended him for the burglary. Ron claimed he needed to sell the goods so that he would have money for college tuition.

   What sentence would you give Ron?

Activity 2

What sentence would you give each of the following defendants? What factors would be most important to you? What other types of information would you want to know to make a more informed sentencing decision?

1. Miss Colby, a 32-year-old single mother, was convicted of reckless driving. On January 23, she was driving while intoxicated along State Street and hit a parked fire truck. The fire department was responding to an emergency medical call, attempting to transport an elderly man who had suffered a heart attack to the hospital. Because of the accident, the man could not be transported until another transport vehicle arrived. Miss Colby was originally charged with driving while intoxicated, but the prosecutor allowed her to plead to reckless driving.

2. Daniel Driver, 35 years old, was convicted on felony child molestation charges. He was on parole for similar charges at the time of the current offense. Mr. Driver is divorced, works as a computer consultant for an electronics firm, and has been described as an "active churchgoer."

3. Maria Campo, 40, pleaded guilty to two counts of passing bad checks. Ms. Campo had been purchasing new furniture for her apartment, paying with checks for which she had no funds. She has two previous convictions for forgery.

4. Thomas "Ziggy" Petruzzelli, 16, was convicted on involuntary manslaughter charges. The fight that led to the stabbing happened on July 4 outside a convenience store. Ziggy was standing outside the store asking adults to buy him a pack of cigarettes-something he could not do as a minor. Bruce Pearl, 33, agreed to buy the cigarettes, but when Pearl came back outside the store, the two began arguing. Ultimately, Ziggy's father got involved, intervening with a two-by-four. His father is currently awaiting trial on an assault with a deadly weapon charge.

Activity 3

Robert Jones, son of Debbie and Tom Jones, was murdered on his way home from work. Darrin Alexander was quickly apprehended near the scene of the crime, was identified by multiple eyewitnesses, and confessed to the crime. At trial, the jury took only 48 minutes to reach a guilty verdict in this death penalty case.

Robert Jones's parents had completed a written victim-impact statement and had prepared oral statements. However, the judge did not allow them to speak. Despite their objections, the sentencing phase of the trial occurred without their input. Alexander had 12 witnesses speak on his behalf. The jury, after considering the aggravating and mitigating factors in the case, decided to sentence Alexander to life imprisonment rather than to death.

Some victim advocates would argue that this would not have occurred if there existed a federal constitutional amendment that protected crime victims. Victim advocates believe that such an amendment would give victims complete protection of their rights.

Lawyers are split on their support for such an amendment. Some argue against it because it might put a halt to plea-bargaining, it would overburden the system, courts are ill equipped to handle such a radical change, and it would give victims too much veto power. Others, however, support the amendment, arguing that it would protect victims from such harm as described above, would give victims a voice in all court proceedings, would lessen the traumatizing impacts of crime, and would make the system more balanced. There are many additional arguments both for and against the amendment.

What do you think? This student activity requires you to take a position in support of or against this constitutional amendment. Make a strong argument for your position.

_____

_____

_____

_____

_____

_____

Activity 4

LIBRARY extra

Visit **Library Extra 11–6**. This link will take you to the report "A Broken System: Error Rates in Capital Cases, 1973–1995." Write a summary of the information provided in the report in the space below.

_____

_____

_____

_____

_____

_____

Internet Activity

Visit the Death Penalty Information Center at http://www.deathpenaltyinfo.org. Review the various "Information Topics" provided by the site. Look at each of the subareas (under Information Topics), including those under "General," "Issues," "Special Topics," and "In-Depth Reports." Provide a brief description of the kinds of material each subarea contains. Which of these subareas do you find the most interesting? Why? Your instructor may request that you submit your findings.

_____

_____

_____

_____

_____

_____

Distance Learning Activity

In the space below, take a position on the death penalty. Visit three or four websites to search for evidentiary support for your position. The following pages will be helpful: (1) ACLU's Death Penalty page: http://www.aclu.org/death-penalty; (2) Amnesty International Death Penalty Campaign: http://www.web.amnesty.org/rmp/dplibrary.nsf/index?openview; (3) Death Penalty Focus: http://www.deathpenalty.org; (4) Death Penalty Information Center: http://www.deathpenaltyinfo.org. If your instructor asks you to do so, participate in a class debate on the issue.

_____

_____

_____

_____

_____

_____

Student Study Guide Questions

True or False

____ 11-1. Deterrence is based on the idea of "an eye for an eye."

____ 11-2. Mitigating circumstances result in harsher sentences under the determinate model.

____ 11-3. Sentencing philosophies are manifestly intertwined with issues of religion, morals, values, and emotions.

____ 11-4. The overall goal of deterrence is crime prevention.

F 11-5. Presumptive sentencing guidelines eliminate judicial discretion.

____ 11-6. Most judges ignore the presentence investigation report writer's recommendations.

____ 11-7. Very few states currently use capital punishment as a sentencing option.

____ 11-8. Justifications for the death penalty are collectively referred to as the retentionist position.

F 11-9. Truth in sentencing means that before sentencing, probation officers present their investigation reports based on the truths they uncovered.

____ 11-10. General deterrence is a goal of criminal sentencing that seeks to prevent a particular offender from engaging in repeat criminality.

Multiple Choice

11-11. Modern sentencing practices are influenced by which of the following goals?
   a. retribution
   b. incapacitation
   c. deterrence
   d. rehabilitation
   e. all of the above

11-12. Which official is responsible for conducting presentence investigations in most jurisdictions?
   a. judge
   b. defense attorney
   c. prosecutor
   d. probation or parole officer

11-13. What philosophy of sentencing seeks to prevent others from committing crimes similar to the one for which an offender is being sentenced?
   a. rehabilitation
   b. retribution
   c. deterrence
   d. incapacitation

11-14. The retribution goal of sentencing corresponds to what model of sentencing?
   a. just deserts model
   b. medical model
   c. restoration model
   d. psychological healing model

11-15. _____ sentencing relies heavily upon a judge's discretion to choose among types of sanctions and set upper and lower limits on the length of prison stays.
   a. Intermediate
   b. Indeterminate
   c. Determinate
   d. Deterrent

11-16. Much of the philosophical basis of today's victims' movement can be found in the _____ model.
   a. restorative justice
   b. retribution
   c. restitution
   d. none of the above

11-17. The future of the death penalty rests primarily with
   a. the president.
   b. state legislatures.
   c. Congress.
   d. all of the above.

11-18. A study of the efficacy of victim-impact statements found that judicial sentencing decisions were _____ affected by them.
   a. greatly
   b. rarely
   c. modestly
   d. never

11-19. Which of the following is not one of the retentionist justifications for the death penalty?
   a. deterrence
   b. revenge
   c. just deserts
   d. protection

11-20. This U.S. Supreme Court case created the two-step trial procedure that separated the determination of guilt and sentencing stages.
   a. *Gregg* v. *Georgia*
   b. *Poyner* v. *Murray*
   c. *Furman* v. *Georgia*
   d. none of the above

Fill-In

11-21. A _____ is an examination of a convicted offender's background prior to sentencing.

11-22. _____ is an attempt to have a close correspondence between the sentence imposed and the actual time served.

11-23. The attempt to reform a criminal offender is called _____.

11-24. _____ is a goal of criminal sentencing that attempts to prevent a particular offender from engaging in repeat criminal behavior.

11-25. A sentence of two to 12 years is an example of _____.

11-26. _____ is the act of taking revenge upon a criminal perpetrator.

11-27. _____ is a model for criminal punishment that sets one particular punishment, or length of sentence, for each specific type of crime.

11-28. The amount of time deducted from time to be served in prison on a given sentence based upon good behavior while in prison is called _____.

11-29. _____ are factors surrounding an offense that could result in a harsher sentence.

11-30. A _____ is a criminal offense punishable by death.

Crossword Puzzle

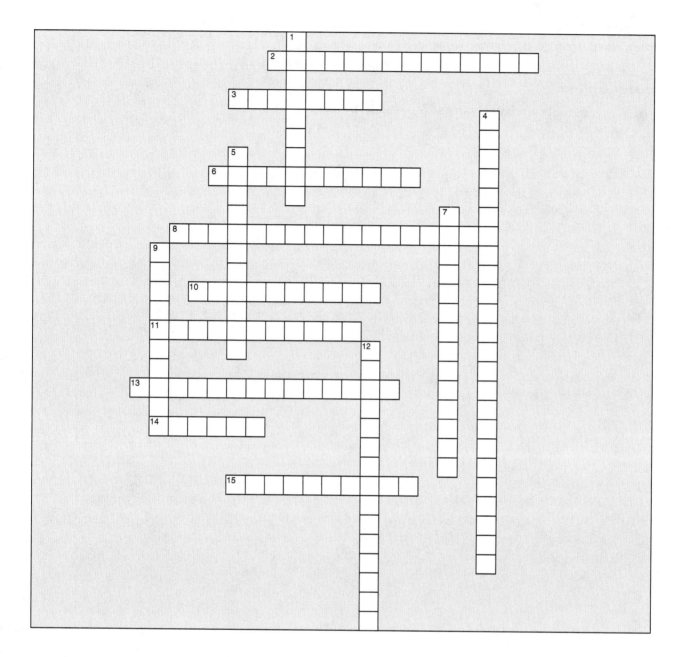

Across

2. An offense that is punishable by death.
3. The amount of time for good behavior deducted from time to be served in prison on a given sentence.
6. Also called fixed sentencing.
8. Also called the death penalty.
10. Not aggravating, but _____ circumstances.
11. To make the victim whole again.
13. The use of imprisonment or other means to reduce the likelihood that an offender will be capable of committing future offenses.
14. The sentencing principle based upon concerns for social equality.
15. The imposition of a criminal sanction by a judicial authority.

Down

1. Sentencing scheme that allows no leeway in the nature of the sentence.
4. Prior to sentencing, a probation officer usually conducts one of these.
5. "An eye for an eye."
7. An attempt to change the offender.
9. A goal of criminal sentencing that seeks to inhibit criminal behavior through the fear of punishment.
12. A sentencing principle that holds that the severity of sanctions should bear a direct relationship to the seriousness of the crime committed.

Word Search Puzzle

```
M I T I G A T I N G C I R C U M S T A N C E S I O R T N N C
I A T E S V A I G N I C N E T N E S D E R U T C U R T S T T
V T E N U C R E N A E N I C R B E N N T I T R T N E R T R V
E T R S E E V S G D E O N T D E N M E J T A M B E R N N N R
M E S E C I I P S E E I S A I I S D I N G O R T C I N N E R
I V M T O I C T T C E T M E E E T T E T N A R N T Y I U P R
T S G S C N T S G N I A E T N T C N O C D T I E C S J R L E
N G E U M C I U N E I G S R I D A U G R L O D C E A O L N O
I E N N D N M A I R U I R N M I N D S N A E O C N P E D R E
A N T A A P I V C R P T I E A I E T M A T T N G O R M A N D
G E R I N P M V N E N S C O S A N G C E N A I R I T L A E P
C R U E I A P T E T S E N N E N T A R E T R T O L E E T A Y
T A T E R I A E T E O V A A T E E R T S L I C A N C E S T E
N L H A C I C I N D C N R E I O E F M E O E E C I R T I T S
O D I D T A T N E C I I E S A N O U F N S E O T M E U C I U
I E N R A N S G S I A E V G C J C S A O E E S I N Q T T T E
T T S S N R T C Y F L C I E S R G L S T L U N T E C G I E N
A E E S R F A E R I D N T A I H I R N G J A N T T L I E E Y
T R N I S N T I O C E E N C I T I O R E T D T A E D C C V R
I R T E C I E T T E B T G E Y I I T V E A S T I R N T T G E
C E E L T O M R A P T N C E E T S I S G T C Q V P N C G T N
A N N T I T E L D S I E E I U N T E N I I D N E G A L I N G
P C C B R N N I N T Y S T B T A N R T I O P M N T T C S N M
A E I N I A T O A M R E I R R T L N T R F R N E T P T I G G
C N N I C S I V M E S R T O E C R E N T I E T E I G C G M C
N R G N T R A I N I T P T N I L T E R I E S R N L I N D T V
I G E C E R T N I E R S C A P I T A L P U N I S H M E N T C
R R F E G T I I R T E I G N I C N E T N E S E U M E T E C A
E N A G E N N T E R N O I T A T I L I B A H E R T E I N I C
A M A E D T N N I G I Y E T R P J U S T D E S E R T S U A S
```

Aggravating Circumstances
Capital Offense
Capital Punishment
Determinate Sentencing
Deterrence
Equity
Gain Time
General Deterrence
Good Time
Incapacitation
Indeterminate Sentencing
Just Deserts
Mandatory Sentencing

Mitigating Circumstances
Presentence Investigation
Proportionality
Rehabilitation
Restoration
Restorative Justice
Retribution
Sentencing
Social Debt
Specific Deterrence
Structured Sentencing
Truth in Sentencing
Victim Impact Statement

Probation, Parole, and Community Corrections

LEARNING OBJECTIVES

After reading this chapter, you should be able to:

■ Explain the difference between probation and parole, and describe the advantages and disadvantages of each

■ Describe in detail the legal environment surrounding the use of probation and parole, and know the names of significant court cases

■ Describe the federal probation system

■ Explain the nature of the job of probation and parole officers

■ List the advantages of intermediate sanctions over more traditional forms of sentencing

■ Describe the likely future of probation and parole

Chapter Summary

Chapter 12 discusses many issues important to understanding **community-based corrections**. This chapter focuses primarily on probation and parole. However, there is also a discussion of intermediate sanctions.

Probation is a sentence of imprisonment that is suspended. Offenders, if they abide by the specific and **general conditions** of probation, will serve their entire sentences in the community. This provides them with the opportunity to continue to work or remain in school, maintain family and social ties, and use the treatment programs available in the community. Chapter 12 discusses the history of probation in the United States and describes it as the most common form of criminal sentencing today. There are close to four million offenders currently on probation, and even offenders convicted of serious crimes are eligible for probation.

Parole is often mistaken for probation, but the two sentences are different. When sentencing an offender to probation, a judge makes the decision that a prison sentence should be suspended and the offender should serve his or her sentence in the community. An offender is on parole when he or she first serves time in prison and then is conditionally released by the paroling authority. However, similar to the constraints put on the probationer, the parolee must abide by general and **specific conditions** or face **revocation** of parole.

The text then describes the advantages and disadvantages of probation and parole. Advantages include lower cost than imprisonment, increased employment opportunities, opportunity to pay **restitution**, opportunity to receive community support, the reduced risk of criminal socialization, and the increased use of community services and opportunities for rehabilitation. Disadvantages include concerns about the lack of punishment, increased risk to the community, and increased social costs.

The legal environment of probation and parole is interesting because convicted offenders have fewer legal protections than someone accused of a crime. For example, the Supreme Court has decided that probation officers may conduct searches without a warrant or without probable cause (*Griffin* v. *Wisconsin*). Parole boards do not have to specify the evidence used in denying parole (*Greenholtz* v. *Nebraska*), and incriminating statements to a probation officer may be used as evidence if the probationer does not specify a right against self-incrimination (*Minnesota* v. *Murphy*). It is important to note, however, that probationers and parolees have some legal protections. The important *Gagnon* v. *Scarpelli* and *Morrissey* v. *Brewer* decisions declared that probationers and parolees deserve procedural safeguards when their probation or parole is being revoked.

The last section of Chapter 12 describes intermediate and innovative sentences. Judges have a wide variety of intermediate sanctions at their disposal. A **split sentence** requires the convicted person to serve a period of confinement in a facility followed by a period of probation. Similar to this type of sentence, **shock probation** (or **shock parole**) involves sentencing an offender to prison but then allowing him or her to be released early to probation. The first part of a split sentence is typically spent in a jail, and the first part of a shock probation sentence is spent in prison. **Shock incarceration** is a sentence to a military-style boot camp prison. **Intensive supervision** involves frequent face-to-face contacts between the probationary client and probation officers. Other intermediate sanctions discussed in Chapter 12 include **mixed sentences**, **community service**, and **home confinement**.

Key Concepts

Caseload: The number of probation or parole clients assigned to one probation or parole officer for supervision.

Community Corrections: The use of a variety of officially ordered program-based sanctions that permit convicted offenders to remain in the community under conditional supervision as an alternative to active prison sentences. Also called *community-based corrections*.

Community Service: A sentencing alternative that requires offenders to spend at least part of their time working for a community agency.

Conditions of Parole (Probation): The general and special limits imposed upon an offender who is released on parole (or probation). General conditions tend to be fixed by state statute, while special conditions are mandated by the sentencing authority (court or board) and take into consideration the background of the offender and the circumstances of the offense.

Home Confinement (House arrest): Individuals ordered confined to their homes are sometimes monitored electronically to ensure they do not leave during the hours of confinement. Absence from the home during working hours is often permitted.

Intensive Probation Supervision (IPS): A form of probation supervision involving frequent face-to-face contact between the probationer and the probation officer.

Intermediate Sanctions: The use of split sentencing, shock probation or parole, shock incarceration, community service, intensive supervision, or home confinement in lieu of other, more traditional, sanctions, such as imprisonment and fines. Also called *alternative sanctions*.

Mixed Sentence: A sentence that requires that a convicted offender serve weekends (or other specified periods of time) in a confinement facility (usually a jail) while undergoing probation supervision in the community.

Parole: The status of an offender who has been conditionally released from prison by a paroling authority before the expiration of his or her sentence, is placed under the supervision of a parole agency, and is required to observe conditions of parole.

Parole Board: A state paroling authority. Most states have parole boards that decide when an incarcerated offender is ready for conditional release. Some boards also function as revocation hearing panels. Also called *parole commission*.

Parole Revocation: The administrative action of a paroling authority removing a person from parole status in response to a violation of lawfully required conditions of parole, including the prohibition against committing a new offense, and usually resulting in a return to prison.

Parole (Probation) Violation: An act or a failure to act by a parolee (or probationer) that does not conform to the conditions of his or her parole (or probation).

Probation: A sentence of imprisonment that is suspended. Also, the conditional freedom granted by a judicial officer to an adjudicated adult or juvenile offender, as long as the person meets certain conditions of behavior.

Probation Revocation: A court order in response to a violation of conditions of probation, taking away a person's probationary status and usually withdrawing the conditional freedom associated with that status.

Restitution: A court requirement that an alleged or convicted offender pay money or provide services to the victim of the crime or provide services to the community.

Revocation Hearing: A hearing held before a legally constituted hearing body (such as a parole board) to determine whether a probationer or parolee has violated the conditions and requirements of his or her parole or probation.

Shock Incarceration: A sentencing option that makes use of "boot camp"–type prisons to impress upon convicted offenders the realities of prison life.

Shock Probation: The practice of sentencing offenders to prison, allowing them to apply for probationary release, and enacting such release in surprise fashion. Offenders who receive shock probation may not be aware of the fact that they will be released on probation and may expect to spend a much longer time behind bars.

Split Sentence: A sentence explicitly requiring the convicted offender to serve a period of confinement in a local, state, or federal facility followed by a period of probation.

Key Cases

Bearden v. *Georgia*: Probation cannot be revoked for failure to pay a fine and make restitution if it cannot be shown that the defendant was responsible for the failure. Alternative forms of punishment must be considered and be shown to be inadequate before the defendant can be incarcerated (*Bearden* v. *Georgia*, 461 U.S. 660, 103 S.Ct. 2064, 76 L.Ed. 2d 221 [1983]).

Escoe v. *Zerbst*: Probation "comes as an act of grace to one convicted of a crime" and the revocation of probation without hearing or notice to the probationer was acceptable (*Escoe* v. *Zerbst*, 295 U.S. 490 [1935]).

Gagnon v. *Scarpelli*: Extended the due process rights granted to parolees in *Morrissey* (see below) to probationers, and also required that two hearings be held before probation can be revoked—a preliminary hearing and a final hearing. Also provided some indigence relief to probationers facing revocation hearings (*Gagnon* v. *Scarpelli*, 411 U.S. 778 [1973]).

Greenholtz v. *Nebraska*: Parole boards do not have to specify the evidence used in deciding to deny parole (*Greenholtz* v. *Inmate of Nebraska Penal and Correctional Complex*, 442 U.S. 1 [1979]).

Griffin v. *Wisconsin*: Probation officers may conduct searches of a probationer's residence without a search warrant or probable cause (*Griffin* v. *Wisconsin*, 483 U.S. 868, 107 S.Ct. 3164 [1987]).

Mempa v. *Rhay*: Both notice and a hearing are required in order to revoke probation (*Mempa* v. *Rhay*, 389 U.S. 128 [1967]).

Minnesota v. *Murphy*: A probationer's incriminating statements to a probation officer may be used as evidence if the probationer did not specifically claim a right against self-incrimination (*Minnesota* v. *Murphy*, 465 U.S. 420, 104 S.Ct. 1136, 79 L.Ed. 2d 409 [1984]).

Morrissey v. *Brewer*: Procedural safeguards are required in revocation hearings involving parolees: (1) There must be written notice of alleged violations; (2) evidence of the violation must be disclosed; (3) a neutral and detached body must constitute the hearing authority; (4) the parolee should have the chance to appear and offer a defense, including testimony, documents, and witnesses; (5) the parolee has the right to cross-examine witnesses; and (6) a written statement should be provided to the parolee at the conclusion of the hearing that includes the body's decision, the testimony considered, and reasons for revoking parole if such occurs (*Morrissey* v. *Brewer*, 408 U.S. 471 [1972]).

Pennsylvania Board of Probation and Parole v. *Scott*: The Supreme Court declined to extend the exclusionary rule to searches by parole officers (*Pennsylvania Board of Probation and Parole* v. *Scott* 524 U.S. 357 [1998]).

U.S. v. *Knights*: This case expanded the search authority normally reserved for probation and parole officers to police officers in certain circumstances (*U.S.* v. *Knights*, No. 00-1260 [U.S. Supreme Court, decided December 10, 2001]).

Learning Tips

Taking Notes

Pay special attention to key words. Names, vocabulary words, and quotations are examples of key words. Focusing on key words will eliminate excess material from cluttering your notes. More important, key words are wonderful review mechanisms because they help you recall images.

REMEMBER

The *Griffin* v. *Wisconsin* case is an important decision affecting the rights of probationers. Recall that Chapter 7 discussed the *Weeks* v. *United States* and *Mapp* v. *Ohio* cases. These cases pertain to Fourth Amendment protections against unreasonable searches and seizures. Remember that the exclusionary rule is the understanding that incriminating information must be seized according to constitutional specifications of due process or it will not be allowed as evidence in criminal trials. Because of the *Griffin* v. *Wisconsin* court decision, the exclusionary rule does not apply to probation officers.

Reviewing Notes

Because short-term memory is indeed short, it is important to review your class notes as soon as possible, especially within 24 hours. Extensively review your notes, correct misspellings, write out abbreviations, insert any information you were unable to write in your notes during the class, and write as legibly as possible. Not only can these strategies save valuable time when studying for tests, but they also help transfer information from short-term to long-term memory.

CJ Today on the World Wide Web

Web links to organizations and agencies related to the material in Chapter 12 include:

WEBSITE TITLE	URL
Alternative Dispute Resolution Resources, Mediation Essays and Web Page Hosting for Mediators	http://adrr.com
Electronic monitoring	http://www.housearrest.com
Institute for Dispute Resolution	http://www.cpradr.org
Justice Concepts Incorporated	http://www.justiceconcepts.com
Mediation Works, Inc.	http://www.mwi.org
National Center on Institutions and Alternatives	http://www.igc.org/ncia
The Sentencing Project	http://www.sentencingproject.org
Victim-Offender Reconciliation Program Resources	http://www.vorp.com
American Probation & Parole Association (APPA)	http://www.appa-net.org
International Community Corrections Association	http://www.iccaweb.org

Student Activities

Activity 1

According to the Bureau of Justice Statistics study discussed at the beginning of Chapter 12, 5% of murderers and 21% of sexual offenders are sentenced to probation. Do you think that murderers and sexual offenders should be sentenced to probation? Why or why not? What factors contribute to courts relying on probation for these types of offenders? Are there any offenses for which you would exclude probation as a sentencing option? Explain your answer.

_____

_____

_____

_____

_____

_____

Activity 2

One of the significant pressures affecting the criminal justice system is overcrowding in the prison system. Most prisons operate above capacity, and some state systems are under court mandate to reduce overcrowding. At the same time, however, many states are considering abolishing parole. Parole has traditionally been one mechanism that can reduce overcrowding by allowing the early release of inmates. Do you think parole should be eliminated? Why or why not? Are there other mechanisms that states can use to reduce prison populations? Explain your answer.

_____

_____

_____

_____

_____

_____

Activity 3

Visit **Library Extra 12–2** and read the publication on trends in state parole. In the space below, describe the major trends identified. What trends do you think will influence parole in the next ten years? Explain your answer.

LIBRARY extra

_____

_____

_____

_____

_____

_____

Activity 4

Locate a probation or parole agency in your state. Visit or call that agency, and interview an officer in each agency. Find out about the types of intermediate sanctions available in your state. In the space provided below, describe at least three of the intermediate sanction programs available.

_____

_____

_____

_____

_____

Internet Activity

Visit the American Probation and Parole Association at http://www.appa-net.org. Use the site map on the home page to locate APPA position statements. What topics do these statements cover? Select three or four position statements and read and summarize them. Your instructor may request that you submit your findings.

_____

_____

_____

_____

_____

_____

Distance Learning Activity

Visit the Dispute Resolution Resources webpage at http://adrr.com. This website provides essays on mediation and dispute resolution. Read one of the essays posted and provide a summary of its key ideas. If your instructor asks you to do so, organize a class discussion that provides an opportunity to compare and contrast the findings from the different essays.

_____

_____

_____

_____

_____

_____

Student Study Guide Questions

True or False

_____ 12-1. When using shock probation, the judge sentences an offender to a prison term then suspends the sentence before the offender actually starts to serve the sentence in a jail or prison.

_____ 12-2. Community service is a sentencing alternative that requires offenders to spend at least part of their time working for a community agency.

_____ 12-3. A split sentence requires an offender to serve at least part of his or her sentence in a jail or prison, followed by a longer period on probation.

_____ 12-4. Restitution is a court requirement that an offender pay money or provide services to the victim of the crime or provide services to the community.

_____ 12-5. Parole is the status of an offender conditionally released from a prison by a paroling authority prior to the expiration of the sentence.

_____ 12-6. Probation is the conditional freedom granted by a judicial officer to an adjudicated adult or juvenile offender after a period of incarceration.

_____ 12-7. Few states use parole boards to decide when an incarcerated offender is ready for conditional release; most of that function has been taken over by prison wardens.

_____ 12-8. If a judge orders that a convicted offender's sentence be suspended and places the offender on probation, no further steps can be taken to reinstate the suspended prison time regardless of the offender's behavior while on probation.

_____ 12-9. The number of probation and parole clients assigned to a probation or a parole officer for supervision is referred to as the officer's caseload.

_____ 12-10. Any act or failure to act by a probationer (or parolee) that does not conform to the conditions of probation (or parole) is a violation.

Multiple Choice

12-11. Probation and parole
   a. are essentially the same and are terms that are used interchangeably.
   b. use different supervision techniques but are usually administered by the same office.
   c. are sentences handed down by the courts.
   d. are distinctly different forms of community corrections administered by different authorities.

12-12. The man known as the first probation officer, a Boston shoemaker, was
   a. John Howard.
   b. Ben Franklin.
   c. Thomas Mott Osborne.
   d. John Augustus.

12-13. In the 1973 case of *Gagnon* v. *Scarpelli*, the U.S. Supreme Court
   a. affirmed the privilege against self-incrimination revocation hearings.
   b. extended the holding in *Morrissey* v. *Brewer* to include probationers.
   c. stressed the rehabilitative nature of probation.
   d. ruled against the use of hearsay evidence in probation revocation hearings.

12-14. Parole boards grant _____ parole.
   a. mandatory
   b. conditional
   c. discretionary
   d. limited

12-15. In what case did the court rule that the search authority of probation and parole officers might be extended to police officers in certain situations?
   a. *U.S.* v. *Knights*
   b. *Mempa* v. *Rhay*
   c. *Griffin* v. *Wisconsin*
   d. *Pennsylvania Board of Probation and Parole* v. *Scott*

12-16. In the event of a technical violation of probation, the _____ would be responsible for initiating violation proceedings.
   a. police officer
   b. probation officer
   c. judge
   d. prosecutor

12-17. In the 1983 case of *Bearden* v. *Georgia*, the U.S. Supreme Court determined that
   a. a restitution order cannot be vacated through a filing of bankruptcy.
   b. probation cannot be revoked for failure to pay a fine and make restitution if it can be shown that the defendant was not responsible for the failure.
   c. a probationer's incriminating statements made to a probation officer may be used as evidence against him or her.
   d. probation "comes as an act of grace to one convicted of a crime."

12-18. _____ allows for a three- to six-month regimen of military drill, drug treatment, exercise, and academic work in return for having several years removed from an inmate's sentence.
   a. "Good time" law
   b. Shock incarceration
   c. Intensive parole
   d. Intensive probation

12-19. All of the following are considered advantages of probation and parole except
   a. relative lack of punishment.
   b. reduced risk of criminal socialization.
   c. lower cost.
   d. increased employment opportunities.

12-20. In the 1967 case of _____, the U.S. Supreme Court determined that both notice of the charges and a hearing are required in order to revoke an offender's probation.
   a. *Gagnon* v. *Scarpelli*
   b. *Morrissey* v. *Brewer*
   c. *Mempa* v. *Rhay*
   d. *Griffin* v. *Wisconsin*

Fill-In

12-21. _____ are state-ordered limits imposed on all offenders who are released on either probation or parole.

12-22. _____ is the practice of sentencing offenders to prison, allowing them to apply for probationary release, and enacting such release in a surprise fashion.

12-23. A _____ is used to decide if an offender has violated the terms of his or her probation or parole by committing a new offense or failing to live up to the conditions of probation or parole.

12-24. Split sentencing, shock probation and parole, home confinement, shock incarceration, and community service are all examples of _____.

12-25. _____ is also called house arrest.

12-26. A _____ requires an offender to serve a period of confinement in a local, state, or federal facility followed by a period of probation.

12-27. _____ makes use of "boot camp"-type prisons to impress upon convicted offenders the realities of prison life.

12-28. A _____ requires that a convicted offender serve weekends in jail while on supervised probation in the community during the week.

12-29. _____ is a sentencing alternative that requires offenders to spend at least part of their time working for a community agency.

12-30. _____ is a form of probation supervision involving frequent face-to-face contacts between the probationary client and probation officers.

Crossword Puzzle

Across

1. Like "boot camp."
3. A hearing to determine whether a probationer has violated probation.
5. A sentence that requires offenders to spend time working for a community agency.
8. A court requirement that an alleged or convicted offender pay money or provide services to the victim.
10. Also called community-based corrections.
12. An act or a failure to act by a probationer that does not conform to the conditions of his or her probation.
13. A suspended sentence.
14. IPS.

Down

2. Also called house arrest.
4. Also called alternative sanctions.
6. Shock _____.
7. A sentence explicitly requiring the convicted offender to serve a period of confinement in a local, state, or federal facility followed by a period of probation.
9. The state paroling authority.
10. The number of clients assigned to a probation officer.
11. _____ v. *Scarpelli*.

Word Search Puzzle

```
O E A X M E S N O I T U T I T S E R O O B B O P E P S R A S
T N O S G E L O R A P F O S N O I T I D N O C H B N E I I B
O E I R N N T P T D A S H O C K P R O B A T I O N V C N O H
G D X S I S I N O E A S T B E I V S O E O T A A N I P T N A
E N N I I P I R A A A T O N E O T O N A M T T S P I I E T O
M I Y S E E S I A V M O I E T U S S I M C N A L O E N N P L
O P T E R N E O V E N A E N E M N I P S M S I A X I E S O I
N N I E I O P P P E H I O S E S V O N V I O O L A M E I E C
O Y B R M S R R E P M N H N I N E S A S T N O R E O E V O N
L N O N E C P M N H T E O I O S T M P I O S H N E L R E E O
S C B N F V O L T E E C I I C I S A S N S U I N O L O P O L
P N I N N O O N I O N I A P T E T O I S P F S P A E R R K I
A T D O S D A O E T R V A E H A I A O V N O R N L B P O I E
N K T E P A I O R C S R I N S O C O B O A O O O E N R B G A
R O C N N E I R D H O E O E L E D O C O B S R O T Y S A N O
I D X V I E S I E L I S N A E M N E V A R A I T A P R T O R
N P N T E O R O E B T Y I T U D M O T E P P T E O O H I O R
N R T N E S C B D R E T O E E O B I M C R N A T N I A O I C
S E M E N O O I P O O I I N H N O T I A P T I V E I T N B R
N S C R M A O L A O I N I C D N C I X T M N T A I T R S N O
S R D E R I O E E C R U O A R T I E E R C A N E M D N U I E
I S C D S R O S N O L M E E E S E E D A T R M B R A R P R R
R L N O T R V S O B E M V O N C N M S S O S P I O O I E T T
A E I R R I T N E A P O S U R T F B E O S O B C O L T R E U
E S X O E N S N M D C C N T O R E E N D P O C U D E T V H I
C N L T E A O R P A B R O C V E M S T D A R E E I S E I C H
A O E T E T N T T I E X L S C P N R E C O E Y O U A I S C E
S C R E L N O I E A P N N A E E E I N N O L E N S C C I N S
I P N I S I O R A A R T B P R A E I C U I R O N B C A O P A
E I E D O N B I P P V R R O C S O N E T R A C C N C S N T E
```

Caseload

Community Service

Conditions of Parole

Home Confinement

Intensive Probation Supervision

Mixed Sentence

Parole

Parole Board

Probation

Probation Revocation

Restitution

Revocation Hearing Shock Probation

Split Sentence

Prisons and Jails

chapter 13

OUTLINE

Introduction
Early Punishments
The Emergence of Prisons
Prisons Today
Jails
Private Prisons

LEARNING OBJECTIVES

After reading this chapter, you should be able to:

- Describe the nature and history of early punishments and their impact on modern correctional philosophy

- Outline the historical development of prisons

- Discuss the major characteristics and purpose of today's prisons

- Describe the prison population in America today

- Describe the just deserts model, and explain how it has led to an increased use of imprisonment and to prison overcrowding

- Discuss how changes in the rate of criminal offending relate to changes in the rate of imprisonment over the last decade

- Explain the role that jails play in American corrections, and discuss the issues that jail administrators currently face

- Describe the role of private prisons today, and predict their future

Chapter Summary

Chapter 13 discusses four areas related to imprisonment in the United States: early punishments, prisons today, jails, and private prisons.

The massive institutions that house many inmates today are a relatively new invention. Most early punishment was corporal punishment, attempting to satisfy the doctrine of **lex talionis**. Chapter 13 describes various types of corporal punishment, including flogging, mutilation, branding, public humiliation, workhouses, and exile.

Prisons first emerged in the early 1790s when Pennsylvania Quakers sought an alternative to corporal punishment. The **Pennsylvania system** made use of solitary confinement and also encouraged rehabilitation. The Pennsylvania system dominated prison construction until the 1820s. One of the first prisons to abandon the Pennsylvania model was Auburn prison in 1825, marking the beginning of the mass prison era. The Auburn style consisted of building mass prisons, where prisoners were held in congregate fashion and required to maintain silence.

The text describes several other historical eras in prison development. For example, it discusses how Captain Alexander Maconochie and Sir Walter Crofton influenced the practices at Elmira Reformatory. The reformatory era of prisons (1876–1890) gave way to the industrial prison era (1890–1935). During this era, prisons attempted to capitalize on convict labor. However, states had to limit the use of prison industries because of the **Ashurst-Sumners Act**. Punishment and security were the focus of the punitive era (1935–1945), but interest in reformation and rehabilitation of offenders grew in the era of treatment (1945–1967). Similarly, the community-based format era (1967–1980) attempted to decarcerate offenders and treat them in the community. This era was followed by the warehousing/overcrowding era (1980–1995)—a period during which the number of incarcerated inmates nearly tripled. Finally, the current era is referred to as the just deserts era (1995–present).

Today, there are more than 1,500 state and federal prisons in operation. The number of inmates is close to 1.5 million, and most prisons are operating above capacity. There are more men than women in prison, and there are significant disparities by race. For example, the incarceration rate for African-Americans is ten times greater than the figure for whites. More than 350,000 people are employed in the maximum-, medium-, and minimum-security prisons across the country.

Jails are another type of confinement facility discussed in Chapter 13. Jails, the responsibility of local governments, generally house either pretrial detainees or offenders with a sentence of a year or less. There are approximately 630,000 persons in the 3,365 jails in the United States. This section of the text also discusses women as the largest growth group in jails nationwide. Women in jails pose unique challenges to jail administrators because most jurisdictions do not have separate housing for female inmates. The text also discusses the fact that many jurisdictions are using citizen volunteer programs, jail boot camps, and regional jail systems.

The last section of Chapter 13 discusses private prisons. An increasing number of jurisdictions are contracting with private firms to provide their confinement responsibilities. Currently, there are more than 85,000 inmates housed in facilities run by private companies. Legal issues, and the relationship between the state-run and privately managed facilities, are interesting issues that have emerged since the privatization of prisons began.

Key Concepts

ADMAX: Administrative maximum. The term is used by the federal government to denote ultra-high-security prisons.

Ashurst-Sumners Act: Federal legislation of 1935 which effectively ended the industrial prison era by restricting interstate commerce in prison-made goods.

Auburn System: A form of imprisonment developed in New York State around 1820 that depended upon mass prisons, where prisoners were held in congregate fashion requiring silence. This style of imprisonment was a primary competitor with the Pennsylvania system.

Classification System: A system used by prison administrators to assign inmates to custody levels based on offense history, assessed dangerousness, perceived risk of escape, and other factors.

Design Capacity: The number of inmates a prison was intended to hold when it was built or modified. Also called *bed capacity.*

Direct-Supervision Jail: A temporary confinement facility that eliminates many of the traditional barriers between inmates and correctional staff. Physical barriers in direct-supervision jails are far less common than in traditional jails, allowing staff members the opportunity for greater interaction with, and control over, residents. Also called *new-generation jail; podular-direct jail.*

Industrial Prison: A correctional model intended to capitalize on the labor of convicts sentenced to confinement.

Jail: A confinement facility administered by an agency of local government, typically a law enforcement agency, intended for adults but sometimes also containing juveniles, which holds persons detained pending adjudication and/or persons committed after adjudication, usually those sentenced to a year or less.

Justice Model: A contemporary model of imprisonment based upon the principle of just deserts.

Lex Talionis: The law of retaliation, often expressed as "an eye for an eye" or "like for like."

Medical Model: A therapeutic perspective on correctional treatment that applies the diagnostic perspective of medical science to the handling of criminal offenders.

Nothing-Works Doctrine: The belief, popularized by Robert Martinson in the 1970s, that correctional treatment programs have had little success in rehabilitating offenders.

Operational Capacity: The number of inmates a prison can effectively accommodate based on management considerations.

Pennsylvania System: A form of imprisonment developed by the Pennsylvania Quakers around 1790 as an alternative to corporal punishments. This style of imprisonment made use of solitary confinement and encouraged rehabilitation.

Prison: A state or federal confinement facility that has custodial authority over adults sentenced to confinement.

Prison Capacity: The size of the correctional population an institution can effectively hold. There are three types of prison capacity: rated, operational, and design. *Source*: Bureau of Justice Statistics, *Prisoners in 1998* (Washington, D.C.: BJS, 1999), p. 7.

Private Prison: A correctional institution operated by a private firm on behalf of a local or state government.

Privatization: The movement toward the wider use of private prisons.

Rated Capacity: The number of inmates a prison can handle according to the judgment of experts.

Recidivism: The repetition of criminal behavior. In statistical practice, a recidivism rate may be any of a number of possible counts or instances of arrest, conviction, correctional commitment, or correctional status change related to repetitions of these events within a given period of time.

Reformatory Style: A late-nineteenth-century correctional model based upon the use of the indeterminate sentence and the belief in the possibility of rehabilitation, especially for youthful offenders. The reformatory concept faded with the emergence of industrial prisons around the turn of the century.

REMEMBER

Lex talionis is closely associated with the term *retribution*, discussed in Chapter 11. Remember that the five goals of sentencing are retribution, incapacitation, deterrence, rehabilitation, and restoration. Retribution means "an eye for an eye," incapacitation is isolation from the community (usually in prison or jail), deterrence focuses on prevention, rehabilitation seeks to treat and change the offender, and restoration is designed to help the victim of crime.

Regional Jail: A jail that is built and run using the combined resources of a variety of local jurisdictions.

State-Use System: A system of inmate labor in which items produced by inmates may be sold only by or to state offices. Items that only the state can sell include such things as license plates and hunting licenses, while items sold only to state offices include furniture and cleaning supplies.

Warehousing: An imprisonment strategy that is based upon the desire to prevent recurrent crime but that has abandoned all hope of rehabilitation.

Workhouse: An early form of imprisonment intended to instill habits of industry in the idle. Also called *bridewell*.

Work-Release: A prison program through which inmates are temporarily released into the community in order to meet job responsibilities.

Learning Tips

Attending Class

One of the most important things that you can do to ensure success is to attend class. You may think that attending class is not necessary because you have a friend, a roommate, or a neighbor who attends and allows you to copy the notes. However, it is important to have your own notes that you created by attending the lectures. This will help you learn and retain the information more effectively and will make it easier for you to prepare for examinations.

Active Learning

Attending class is important, but it is also imperative that you try to be actively engaged in the lecture. Get to class early so that you can find a seat and are ready to focus on the material. Try to sit near the front of the class and do not sit near students who are constantly talking or shuffling in their seats. Try not to daydream. Stay focused on the professor's lecture, ask questions, and take clear and complete notes.

CJ Today on the World Wide Web

Web links to organizations and agencies related to the material in Chapter 13 include:

WEBSITE TITLE	URL
American Correctional Association	http://www.corrections.com/aca
American Jail Association	http://www.corrections.com/aja
Correctional News Online	http://www.correctionalnews.com
Corrections (NCJRS)	http://virlib.ncjrs.org/Corrections.asp
Federal Bureau of Prisons	http://www.bop.gov/bopmain.html
The Other Side of the Wall	http://www.prisonwall.org
Prison Diaries	http://www.npr.org/programs/atc/ prisondiaries
Prison Industry Links	http://www.corrections.com/industries
National Juvenile Detention Association	http://www.njda.com
Prison Legal News	http://www.prisonlegalnews.org

Student Activities

Activity 1

Consider the following case. Michael Faye was an 18-year-old American living with his parents in Singapore when he was arrested for spray-painting cars during ten days of vandalism. He confessed to these crimes but later said that his confession was coerced by police officials who severely beat him. He was convicted and sentenced to four strokes with a rattan cane-a punishment in which the prisoner is flogged, tearing open the skin and producing permanent scars. Was his punishment a violation of Michael Faye's rights? Remember that his crime took place in Singapore, a legal system that balances individual and community rights very differently from our own. Indeed, more than 1,000 prisoners are caned per year in Singapore. Do you think we should use similar types of punishment in the United States? Would you recommend the use of any of the other early punishments described in Chapter 13? Why?

_____

_____

_____

_____

_____

_____

_____

Activity 2

Visit **Library Extra 13–3**. This link provides a discussion of internal prison classification systems. Summarize the major findings from this study.

LIBRARY extra

_____

_____

_____

_____

_____

_____

Activity 3

Collect data to answer the following questions about the prisons in the state where your campus is located. How many inmates are incarcerated in the state? How many prisons are there? How many maximum-security? Medium? Minimum? How has the number of prisoners changed over time? Present the data you collected in the space below, and then discuss how the data on your state system are similar to and different from the national data presented in Chapter 13.

_____

_____

_____

_____

_____

_____

Activity 4

Many private companies, such as Corrections Corporation of America and Corrections Concepts, have been able to convince legislators to turn over the operation of some prisons (or prison functions) to private companies. Do you think the use of private companies to run state prison systems is a good idea? What are some problems with using private companies? Do you think the prisons run by private companies will be more effective than state-run prisons? Explain your answer.

_____
_____
_____
_____
_____
_____
_____

Internet Activity

Visit the *Corrections Connection* on the World Wide Web (http://www.corrections.com). View (and click on) the topics in the "Hot Topics" section. Write a brief summary of three different items. Your instructor may request that you submit these summaries.

_____
_____
_____
_____
_____
_____

Distance Learning Activity

Visit the *Correctional News* website or some other major industry legal publication (see *Correctional News Online*: http://www.correctionalnews.com or *Prison Legal News*: http://www.prisonlegalnews.org). In the space below, summarize one of the articles or cases posted on the website. If your instructor asks you to do so, share your summary with other students in the class and participate in a class discussion about the issues that students wrote about.

_____
_____
_____
_____
_____
_____

Student Study Guide Questions

True or False

____ 13-1. A state or federal confinement facility that has custodial authority over adults sentenced to confinement for less than one year is called a prison.

____ 13-2. Under *lex talionis* the convicted offender was sentenced to a punishment that most closely approximated the original injury.

____ 13-3. An overview of various approaches to correctional treatment suggests that programs focused on rehabilitation should be abolished.

____ 13-4. Most deaths that occur in jails are the result of natural causes.

____ 13-5. The movement toward the wider use of private prisons is called corporationalization.

____ 13-6. Prisons that flourished during the industrial prison era, and whose intent was to capitalize on the labor of convicts sentenced to confinement, were part of the reformatory concept.

____ 13-7. The just deserts model was a late-nineteenth-century correctional model based upon the use of the indeterminate sentence and belief in the possibility of rehabilitation of offenders.

____ 13-8. At one time, England used hulks to house convicted offenders and send them into exile.

____ 13-9. The 1935 Taft-Hartley Act effectively ended the industrial prison era by restricting interstate commerce in prison-made goods.

____ 13-10. Direct supervision jails are temporary confinement facilities that eliminate many of the traditional barriers between inmates and correctional staff.

Multiple Choice

13-11. The term used by the federal government to denote ultra-high-security prisons is
   a. ULTRAMAX.
   b. SUPERMAX.
   c. ADMAX.
   d. MAXIMAX.

13-12. The group that most influenced the beginnings of the American prison experience was the
   a. Pilgrims.
   b. Quakers.
   c. Catholic Church.
   d. Salvation Army.

13-13. The first American penitentiary, opened in the late 1700s in Philadelphia, was called
   a. Alcatraz.
   b. Huntsville Prison.
   c. Walnut Street Jail.
   d. Eastern Penitentiary.

13-14. One of the first attempts at parole, as practiced by Ireland's Sir Walter Crofton, allowed offenders to earn a conditional release by meeting certain objectives. Release was granted under a
   a. good behavior rule.
   b. Marx system.
   c. mark system.
   d. ticket of leave.

13-15. The feature of Eastern and Western penitentiaries that most clearly characterized the nineteenth-century Pennsylvania correctional philosophy was
   a. corporal punishment.
   b. solitary confinement.
   c. congregate cellblocks.
   d. the whipping post.

13-16. Auburn prison, established in 1823 in New York State, attempted to reform prisoners by
   a. enforcing the "codes of confinement."
   b. torturing them.
   c. forced labor and use of the silent system.
   d. use of the pleasure-pain principle.

13-17. *Lex talionis* is a Latin term that means
   a. "the law of the king."
   b. "the law of retaliation."
   c. "the law of the dead."
   d. "the law of the land."

13-18. The 1981 U.S. Supreme Court case of *Rhodes* v. *Chapman* dealt with the issue of prison overcrowding and held that
   a. placing two inmates in one cell is cruel and unusual punishment.
   b. placing two inmates in one cell is not cruel and unusual punishment.
   c. inmates must show that prison officials exhibited "deliberate indifference" by not dealing with overcrowding sooner.
   d. inmates have a reasonable expectation of privacy that is violated by having to share a cell with another inmate.

13-19. _____ house the most serious offenders and are characterized by double and triple security patterns.
   a. Maximum-security prisons
   b. Reformatories
   c. Medium-security prisons
   d. Minimum-security prisons

13-20. The number of inmates a prison was intended to hold when it was built or modified is its
   a. prison capacity.
   b. rated capacity.
   c. operational capacity.
   d. design capacity.

Fill-In

13-21. The _____ was a form of imprisonment developed by the Quakers that made use of solitary confinement and resulted in the nation's first penitentiary.

13-22. _____ is the repetition of criminal behavior.

13-23. The _____ was a form of early imprisonment designed to instill a work ethic in the idle.

13-24. The _____ held that treatment programs have little rehabilitative success.

13-25. The _____ is a form of inmate labor in which items produced by inmates are salable only to state agencies.

13-26. _____ is a prison program through which inmates are temporarily released into the community in order to meet job responsibilities.

13-27. _____ is an imprisonment strategy based upon the desire to prevent recurrent crime but which has abandoned any hope of rehabilitation.

13-28. The _____ of imprisonment is characterized by a belief that offenders are sick and can be cured through behavioral and other forms of therapy.

13-29. The _____ is a contemporary model of imprisonment based on the social philosophy of just deserts. **(justice model, p. 553)**

13-30. A _____ jail is built and run using the combined resources of a variety of local jurisdictions. **(regional, p. 573)**

Crossword Puzzle

Across

1. Also called administrative maximum.
2. The form of imprisonment developed in New York.
4. The number of inmates a prison was intended to hold when it was built or modified.
5. Also called new generation or podular jails.
6. A form of imprisonment developed by the Quakers.
8. A short-term confinement facility.
10. Model based on just deserts.
11. The repetition of criminal behavior.
12. The number of inmates a prison can effectively accommodate based upon management considerations.
13. The belief popularized by Robert Martinson.
14. The number of inmates an institution can effectively hold.

Down

1. Act that ended the industrial prison era.
3. A correctional model intended to capitalize on the labor of convicts.
7. The movement toward the wider use of private prisons.
9. The law of retaliation.

Word Search Puzzle

```
A O P C O S R V K R E G I O N A L J A I L R T H N A O H I A
E A E P I N T H A R M O E R O O C R S I N O I L A T X E L W
T M O E I A T E P D E E U T N Y T I C A P A C N O S I R P E
A E A T F S R A Y R M F T H I G X N N E I O I I S R H O I T
G N O U Y M S I R N I A O S T E N A A S T R V J E C L I E L
E I A S A O S I L E E M X R Y E A I U S A L S I I A Y A Y I
O R U N O E A N L N C S N T M S J A S J D I I O D T E T N L
R T C E M T L D S R C I O L C A N T I U M N L T I T I W N A
L C D L P L A U N T S V I D M U T O A Y O U H C K C A S Z T
R O V N R A C S C I L I T I R E P O I S E H A E A Z T L R T
S D A D A S S T T S I D A I D L D V R T A P E P C D D I S E
E S D R T N T R M J J I Z R Y N I I N Y A I A R E L M D I T
I K A G R C T I S R U C I O O D S D C C S C M S A I A R C O
P R I N N R Y A S S S E T D N I O T L A D T I N A W S I T T
O O T E Y T S L T E T R A R D T C A S E L G Y F J S U T Y O
S W I I R S T P E D I C V S P O N E T T N M K L I N S I T I
V G S P A I I R A O C I I A U O N A A C S A O N E S C R A A
T N D V O Y H I M S E D R P I R R O A O O E E D A E S I M T
T I O S O J I S I L M P P T I I P P S M N V A M E O R A R A
I H R M L F N O R R O N A R H D A R M I N C L I I L S I L E
A T L W A O D N L U D R C A E C A D B V R T C A D I R E W C
A O F R R S A P R P E I Y H I S A P T O S P P C S F S E N I
C N T O C R T O L P L C R T D R U A W L A Y E N T U A E R A
L S T I A N A S O C P O Y T E R I L I L U I L T O T G I R F
L I A J N O I S I V R E P U S T C E R I D E A H A Y S P E T
E T N F A T A L T P R I S O N I P N R D A E K E R V B C D R
V O A D C M L X U A C I N T O D B N R C P R O T V S I W I J
O C L V T S N C Y M N V D N C N N E H S O C A L A R M R O R
M E T S Y S N R U B U A C O E R T P O W A C H T E S T T P N
L A S H U R S T S U M N E R S A C T C P I H M I X U L E E L
```

ADMAX
Ashurst-Sumners Act
Auburn System
Classification System
Design Capacity
Direct-Supervision Jail
Industrial Prison
Justice Model
Lex Talionis
Medical Model
Nothing-Works Doctrine

Operational Capacity
Prison
Prison Capacity
Private Prison
Privatization
Rated Capacity
Recidivism
Reformatory Style
Regional Jail
Warehousing
Workhouse

Prison Life

LEARNING OBJECTIVES

After reading this chapter, you should be able to:

- Describe the realities of prison life and subculture from the inmate's point of view

- Explain the concept of prisonization

- Illustrate the significant differences between men's prisons and women's prisons

- Describe the realities of prison life from the correctional officer's point of view

- Describe the causes of prison riots, and list the stages through which most riots progress

- Explain the nature of the hands-off doctrine, and discuss the status of that doctrine today

- Discuss the legal aspects of prisoners' rights, and explain the consequences of precedent-setting U.S. Supreme Court cases in the area of prisoners' rights

- Explain the balancing test established by the U.S. Supreme Court as it relates to the rights of prisoners

- Explain state-created rights within the context of corrections

- Describe the major problems and issues that prisons face today

Chapter Summary

Chapter 14 describes life in prison. The text focuses on the various social realities that coexist among correctional officers and inmates in male and female institutions, including prison riots, prisoners' rights, and other issues facing prisons today.

The discussion of the realities of the male inmate's world revolves around the discussion of **total institutions** and **prison subcultures**. Since inmates share all aspects of their lives on a daily basis, prison life is shaped by both the official structure and rules and the values and behavioral patterns of the inmates. New inmates undergo a process of **prisonization**, learning the values, language (**prison argot**), and rules of the institution. The text also describes nine inmate types who occupy various positions in the prison hierarchy.

Chapter 14 also describes the realities of life in prison for women. Although accounting for only 6.6% of the U.S. prison inmate population, the number of women in prison is growing rapidly. Two important factors contributing to this growth are female involvement in drug and drug-related offenses and the demise of the "chivalry factor." Although there is some disagreement among scholars attempting to describe the social structure of women's prisons, many researchers find that females are more likely to be involved in prison "families." Also, the amount and type of violence in female institutions is significantly different from that in male institutions. The text describes several types of female inmates, including the "square," the "cool," the "life," and "crack kids."

Correctional officers also undergo a socialization process into the prison culture. Due to overcrowded prisons and limitations in the number of staff, the primary mission of correctional officers is custody and control. The text describes six types of correctional officers and how they relate to inmates. The field of corrections is growing and is undergoing significant changes. Among the efforts to adapt to these changes is the professionalization of correctional officers.

Chapter 14 also discusses prison riots, emphasizing the explosive decade of prison riots. Several significant riots occurred between 1970 and 1980, beginning with the Attica riots and ending with the Santa Fe prison riots. Research indicates that the causes of prison riots include an insensitive prison administration and neglected inmates' demands, the lifestyles most inmates are familiar with on the streets, dehumanizing prison conditions, the way that riots regulate inmate society and redistribute power, and the power vacuums created by a variety of factors. The text also discusses the five typical stages of a riot and the control of riots.

Chapter 14 provides an examination of the legal rights of inmates. Historically, courts have adhered to a policy of nonintervention with regard to prison management. However, this **"hands-off doctrine"** was abandoned in the late 1960s. Courts have since provided precedent in many areas important to life in prison, including communications, religious practice, visitation, legal access to courts, privacy, medical care, and disciplinary proceedings. The **balancing test** is the important test applied to these areas of prison life. This test, articulated in the *Pell* v. *Procunier* decision, attempts to weigh the rights of an individual against the authority of states to make laws or otherwise restrict a person's freedom.

Chapter 14 concludes with a discussion of three issues facing prisons today. First, it discusses AIDS in prisons, describing the number of inmates infected and some of the strategies in place to reduce the transmission of this disease. Second, it discusses the growing geriatric offender population. With longer sentences, and the "graying" of the population, administrators must implement policies to deal with the special needs of geriatric and long-term inmates. Third, the special needs of mentally ill inmates are discussed.

Key Concepts

Balancing Test: A principle developed by the courts and applied to the corrections arena by *Pell* v. *Procunier* (1974), which attempts to weigh the rights of an individual as guaranteed by the Constitution against the authority of states to make laws or otherwise restrict a person's freedom in order to protect the state's interests and its citizens.

Civil Death: The legal status of prisoners in some jurisdictions who are denied the opportunity to vote, hold public office, marry, or enter into contracts by virtue of their status as incarcerated felons. While civil death is primarily of historical interest, some jurisdictions still limit the contractual opportunities available to inmates.

Grievance Procedure: A formalized arrangement, usually involving a neutral hearing board, whereby institutionalized individuals have the opportunity to register complaints about the conditions of their confinement.

Hands-Off Doctrine: A policy of nonintervention with regard to prison management that U.S. courts tended to follow until the late 1960s. For the past 30 years, the doctrine has languished as judicial intervention in prison administration dramatically increased, although there is now some evidence that a new hands-off era is approaching.

Prison Argot: The slang characteristic of prison subcultures and prison life.

Prisonization: The process whereby newly institutionalized offenders come to accept prison lifestyles and criminal values. Although many inmates begin their prison experience with only a few values that support criminal behavior, the socialization experience they undergo while incarcerated leads to a much wider acceptance of such values.

Prison Subculture: The values and behavioral patterns characteristic of prison inmates. Prison subculture has been found to have surprising consistent across the country.

Total Institution: An enclosed facility, separated from society both socially and physically, where the inhabitants share all aspects of their lives daily.

Key Cases

Block v. *Rutherford*: In the interests of security, jails can prohibit all visits from friends and relatives (*Block* v. *Rutherford*, 486 U.S. 576 [1984]).

Bounds v. *Smith*: Not only confirmed the right of prisoners to have access to the courts and to legal assistance but also required states to assist inmates in the preparation and filing of legal papers. This assistance can be given through trained personnel or through the creation and availability of a law library for inmates (*Bounds* v. *Smith*, 430 U.S. 817, 821 [1977]).

Cruz v. *Beto*: Inmates must be given a "reasonable opportunity" to pursue their religious faith even if it differs from traditional forms of worship (*Cruz* v. *Beto*, 405 U.S. 319 [1972]).

Estelle v. *Gamble*: Requires prison officials to provide for inmates' medical care, and established the concept of "deliberate indifference" in determining whether prison administrators are meeting the medical needs of prisoners (*Estelle* v. *Gamble*, 429 U.S. 97 [1976]).

Helling v. *McKinney*: Inmate sued due to involuntary exposure to secondhand cigarette smoke. The Court indicated that prison officials are responsible not only for "inmates' current serious health problems" but also for maintaining environmental conditions under which health problems might be prevented (*Helling* v. *McKinney*, 113 S.Ct. 2475, 125 L.Ed. 2d 22 [1993]).

Houchins v. *KQED*: News personnel cannot be denied correspondence with inmates, but they have no constitutional right to interview inmates or inspect correctional facilities beyond what is available to the general public (*Houchins* v. *KQED, Inc.*, 438 U.S. 11 [1978]).

Hudson v. *Palmer*: The need for prison officials to conduct thorough and unannounced searches precludes inmates' right to privacy in personal possessions (*Hudson* v. *Palmer*, 468 U.S. 517 [1984]).

Johnson v. *Avery*: Inmates have a right to consult "jailhouse lawyers" for advice if assistance from trained legal professionals is not available (*Johnson* v. *Avery*, 393 U.S. 483 [1968]).

Jones v. *North Carolina Prisoners' Labor Union*: Prisons must establish some formal opportunity for the airing of inmates' grievances (*Jones* v. *North Carolina Prisoners' Labor Union, Inc.*, 433 U.S. 119, 53 L.Ed. 2d 629, 641 [1977]).

Katz v. *U.S.*: The Court, in this case, stated that when a person makes an effort to keep private, even in a public place, it requires a judicial decision, in the form of a warrant issued upon probable cause, to unveil (*Katz* v. *U.S.*, 389 U.S. 347, 88 S.Ct. 507, 19 L.Ed. 2d 576 [1967]).

Newman v. *Alabama*: Found Alabama's prison medical services to be so inadequate as to be "shocking to the conscience" (*Newman* v. *Alabama*, 349 F.Supp. 278 [M.D. Alabama, 1972]).

Overton v. *Bazzetta*: The Court held that new visitation restrictions to counter prison security problems were acceptable. (*Overton* v. *Bassetta*, No. 02-94 [U.S. Supreme Court, decided June 16, 2003]).

Pell v. *Procunier*: Supreme Court established a "balancing test" to guide prison authorities in determining what rights an inmate should have. Inmates should have the same rights as nonincarcerated citizens, provided that the legitimate needs of the prison for security, custody, and safety are not compromised (*Pell* v. *Procunier*, 417 U.S. 817, 822 [1974]).

Pennsylvania Department of Corrections v. *Yeskey*: The Supreme Court held that the Americans with Disabilities Act of 1990 applies to prisons and prison inmates (*Pennsylvania Department of Corrections* v. *Yeskey*, 524 U.S. 206, 209 [1998]).

Ruiz v. *Estelle*: Challenged the structure of the Texas prison system and specifically required major changes in the handling of inmates' medical care. The Court ordered an improvement in record keeping, physical facilities, and general medical care while it continued to monitor the progress of the department (*Ruiz* v. *Estelle*, 503 F.Supp. 1265 [S.D. Texas, 1980]).

Sandin v. *Conner*: An apparent return to the hands-off doctrine, as the Court rejected the argument that any state action taken for a punitive reason encroaches upon a prisoner's constitutional right to be free from the deprivation of liberty (*Sandin* v. *Conner*, 63 U.S.L.W. 4601 [1995]).

Wolff v. *McDonnell*: Sanctions cannot be levied against inmates without appropriate due process. Beginning of concept of "state-created liberty interests" (*Wolff* v. *McDonnell*, 94 S.Ct. 2963 [1974]).

Learning Tips

Multiple-Choice Questions

Multiple-choice questions can be very confusing and challenging, but the following four-step process will assist you in tackling these types of questions. First, check to see how many answers you are supposed to choose for each question. Second, read and answer the questions without looking at the test answers. If your answer matches one of the test answers, choose it. This will avoid additional confusion by the other test answers. Third, if you don't know the exact answer, read each choice because answers are often quite similar. Fourth, skip questions that you cannot answer immediately and go back to them when you have time.

Multiple-Choice Answers

Whenever you are not penalized for wrong answers on multiple-choice questions and you are completely unable to answer the question, there are three ways to choose the best answer. One strategy is to eliminate any answer you know to be wrong and guess from the remaining choices. Another strategy is to assess if two answers are very similar, except for a couple of words, and to choose one of these two answers. A third strategy: If it is a question involving numbers and the answers are listed in numerical order, choose an answer that lies in the middle.

CJ Today on the World Wide Web

Web links to organizations and agencies related to the material in Chapter 14 include:

WEBSITE TITLE	URL
Prison Legal News	http://www.prisonlegalnews.org
Stop Prisoner Rape	http://www.spr.org/index.html
Attica Prison Riot	http://www.pbs.org/wgbh/amex/ rockefellers/sfeature/sf_5.html
Weight Lifting and Recreation	http://www.strengthtech.com/index.htm
15 Years to Life	http://www.15yearstolife.com
Prison Life Inside	http://www.inmate.com/inmates/ davidcdc.htm
Pennsylvania Department of Corrections	http://www.cor.state.pa.us

Student Activities

Activity 1

Your text outlines in great detail the adaptation process that inmates go through when entering a prison setting and describes the prisonization process. How are these adaptations similar to and different from the adaptations that students have to make at a college campus? What subcultures exist on your campus? Is there an argot unique to college campuses?

_____
_____
_____
_____
_____
_____

Activity 2

Mike and his sister Michelle committed several bank robberies together. After they were caught, tried, and convicted, the judge sentenced them both to 25 to 50 years in a maximum-security prison. Their sentencing hearing occurred about two years ago. Recently, they exchanged their first letters describing their lives in prison. What did each of them say? Be sure to discuss the physical characteristics of the prison, what needs are fulfilled by the prison, and the different social realities of prison.

_____
_____
_____
_____
_____
_____

REMEMBER

The policing section discusses two terms that can be related to some of the material described in Chapter 14. First, it describes the police subculture as a particular set of values, beliefs, and acceptable forms of behavior characteristic of American police and with which the police profession strives to imbue new recruits. Socialization into the police subculture commences with recruit training and is ongoing thereafter. Second, it describes the police working personality. This term refers to all aspects of the traditional values and patterns of behavior evidenced by police officers who have been socialized into the police subculture. Inmates and correctional officers belong to subcultures. Moreover, one would expect that correctional officers have a working personality as well.

Activity 3

Visit the Prison Issues Desk at www.prisonactivist.org. Click on the Issues section. This section includes research information and data on issues such as the prison crisis, political prisoners, women and prison, medical neglect in prison, and children in prison. Choose one of these topics, and in the space below write a summary of the information provided.

_____

_____

_____

_____

_____

_____

Activity 4

Contact a local correctional facility (either a prison or a jail). Interview an administrator of that facility about the issues discussed in Chapter 14. How is that facility responding to AIDS? How is it managing the aging inmate population? Mentally ill inmates? In the space below, discuss what you learn.

_____

_____

_____

_____

_____

_____

Internet Activity

LIBRARY extra

Read **Library Extras 14–6** and **14–7**. Describe the medical issues facing corrections officials in the space below. Your instructor may request that you submit this material.

_____

_____

_____

_____

_____

Distance Learning Activity

Write a short essay about life in prison from the perspective of a correctional officer or from the perspective of an inmate. Search the World Wide Web for materials to be included in your essay. The following websites will be helpful: (1) New York State Correctional Officer Informational Page: http://www.geocities.com/MotorCity/Downs/3548, (2) 15 Years to Life: http://www.15yearstolife.com, (3) Prison Life Inside: http://www.inmate.com/inmates/davidcdc.htm. If your instructor asks you to do so, share your essay with other students in the class.

_____

_____

_____

_____

_____

_____

Student Study Guide Questions

True or False

____ 14-1. Few states have substantial capacity for the psychiatric treatment of mentally disturbed inmates.

____ 14-2. In 1935, an Indiana University sociology professor completed a groundbreaking study of prison life when he voluntarily served three months in prison as a participant-observer to discover what being an inmate was really like.

____ 14-3. Prison argot is a secret language prisoners use to communicate that no one except the prisoners knows.

____ 14-4. In all state and federal prison facilities combined, the number of incarcerated male prisoners is greater than the number of females incarcerated by a ratio of slightly more than two to one.

____ 14-5. The "chivalry factor" has led to a recent decline in the number of women sentenced to prison, as more and more judges are reluctant to separate mothers from their children.

____ 14-6. A prisoner's private mail from immediate family members may be not be opened and censored by prison authorities.

____ 14-7. Prison riots are generally unplanned and tend to occur spontaneously, the result of some relatively minor precipitating event.

____ 14-8. Most male sexual aggressors in prisons do not consider themselves heterosexual.

____ 14-9. Inmates have a right to consult "jailhouse lawyers" for advice if the prison does not provide assistance from trained legal professionals.

____ 14-10. The U.S. Supreme Court case of _Hudson_ v. _Palmer_ asserts that the need for prison officials to conduct thorough and unannounced searches is greater than inmates' right to privacy in personal possessions.

Multiple Choice

14-11. _____ develop independently of the plans of prison administrators.
   a. Prison subcultures
   b. Total institutions
   c. Women's prisons
   d. Parole boards

14-12. The _____ established by the U.S. Supreme Court in _Pell_ v. _Procunier_ has served as a guideline generally applicable to all prison operations.
   a. either-or doctrine
   b. balancing test
   c. writ of _habeas corpus_
   d. prisonization process

14-13. Correctional officers are generally considered to be part of the _____ staff.
  a. professional
  b. administrative
  c. custodial
  d. treatment

14-14. The policy followed by the courts until the 1960s in refusing to hear inmate complaints about the conditions of incarceration and the constitutional deprivations of inmate life was called the
  a. fingers-crossed model.
  b. bloody codes.
  c. hands-off doctrine.
  d. inmate code.

14-15. The hands-off doctrine ended when the federal court declared that the entire prison system in the state of _____ was in violation of the constitutional ban against cruel and unusual punishment.
  a. Arkansas
  b. New Mexico
  c. Indiana
  d. New York

14-16. An inmate who is quick to fight and fights like a wild man is referred to as
  a. the opportunist.
  b. the mean dude.
  c. the hedonist.
  d. the retreatist.

14-17. In *The Society of Captives*, Gresham Sykes claims that prisoners are deprived of all of the following except
  a. liberty.
  b. goods and services.
  c. homosexual relationships.
  d. autonomy.

14-18. All of the following are listed as contributing to the "graying" of America's prison population except
  a. increasing crime among those over 50.
  b. the gradual aging of the society from which prisoners come.
  c. a trend toward longer sentences.
  d. the reduction in the number of older habitual offenders in prison.

14-19. Inmates adopt a series of lifestyles in an attempt to survive the prison experience. _____ build their lifestyle around the limited pleasures that can be had within the confines of prison.
  a. Mean dudes
  b. Hedonists
  c. Opportunists
  d. Retreatists

14-20. Correctional officers can be classified according to certain categories. If an officer tries to fraternize with inmates, attempting to be "one of the guys," he or she would be classified as a(n)
  a. dictator.
  b. friend.
  c. merchant.
  d. indifferent.

Fill-In

14-21. _____ is the slang characteristic of prison subcultures and prison life.

14-22. _____ are enclosed facilities where the inhabitants share all aspects of their lives.

14-23. _____ is the case that required that inmates be given a "reasonable opportunity" to pursue their religious faith even if it differs from traditional forms of worship.

14-24. _____ are formalized arrangements prisoners have to register complaints about the conditions of their confinement.

14-25. The _____ attempts to weigh the constitutional rights of an individual against the authority of the state to make laws to protect its interests and its citizens.

14-26. The values and behavioral patterns characteristic of prison inmates comprise the _____.

14-27. The _____ was a policy of nonintervention with regard to prison management that American courts tended to follow until the late 1960s.

14-28. _____ is the process whereby institutionalized individuals come to accept prison lifestyles and criminal values.

14-29. _____ is the legal status of prisoners in some jurisdictions who are denied the opportunity to vote, hold public office, marry, or enter into contracts by virtue of their status as incarcerated felons.

14-30. The legislation that attempts to restrict the number of suits files by inmates is _____.

Crossword Puzzle

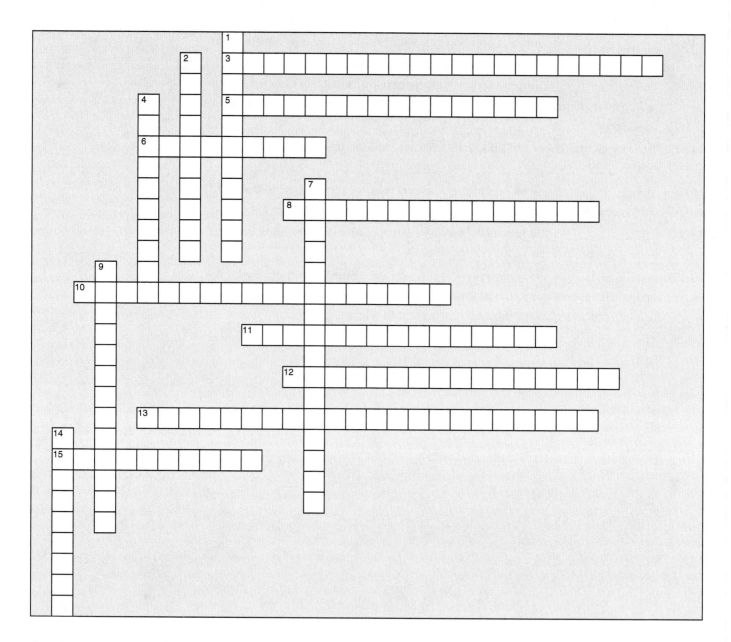

Across

3. Standard set by *Cruz* v. *Beto*.
5. *Hudson* v. *Palmer* focuses on this issue.
6. Test established by *Pell* v. *Procunier*.
8. An inmate lawyer.
10. The official way prisoners can complain about the conditions of their confinement.
11. Case that started the concept of state-created liberty interests.
12. Enclosed facilities, separated from society both socially and physically, where the inhabitants share all aspects of their lives daily.
13. Standard set by *Estelle* v. *Gamble*.
15. *Block* v. _____.

Down

1. The language of inmates.
2. Prisoners are denied the opportunity to vote and hold public office; this is called _____.
4. The values and behavioral patterns of prison inmates.
7. A policy of nonintervention by prison management.
9. The process whereby newly institutionalized offenders come to accept prison lifestyles and criminal values.
14. *Pell* v. _____.

Word Search Puzzle

```
V I S I T A T I O N S P O E O D S F E O V L N A I E R Z L I
P T E F D I C T L F V A R N A L R S N I I N A R T N E T E T
A R A O P T S L D F A U O N H B J U V C I A I T E E I S I T
N E T C I Z P H U A T A U D T N A S O U P D M A O Y F N B R
B E I A T B E R E L P E L Y G I Z A A T L O A C N I I L S N
R E Y W A L E S U O H L I A J T N B A C R C B R O F T U I I
S O I L A G N C I T I I E R N A F N N B N B I R O T O D U I
T C V P S B B L P N O A T E A A A T E I I Y I Y S E L Y O I
L S I B P U N L C I E N A N Z H I A O V H E L E R P T P E T
L D E A S L T O B A T I T R R A I Y I N E U L I A I N R C T
D A S R N D F N L T T E C S P A E M I B O I D C N T T E N E
I N N V G R I E V A N C E P R O C E D U R E A U R O E S E V
U S S P I T U M T O I T N E V B E D E E T I T O T S N N R F
R C E W R H V C E C P P T T I A N N N I N R S A C I S G E I
E I I A U A E Y I N S R R S I E E R I L O I L E N N A T F L
I V L U N N S N I S T E I I A A C I U P L I L E I U I E F F
U I T U O D R T T H A E S E H L N P O N R U U T I L R I O
G L V V E S A C I S N B L O O R H O N S S E L S A E T S D D
T D E S N O L O I E O O L L R N E L T H A N A O S C R E N A
G E T E T F D D L T R O I N Y L R I U E E D T S D C A N I E
G A M T L F C D L G E T I T B I T I I I E I F P R N C R E G
C T D I A D N T F N C E L A A U L E O T L A I L B Z I T T O
U H U F N O Y E T I I H N A T Z A L A T S U P E D F N A A E
S T L R S C S L T C E O N I I P I E I E W S T N G E T A R E
R A D C L T I T E N S N O R Y L R N C N O V A N U I O L E F
C R H U E R T I I A I N N W T P T U O I M O O I N U I D B H
T O J N N I F U E L D A R M T Z R D P S E A A N I V L W I R
L Y E A Y N N R F A I D R T R I E S R Y I O T N O R R E L A
T A A P C E E R P B R I A L T O N A S D R R T E I A I C E A
T F I C E L O D T O G R A Y D R F A M Z I P P O S T T O D D
```

Argot
Balancing Test
Civil Death
Deliberate Indifference
Grievance Procedure
Hands-Off Doctrine
Jailhouse Lawyer
Mentally Ill Inmates

Prisonization
Prison Riot
Reasonable Opportunity
Security
Subculture
Total Institution
Visitation

chapter 15

Juvenile Justice

LEARNING OBJECTIVES

After reading this chapter, you should be able to:

- Describe the history and evolution of the juvenile justice system in the Western world

- List and define the categories of children in today's juvenile justice system

- Describe the nature of the problems that juveniles face in the United States today

- Name the important U.S. Supreme Court decisions of relevance to juvenile justice, and describe their impact on the handling of juveniles by the system

- Explain the similarities and differences between the juvenile and adult systems of justice

Chapter Summary

Juvenile crime is a perplexing problem for the criminal justice system. It is perplexing because research indicates that the amount of violent crime committed by juveniles is decreasing but public demand for severe punishments for juveniles has increased. Moreover, the public's desire for a crackdown on juvenile crime, and the demand that juvenile punishments be equivalent to adult punishments, is inconsistent with the underlying philosophy of the juvenile court.

This chapter examines four areas of juvenile justice: First, it examines the historical development of the juvenile justice system; second, it compares the juvenile justice system to the adult system; third, it discusses the juvenile justice system process; and finally, it discusses several criticisms of the juvenile system.

The text discusses the historical beginnings of the juvenile justice system throughout the world and in America and traces this history through several important Supreme Court cases decided in the 1970s and 1980s. The text's examination of the historical evolution of the juvenile justice system begins with a discussion of treatment of juveniles in the earliest times, when they were treated differently from adults. For example, the laws of King Aethelbert made no special provisions for offenders because of age. The common law principle of **parens patriae** is important to an understanding of juvenile justice because it means that the state can assume the role of the parent and take custody of a child.

In America, the criminal justice response to juveniles began in the early nineteenth century with the development of houses of refuge. The **child savers movement** began in the mid-1800s, influencing the development of reform schools. The early model, embodied in the **Chicago Reform School**, focused on emulating family environments to provide security and build moral character, emphasizing traditional values such as hard work. Finally, the text discusses the beginnings of the juvenile court era from early legislation in Massachusetts and New York to the Illinois juvenile law that was modeled by most states and the federal government's Juvenile Court Act. Most legislation included six categories of children subject to the jurisdiction of the juvenile court: **delinquent children, undisciplined children, dependent children, neglected children, abused children,** and **status offenders.**

Chapter 15 also covers several theoretical explanations for juvenile delinquency. This discussion includes Shaw and McKay's **social ecology approach,** Cloward and Ohlin's **opportunity theory**, and Sykes and Matza's **neutralization techniques**. Moreover, the text discusses two significant research efforts to identify the determinants of delinquency. First, the text discusses research conducted by Marvin Wolfgang that traced the delinquent behavior of a birth **cohort** in Philadelphia. Second, it discusses the Program of Research on the Causes and Correlates of Juvenile Delinquency and its three coordinated projects.

Chapter 15 also provides an excellent overview of several important Court decisions affecting juveniles. The most significant is *In re Gault*. This decision guaranteed several procedural rights to juveniles including the right to have notice of the charges, the right to counsel, the right to confront and cross-examine witnesses, and the right to appeal. Other cases discussed include *In re Winship, McKeiver* v. *Pennsylvania, Breed* v. *Jones, Kent* v. *United States,* and *Schall* v. *Martin*. Juveniles, however, are not provided all the protections guaranteed to adult defendants. For example, juveniles do not have a constitutional right to a jury trial.

The juvenile justice system, as a process, involves four stages: intake, adjudication, **disposition,** and **postadjudication review. Intake** involves the filing of a juvenile petition by some party, such as the police, alleging illegal behavior by the juvenile. **Adjudication** is the trial process for juveniles. Adjudicatory hearings are similar to the adult trial, but with some exceptions. A **dispositionary hearing**, similar to an adult sentencing hearing, occurs to determine the action the court should take against a juvenile. Judges have several options at disposition, including outright release, probation, or confinement to a secure institution.

Chapter 15 concludes by considering the future of the juvenile justice system, acknowledging that it will increase penalties, reduce privacy, and eliminate diversionary opportunities for juveniles.

Key Concepts

Abused Child: A child who has been physically, sexually, or mentally abused. Most states also consider a child who is forced into delinquent activity by a parent or guardian to be abused.

Adjudicatory Hearing: The fact-finding process wherein the juvenile court determines whether there is sufficient evidence to sustain the allegations in a petition.

Cohort: A group of individuals sharing similarities of age, place of birth, and residence.

Delinquency: In the broadest usage, juvenile actions or conduct in violation of criminal law, juvenile status offenses, and other juvenile misbehavior.

Delinquent Child: A child who has engaged in activity that would be considered a crime if the child were an adult. The term *delinquent* is used to avoid the stigma associated with the term *criminal*.

Dependent Child: A child who has no parents or whose parents are unable to care for him or her.

Dispositional Hearing: The final stage in the processing of adjudicated juveniles, in which a decision is made on the form of treatment or penalty that should be imposed on the child.

Intake: The first step in decision making regarding a juvenile whose behavior or alleged behavior is in violation of the law or could otherwise cause a juvenile court to assume jurisdiction.

Juvenile Disposition: The decision of a juvenile court, concluding a disposition hearing, that an adjudicated juvenile be committed to a juvenile correctional facility; be placed in a juvenile residence, shelter, or care or treatment program; be required to meet certain standards of conduct; or be released.

Juvenile Justice System: Government agencies that function to investigate, supervise, adjudicate, care for, or confine youthful offenders and other children subject to the jurisdiction of the juvenile court.

Juvenile Petition: A document filed in juvenile court alleging that a juvenile is a delinquent, a status offender, or a dependent and asking that the court assume jurisdiction over the juvenile or that an alleged delinquent be transferred to a criminal court for prosecution as an adult.

Neglected Child: A child who is not receiving the proper level of physical or psychological care from his or her parent(s) or guardian(s) or who has been placed for adoption in violation of the law.

Opportunity Theory: A perspective that sees delinquency as the result of limited legitimate opportunities for success available to most lower-class youth.

Parens Patriae: A common law principle that allows the state to assume a parental role and to take custody of a child when he or she becomes a delinquent, is abandoned, or is in need of care that the natural parents are unable or unwilling to provide.

Social Ecology: A criminological approach that focuses on the misbehavior of lower-class youth and sees delinquency primarily as the result of social disorganization.

Status Offender: A child who commits an act that is contrary to the law by virtue of the juvenile's status as a child. Purchasing cigarettes, buying alcohol, and being truant are examples of such behavior.

Status Offense: An act or conduct that is declared by statute to be an offense, but only when committed by or engaged in by a juvenile, and that can be adjudicated only by a juvenile court.

Teen Court: An alternative approach to juvenile justice in which juvenile offenders are judged and sentenced by a jury of their peers.

Undisciplined Child: A child who is beyond parental control, as evidenced by his or her refusal to obey legitimate authorities, such as school officials and teachers.

Key Cases

Breed v. *Jones*: This case severely restricts the conditions under which transfers from juvenile to adult court may occur. Such transfers must occur prior to an adjudicatory hearing in juvenile court (*Breed* v. *Jones*, 421 U.S. 519 [1975]).

Illinois v. *Montanez*: In this case the Supreme Court let stand a state court ruling that threw out a voluntary confession made by a juvenile suspect who had been tried as an adult (*Illinois* v. *Montanez*, [1996], certiori denied).

In re Gault: The Court decided that juveniles have a right to notice of charges, a right to counsel, and a right to confront and to cross-examine witnesses and must be provided protection against self-incrimination (*In re Gault*, 387 U.S. 1 [1967]).

In re Winship: Allegations of delinquency must be established beyond a reasonable doubt. Status offenses, however, can be established with the preponderance of the evidence standard (*In re Winship*, 397 U.S. 358 [1970]).

Kent v. *U.S.*: This case ended the hands-off era in juvenile justice and recognized that at least minimal due process must be provided in juvenile court hearings (*Kent* v. *U.S.*, 383 U.S. 541 [1966]).

McKeiver v. *Pennsylvania*: This case held that juveniles do not have the constitutional right to a jury trial (*McKeiver* v. *Pennsylvania*, 403 U.S. 528 [1971]).

Schall v. *Martin*: This case upheld the practice of preventive detention but stated that it cannot be imposed without prior notice, an equitable detention hearing, and a statement by the judge setting the reasons for the detention (*Schall* v. *Martin*, 467 U.S. 253 [1984]).

Learning Tips

Open-Book or Open-Note Exams

While an open-book or open-note test may seem extremely easy, these exams are often the most difficult. Significant preparation is even more imperative with these exams. To eliminate excess time spent flipping through pages of notes or chapters of a book, prepare thoroughly by marking pages, marking tabs, highlighting key words, including an outline in your notes, and knowing the progression of the notes or chapters backward and forward.

Short Answers

Short-answer questions usually ask for a definition or description and the significance of the question relative to the coursework. Problems arise when students go off on tangents and write everything they know on the topic. It is important to stay focused on the question, be brief, and answer the question directly. In addition, be sure to use facts and key words.

CJ Today on the World Wide Web

Web links to organizations and agencies related to the material in Chapter 15 include:

WEBSITE TITLE	URL
American Bar Association's Juvenile Justice Center	http://www.abanet.org/crimjust/juvjus/home.html

REMEMBER

Chapter 15 discusses several significant Supreme Court decisions affecting juveniles. Some important decisions you read about earlier include *Miranda* v. *Arizona*: Persons in custody must be advised of various warnings prior to being subjected to custodial interrogation; *Mapp* v. *Ohio*: The Fourth Amendment's exclusionary rule is applicable to the states through the due process clause of the Fourteenth Amendment; *Gideon* v. *Wainwright*: Extended the right to appointed counsel in state courts to all indigent defendants charged with a felony; and *Argersinger* v. *Hamlin*: The Supreme Court required that adequate legal representation be given to any defendant facing a potential sentence of imprisonment.

WEBSITE TITLE	URL
Center on Juvenile and Criminal Justice (CJCJ)	http://www.cjcj.org/
(NCJRS) Juvenile Court Section Juvenile Justice	http://virlib.ncjrs.org/JuvenileJustice.asp
Juvenile Justice Magazine Online	http://www.juvenilejustice.com
National Council on Crime and Delinquency	http://www.nccd-crc.org
Office of Juvenile Justice and Delinquency Prevention (OJJDP)	http://ojjdp.ncjrs.org
The Juvenile Justice Clearinghouse	http://www.fsu.edu/~crimdo/jjclearinghouse
An Urban Ethnography of Latino Street Gangs	http://www.csun.edu/~hcchs006/gang.html
National Youth Gang Center (NYGC)	http://www.iir.com/nygc

Student Activities

Activity 1

Youth violence has long been a concern for the criminal justice system. In the early 1900s, for example, legislators across the country decided that juvenile delinquents who commit a crime should be treated differently from adult criminals. Thus, the juvenile justice system was created with the important purpose of providing opportunities for juveniles to reform, rather than strictly punishing them for their acts.

However, an increasing number of juveniles, some as young as 13, have been waived out of the juvenile justice system into adult court. Thirteen- and 14-year-old children are being sent to maximum-security prisons. Currently, it appears that the system is more concerned with punishing delinquents than reforming them. After reading about the juvenile justice system in Chapter 15, combined with what you learned about criminal justice in this class, do you think the juvenile justice system should be abolished? Why or why not?

_____

_____

_____

_____

_____

Activity 2

Chapter 15 provides an excellent overview of several important theories designed to explain juvenile delinquency. Social disorganization, opportunity theory, and neutralization techniques are discussed. There are other theories that might be helpful in attempting to explain juvenile delinquency. For example, some critics argue that the reliance on various sources of media by children is a major contributing cause of delinquency. Video games, cartoons, music-especially rap and heavy metal-and violence on television have all been criticized for poisoning the minds of youth. Do you think media images of violence cause children to become delinquents? Why or why not? What types of media images do you think are most harmful to children? Explain your answer. (Note that there is a very large body of research examining the links between viewing violence and committing violence. It may be helpful to visit the World Wide Web or your library to do some background reading on this topic.)

_____

_____

_____
_____
_____
_____

Activity 3

Judge Gayle Garner has the following three juvenile cases on her docket:

1. Jarred Owens is a 17-year-old high school dropout. He has recently been convicted of two burglaries. His criminal record includes three other crimes: two shoplifting incidents and a theft. His parents are frustrated with his behavior and admit to having trouble controlling him. Jarred's two brothers are well behaved and have no criminal records.

2. Anne Yeerns is 15 years old and was convicted of attempting to steal a car. This was her first offense. However, she is also a runaway. On two prior occasions, she has run away from her father. The first time she went back home after three days, the second time the police brought her back after one week, and this time she claims she was stealing the car to get as far away as possible. Anne's father did not attend the dispositional hearing.

3. Patrick Darvy is 12 years old and was recently initiated into a juvenile gang. He was caught selling drugs; it was his first offense. Patrick lives with his mother, who is divorced. Ms. Darvy is very concerned about recent changes in his behavior and would like the court's help in changing his behavior.

Make a recommendation to Judge Garner for the dispositions of these three cases. Discuss the sentences you would recommend, and provide the rationale for your recommendations.

_____
_____
_____
_____
_____
_____

Activity 4

Near the end of Chapter 15, the text discusses three ongoing efforts directed at reforming the juvenile justice system. These efforts include lessening the degree of privacy, increasing penalties for certain kinds of delinquent acts, and reducing diversionary opportunities for habitual, violent, and serious offenders. The President's Commission on Juvenile Justice would like you to recommend one of these reform efforts. In the space provided below, discuss which one of these reforms you think would have the most positive impact on the juvenile justice system and provide your rationale for excluding the other two reforms.

_____
_____
_____
_____
_____

Internet Activity

Visit the Cybrary at http://www.cybrary.info. Click on the topic "Juvenile Justice," and review the sites that appear. Which of those sites is identified as one of the "Top 100" sites? Are there other juvenile justice sites that you think should be among the "Top 100" identified by the Cybrary? If so, use the feedback link at the bottom of the Cybrary's home page to tell the Cybrary staff what you think. Submit your findings to your instructor if requested to do so.

_____

_____

_____

_____

_____

Distance Learning Activity

Visit the American Bar Association's website on Juvenile Justice Issues at http://www.abanet.org/crimjust/juvjus/jjnews.html. Read one of the essays posted and provide a summary of its key ideas. If your instructor asks you to do so, participate in a class discussion that compares and contrasts the findings from the different essays.

_____

_____

_____

_____

_____

Student Study Guide Questions

True or False

_____ 15-1. Juveniles have a constitutional right to a jury trial.

_____ 15-2. The laws of King Aethelbert created our current juvenile justice system by allowing special allowances for the age of the offender.

_____ 15-3. Gresham Sykes and David Matza developed opportunity theory in the 1960s, arguing that delinquency results from the lack of legitimate opportunities for success available to most lower-class youth.

_____ 15-4. Violence among teenagers and teenage suicide continue to decrease at a rapid rate.

_____ 15-5. Very few juvenile correctional institutions are overcrowded.

_____ 15-6. A delinquent child is one who has no parents or whose parents are unable to care for him or her.

_____ 15-7. Juveniles charged with a status offense have the same procedural rights afforded to adults charged with a criminal offense.

_____ 15-8. If a juvenile is charged as a status offender, his or her guilt must be proved using a preponderance of evidence standard.

____ 15-9. Juvenile trials are open to the public and to the news media.

____ 15-10. If a juvenile is charged with a criminal offense, his or her guilt must be proved beyond a reasonable doubt.

Multiple Choice

15-11. Which of the following was not emphasized by the reform school movement?
a. the worth of hard work
b. wholesome family environments
c. affection necessary to build moral character
d. All of the above were emphasized by the reform school movement.

15-12. Which theory sees delinquency as the result of social disorganization?
a. social ecology
b. opportunity
c. neutralization
d. strain

15-13. Which of the following is not a status offense?
a. truancy
b. running away from home
c. robbery
d. incorrigibility

15-14. What is the evidentiary standard that must be met at a delinquency hearing?
a. preponderance of the evidence
b. beyond a reasonable doubt
c. in most instances
d. the "feel good" standard

15-15. Which of the following U.S. Supreme Court cases ruled that juveniles are entitled to representation by attorneys who must have access to their records when the juveniles are being transferred to adult court?
a. *Breed* v. *Jones*
b. Schall v. Martin
c. Kent v. U.S.
d. Ex parte Crouse

15-16. _____ children are defined as those who do not receive proper care from their parents or guardians.
a. Dependent
b. Neglected
c. Abused
d. Undisciplined

15-17. Teen court is
a. a place where status offenders are given due process.
b. another name of the juvenile justice system.
c. a place where children ages 13–17 are tried.
d. a place where alleged offenders are judged and sentenced by jury of their peers.

15-18. Which step of the juvenile court process is similar to an adult trial?
a. intake
b. adjudication
c. disposition
d. postadjudicatory review

15-19. A common law principle that allows the state to assume a parental role and to take custody of a child who becomes delinquent, is abandoned, or is in need of care that the natural parents are unable or unwilling to provide is
a. arrest.
b. community outreach.
c. *parens patriae*.
d. intake.

15-20. Most states' juvenile court systems were modeled after the court system in this state:
   a. Indiana
   b. Illinois
   c. New York
   d. Ohio

Fill-In

15-21. The term applied to a child in order to avoid the stigma that comes from application of the term *criminal* is _____.

15-22. A child who is beyond parental control, as evidenced by refusal to obey legitimate authorities such as school officials and teachers, is termed a(n) _____.

15-23. _____ theory views delinquency as the result of limited legitimate avenues to be successful.

15-24. A child who has been forced into delinquent activity by a parent or guardian is termed a(n) _____.

15-25. _____ is the principle that allows the state to assume a parental role.

15-26. _____ is the fact-finding process in which the court determines whether or not there is sufficient evidence to sustain the allegations in a petition.

15-27. A document filed in juvenile court alleging that a juvenile is delinquent, a status offender, or a dependent and asking that the court assume jurisdiction over the child is a(n) _____.

15-28. A child who commits an act that is contrary to the law by virtue of the juvenile's status as a child is a(n) _____.

15-29. A child not receiving the proper level of physical or psychological care from parents is a(n) _____.

15-30. A child who has no parent(s) or whose parent(s) is (are) unable to care for him or her is a(n) _____.

Crossword Puzzle

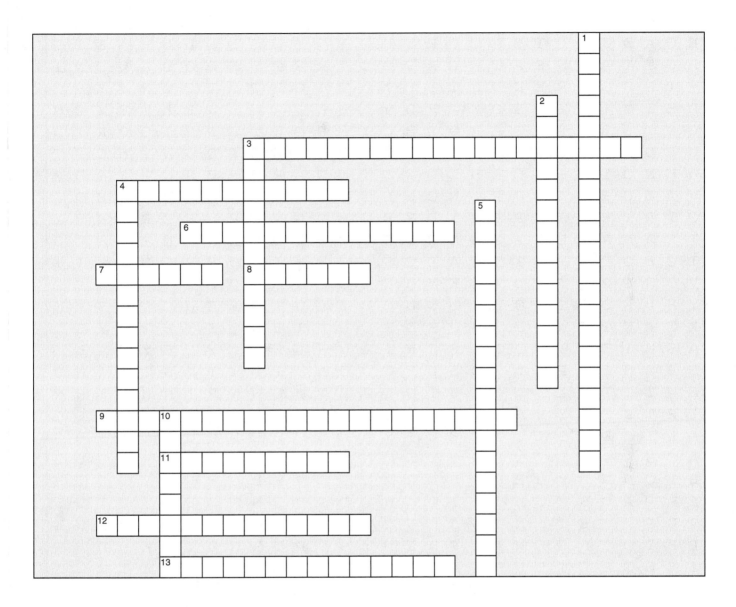

Across

3. The juvenile justice hearing to determine whether there is sufficient evidence to sustain allegations.
4. When a juvenile breaks the law.
6. It means the state assumes responsibility for the welfare of problem children.
7. The first step of the juvenile justice process.
8. A group of individuals sharing similarities of age, blace of birth, and residence.
9. The final stage of the juvenile justice process.
11. An alternative approach to juvenile justice in which juvenile offenders are judged and sentenced by a jury of their peers.
12. Theory that explains delinquency primarily as the result of social disorganization.
13. A child who is not receiving the proper level of physical or psychological care from his or her parents.

Down

1. The system that responds to crimes committed by youthful offenders.
2. Purchasing cigarettes and alcohol and being truant are examples.
3. A child who has been physically, sexually, or mentally abused.
4. A child who has no parents or whose parents are unable to care for him or her.
5. A child beyond parental control.
10. A written request made to a court.

Word Search Puzzle

```
E Q A D J U D I C A T O R Y H E A R I N G L E L L H A E T E
A J I T A H N E A T N E A S G E J R E G T E D O D A U E N I
M T H E O A R E D D J C I L T U T T O H T C I C E R J E S T
D E I Y I U T Y E O N I R D V P E E J R U L R F L T E Y O N
C S T L E N P I T A R O E E C Y P D G D T L D C I O O R I D
U F G S S C C T C T T E N T R U O C N E E T D J N P N C Y T
U H N Q Y N I E C R U I C C J T N U L R U P U H Q P F S H N
V I I U E S L R J P L N O D L T C T V R U A L C U O O E O A
C T R T R C E I P E R T D E E J R D G N U E L E E R O N E Y
T E A N A I L C P O U N E I D S T O L O R H N J N T T I S O
I C E O E H S E I T E A E C S A C H H I E O E E C U L D I T
V O H S G L T Y L T I K Y H B C S J N O I D P I Y N L E S P
Y H L E O I S T O E S L N U C D I L U T C E E U C I E S H N
K T A N T C N C E I G U S D N O D P I C N Q S T H T S Y E L
A S N I D I I O D L O E J N I A U S L L O C Y C E Y C A L T
D B O H O L P A D E S E E O D O A Y I L T T I S T I I N U
S N I T P E I I L C D U I O L P E T O C N N R I N H C T H N
I H T D E D Y H H E U O E T S I O T I E E E E R E N I E G
I L I J D C I I C L C E U I E A N H C D U N D U I O I V D G
A I S U P D L T N D P O D N O N U E N T T T N C T R C D D G
E Y O N N D R U R O E E L R E D D E V E D O E L H Y V D I H
E R P A O E Y U D I L T O O N L P S D U N T F E E I U T U I
O D S I F E T I N I S J C V G E I V E D J I F D U N L I N L
P H I O C S E L N A C E N E D Y S I D T R G O I E E Q D D I
I E D T S E I E N E C A A O L O D L O S P S S L E E T C U I
C I E N S S V E E I D T H L L G L N C O D T U P D K A E A N
E I S I E U U B Y N N P N E C K E D T I D I T N N A N I C T
E I T I J O H O D R D R Y O E E T N E K C E A I C T D D I O
A N B T E N L D L I H C T N E U Q N I L E D T T E N I T H T
O I A P A R E N S P A T R I A E S I C D E T S S I I C A F N
```

Abused Child
Adjudicatory Hearing
Cohort
Delinquency
Delinquent Child
Dependent Child
Dispositional Hearing
Intake
Juvenile Disposition

Juvenile Justice System
Juvenile Petition
Neglected Child
Opportunity Theory
Parens Patriae
Social Ecology
Status Offender
Teen Court
Undisciplined Child

Drugs and Crime

LEARNING OBJECTIVES

After reading this chapter, you should be able to:

■ Discuss the history of drug abuse in America

■ Discuss the history of antidrug legislation in America

■ Identify the different types of drugs that are illegally used in this country, as well as the effects and legal classifications of each

■ Explain the link between drugs and other social problems, including different forms of criminal activity

■ Describe the various efforts to respond to the drug problem, and assess the effectiveness of each

Chapter Summary

The textbook examines the important issue of drugs and crime in Chapter 16. Drug use, drug-related crime, drug laws, and drug-enforcement efforts significantly affect processes of criminal justice. A large proportion of the financial and personnel resources of the criminal justice system is used to respond to the drug problem in the United States. For example, police departments utilize undercover operations to increase the number of arrests of drug offenders, prosecutions for drug offenses overwhelm court dockets, and the number of defendants incarcerated for drug offenses continues to grow.

Chapter 16 begins with an overview of the drug problem. First, it illustrates the importance of the topic by highlighting the specific impacts of drugs on the criminal justice system. The text also provides essential background information with a discussion of the question "What is a drug?" It also examines alcohol abuse and the criminal justice system's response to alcohol-related offenses.

The text then traces the history of drug abuse, covering the use of opium, morphine, and heroin in the 1800s and early 1900s, the response to marijuana in the 1900s, the use of LSD in the 1960s and 1970s, the use of crack cocaine in the 1980s, and the increased use of club drugs in the 1990s. The text further discusses the corresponding history of anti-drug–abuse legislation in the United States. The first significant piece of federal antidrug legislation was the Harrison Act of 1914. The text describes the Marijuana Tax Act of 1937, the Narcotic Control Act of 1956, the Comprehensive Drug Abuse Prevention and Control Act of 1970, and the Anti-Drug Abuse Act of 1988. This latter piece of legislation created the position of drug czar within the Office of National Drug Control Policy.

A detailed explanation of four major drug types, marijuana, cocaine, heroin, and club drugs, follows the discussion of antidrug legislation. The text describes how these drugs are produced, consumed, and trafficked into the United States. Cocaine, for example, is extracted from the leaves of the coca plant, produces intense psychological effects, and typically enters the United States from Peru, Bolivia, Columbia, or Ecuador.

Chapter 16 then examines social problems related to drugs. The chapter discusses the link between drugs and crime and **money laundering**. For example, the link between drugs and crime has at least three dimensions: crimes specifically related to the use or sale of drugs; crimes committed by drug users, such as the addict who commits robberies to maintain his or her habit; and the organized criminal and gang activities that support the drug trade.

Chapter 16 concludes with a discussion of various criminal justice strategies used to respond to the drug problem. These strategies have very different philosophical orientations. On the one hand, several methods focus on the supply side of drug use. Strict enforcement, **forfeiture**, **interdiction**, and crop control efforts concentrate on responding to the problem by attacking the selling and production of drugs through increased efforts by police, courts, and correctional institutions. Strict enforcement efforts include calls for harsher punishments and increasing the number of police officers responding to the problem. Forfeiture involves seizing the assets of individuals involved in drug trafficking, and interdiction involves international efforts to prevent drugs from entering the United States or destroying crops. On the other hand, education, treatment, and counseling efforts focus on prevention and the drug user. For example, project DARE attempts to educate school children, focusing on decision-making skills, peer pressure, and choices. The chapter concludes with a discussion of **legalization** and **decriminalization** efforts.

Key Concepts

Club Drug: A synthetic psychoactive substance often found at nightclubs, bars, "raves," and dance parties. Club drugs include MDMA (ecstasy), ketamine, methamphetamine (meth), GBL, PCP, GHB, and Rohypnol.

Controlled Substance: A specifically defined bioactive or psychoactive chemical substance proscribed by law.

Controlled Substances Act (CSA): Title II of the Comprehensive Drug Abuse Prevention and Control Act of 1970, which established schedules classifying psychoactive drugs according to their degree of psychoactivity.

Curtilage: In legal usage, the area surrounding a residence that can reasonably be said to be a part of the residence for Fourth Amendment purposes.

Decriminalization: The redefinition of certain previously criminal behaviors into regulated activities that become "ticketable" rather than "arrestable."

Drug: Any chemical substance defined by social convention as bioactive or psychoactive.

Drug Abuse: Illicit drug use that results in social, economic, psychological, or legal problems for the user. *Source*: Bureau of Justice Statistics, *Drugs, Crime, and the Justice System* (Washington, D.C.: Bureau of Justice Statistics, 1992), p. 20.

Drug Court: A special state, county, or municipal court that offers first-time substance-abuse offenders judicially mandated and court-supervised treatment alternatives to prison.

Drug Czar: The popular name for the head of the Office of National Drug Control Policy (ONDCP), a federal Cabinet-level position that was created during the Reagan presidency to organize federal drug-fighting efforts.

Forfeiture: The authorized seizure of money, negotiable instruments, securities, or other things of value. Under federal antidrug laws, the authorization of judicial representatives to seize all cash, negotiable instruments, securities, or other things of value furnished or intended to be furnished by any person in exchange for a controlled substance, as well as all proceeds traceable to such an exchange. Also called *asset forfeiture*.

Harrison Act: The first major piece of federal antidrug legislation, passed in 1914.

Interdiction: The interception of drug traffic at the nation's borders. Interdiction is one of the many strategies used to stem the flow of illegal drugs into the United States.

Legalization: Elimination of the laws and associated criminal penalties that prohibit the production, sale, distribution, and possession of a controlled substance.

Money Laundering: The process by which criminals or criminal organizations seek to disguise the illicit nature of their proceeds by introducing them into the stream of legitimate commerce and finance. *Source*: U.S. Department of Treasury, *2000–2005 Strategic Plan* (Washington, D.C.: U.S. Government Printing Office, 2000), p. 1.

Physical Dependence: A biologically based craving for a specific drug that results from frequent use of the substance. Physical dependence on drugs is marked by a growing tolerance of a drug's effects, so that increased amounts of the drug are needed to obtain the desired effect, and by the onset of withdrawal symptoms over periods of prolonged abstinence. Also called *physical addiction*. *Source*: Bureau of Justice Statistics, *Drugs, Crime, and the Justice System* (Washington, D.C.: Bureau of Justice Statistics, 1992), p. 21.

Psychoactive Substance: A chemical substance that affects cognition, feeling, or awareness.

Psychological Dependence: A craving for a specific drug that results from long-term substance abuse. Psychological dependence on drugs is marked by the belief that drugs are needed to achieve a feeling of well-being. *Source*: Bureau of Justice Statistics, *Drugs, Crime, and the Justice System* (Washington, D.C.: Bureau of Justice Statistics, 1992), p. 21.

Racketeer Influenced and Corrupt Organizations (RICO): A federal statute that allows the federal seizure of assets derived from illegal enterprise.

Recreational Drug User: A person who uses drugs relatively infrequently and whose use occurs primarily with friends and in social contexts that define drug use as pleasurable. Most addicts begin as recreational users.

Key Cases

Alexander v. *U.S.*: The Court found that forfeitures under the RICO statute must be limited according to the rules established in *Austin* v. *U.S.* (*Alexander* v. *U.S.*, 113 S.Ct. 2766, 125 L.Ed. 2d 441 [1993]).

Austin v. *U.S.*: This case put limits on the government's authority to seize property, stating that any seizure must not be excessive when compared to the seriousness of the charge (*Austin* v. *U.S.*, 113 S.Ct. 2801, 15 L.Ed. 2d 448 [1993]).

California v. *Greenwood*: In this case the Court held that there is no reasonable expectation of privacy in trash left for collection. It is considered abandoned property (*California* v. *Greenwood*, 486 U.S. 35, 108 S.Ct. 1625 [1988]).

Oliver v. *U.S.*: This case was the first to clearly recognize the term curtilage. Here, the Court ruled that territory within the curtilage of a residence is accorded the same Fourth Amendment protections as that within the walls of the house (*Oliver* v. *U.S.*, 466 U.S. 170 [1984]).

Ratzlaf v. *U.S.*: The Court ruled that no one can be convicted of trying to evade bank-reporting requirements unless authorities can prove that offenders knew they were violating the law (*Ratzlaf* v. *U.S.*, 114 S.Ct. 655, 126 L.Ed. 2d 615 [1994]).

U.S. v. *92 Buena Vista Ave.*: This case established the "innocent owner defense" in forfeiture cases (*U.S.* v. *92 Buena Vista Ave.*, 113 S.Ct. 1126, 122 L.Ed. 2d 469 [1993]).

U.S. v. *Dunn*: The Court held that even if an area is fenced, it is not within the curtilage if sufficiently distant from the household (*U.S.* v. *Dunn*, 480 U.S. 294, 107 S.Ct. 1134 [1987]).

U.S. v. *Oakland Cannabis Buyer's Cooperative*: The Court concluded that the activities of the Cannabis Buyer's Cooperative, which distributed marijuana to patients for medical purposes, were in violation of the U.S. Controlled Substances Act (*U.S.* v. *Oakland Cannabis Buyer's Cooperative*, No. 00-151 (U.S. Supreme Court, decided May 14, 2001).

U.S. v. *Ursery*: The Court rejected claims that civil forfeiture laws constitute double jeopardy (*U.S.* v. *Ursery*, 116 S.Ct. 2135, 135 L.Ed. 2d 549 [1996]).

Learning Tips

Learn about the Library

One of the best learning resources at your disposal is your library. It is important to take advantage of this resource and learn as much as you can about it. Be sure to tour the library to get a feel for its physical layout. Also, surf the library's webpage for information, as well as to identify the databases available online. When you have questions or need information, ask a reference librarian for help and guidance. Taking time to learn about your library now will save you time and frustration when you have to use its resources to write a paper or gather research materials.

Answering Questions on Examinations

Answer the shortest, simplest questions first. This will give you increased confidence for the more difficult questions to follow. In other words, start with the matching, true-or-false, fill-in, and multiple-choice questions. End with essay and short-answer questions. If you get stuck on a question, look for associations or answers in the other test questions.

Most important, budget and monitor your time. Do not spend half of your time on questions that are worth only 20% of the exam. If you are completely stuck, move on.

CJ TODAY on the World Wide Web

Web links to organizations and agencies related to the material in Chapter 16 include:

WEBSITE TITLE	URL
Addiction Resource Guide	http://www.addictionresourceguide.com
Alcohol & Drug Information	http://www.health.org
American Council for Drug Education	http://www.acde.org
Center for Education and Drug Abuse Research	http://cedar.pharmacy.pitt.edu/main.html
Drug Abuse Resistance Education (DARE)	http://www.dare.com
Drug Enforcement Administration (DEA)	http://www.usdoj.gov/dea
Drugs and Crime	http://www.virlib.ncjrs.org/DrugsAndCrime.asp
MADD (Mothers Against Drunk Driving)	http://www.madd.org
National Drug Intelligence Center	http://www.usdoj.gov/ndic
National Institute on Drug Abuse	http://www.nida.nih.gov
The Executive Office for Weed and Seed	http://www.ojp.usdoj.gov/eows

Student Activities

Activity 1

Read the National Drug Control Strategy posted as **Library Extra 16–8**. Describe the strategy in the space below. What aspects of drug enforcement does the strategy focus on? What are its key characteristics?

_____

_____

_____

_____

_____

_____

Activity 2

Historically, political policy on drug enforcement has approached the problem with two different responses. One response is to focus on cracking down on the sellers, increasing the number of arrests, and advocating stricter punishments. The second response focuses on rehabilitating the user with treatment and counseling. Which approach, or combination of approaches, would you recommend as the most effective response to drugs? Discuss how this approach would impact the criminal justice system.

_____

_____

_____

_____

REMEMBER

Chapter 16 describes the Arrestee Drug Abuse Monitoring program (ADAM). The program results are based on self-reports of drug use among people recently arrested. Chapter 2 describes other sources of data used to understand the crime picture in the United States. For example, it describes the Uniform Crime Reports, which provides information on the crimes known by the police. Chapter 2 also discusses the National Crime Victimization Survey, which asks citizens about their victimization experiences.

LIBRARY extra

_____

_____

Activity 3

The war on drugs, fought through the 1980s and early 1990s, focused primarily on a strict enforcement approach. The strict enforcement approach provides police with wide latitude in formulating how best to respond to the drug problem. The United States Supreme Court supported these efforts with several important decisions that limited the rights of individuals. For example, the Supreme Court used several drug cases to redefine Fourth Amendment protections against unreasonable searches and seizures and to redefine Fifth Amendment protections against self-incrimination. Review the legal cases presented in the text. Find three cases discussed earlier in the text that addressed a legal question in a drug case. Describe the facts of the cases, and the Court's rulings, in the space provided below.

_____

_____

_____

_____

_____

Activity 4

A political consulting firm has requested your assistance in writing a memorandum on the legalization of marijuana. Write a memorandum that discusses the advantages and disadvantages of the legalization of marijuana.

_____

_____

_____

_____

_____

Internet Activity

Research drug and alcohol information on the Web using the Cybrary at http://www.cybrary.info. Search the Cybrary listings to find sites that contain suggestions and ideas on how to solve the drug problems facing this country. Describe the various strategies that are proposed. Which do you think are the most useful? Why? Submit your findings to your instructor if requested to do so.

_____

_____

_____

_____

_____

Distance Learning Activity

What is your opinion about the legalization of soft drugs such as marijuana? Visit three or four websites to search for evidentiary support for your position. The following websites should be helpful: (1) American Council for Drug Education: http://www.acde.org; (2) Center for Education and Drug Abuse Research: http://www.cedar.pharmacy. pitt.edu/main.html; (3) Drugs and Crime: http://www.virlib.ncjrs.org/ DrugsAndCrime.asp; (4) Marijuana Policy Project: http://www.mpp.org; (5) National Drug Intelligence Center: http://www.usdoj.gov/ndic; and (6) National Institute on Drug Abuse: http://www.nida.nih.gov. If your instructor asks you to so do, participate in a class discussion about the legalization of drugs.

_____

_____ .

_____

_____

_____

Student Study Guide Questions

True or False

____ 16-1. The limitation model pertains to law enforcement strategies to limit the amount of drugs brought into the United States.

____ 16-2. The Marijuana Tax Act of 1937 created a special assistant to the president on drug issues known as a "drug czar."

____ 16-3. Most federal prisoners are incarcerated for drug offenses.

____ 16-4. In many victimless crimes, society is the ultimate victim.

____ 16-5. Although use of drugs continues to increase, alcohol abuse is declining rapidly.

____ 16-6. Abandoned property is protected under the Fourth Amendment provisions against search and seizure.

____ 16-7. Cocaine is considered a Schedule I drug by the criminal justice system, and crack is considered a Schedule IV drug.

____ 16-8. Because of the Anti-Drug Abuse Act of 1988, an offender who commits a drug-related murder can be sentenced to death.

____ 16-9. Drug abuse has minimum social and personal costs beyond its impact on the criminal justice system.

____ 16-10. Zimring and Hawkins' "legalist" category suggests that drug-control policies are necessary in order to prevent the collapse of social order and of society itself.

Multiple Choice

16-11. Which piece of antidrug legislation created the five schedules used to classify psychoactive drugs?
   a. The Anti-Drug Abuse Act of 1988
   b. The Comprehensive Drug Abuse Prevention and Control Act of 1970
   c. The Boggs Act of 1951
   d. The Narcotic Control Act of 1956

16-12. The Anti-Drug Abuse Act of 1988 accomplished all of the following except
    a. it increased penalties for "recreational" drug use.
    b. it made it difficult for suspected drug dealers to purchase weapons.
    c. it denied federal benefits to convicted drug offenders.
    d. it eliminated the possibility of capital punishment for drug-related murders.

16-13. Which of the following is not a Schedule II drug?
    a. opium
    b. peyote
    c. morphine
    d. codeine
    e. cocaine

16-14. Which U.S. Supreme Court case established the open fields doctrine?
    a. *Hester* v. *United States*
    b. *United States* v. *Dunn*
    c. *California* v. *Greenwood*
    d. *Abel* v. *United States*

16-15. Under the Controlled Substances Act, cough medicine is considered a
    a. Schedule I drug.
    b. Schedule II drug.
    c. Schedule IV drug.
    d. Schedule V drug. (

16-16. Zimring and Hawkins argue that current drug policy is based on three schools of thought. Which of these schools proposes that drug policy be built around a balancing of the social costs of drug abuse?
    a. public health generalist
    b. cost-benefit specifism
    c. legalist
    d. deterrence

16-17. Which of the following pieces of antidrug legislation required drug users to register with the federal government and to pay a tax of $1.00 per year?
    a. The Harrison Act
    b. The Marijuana Tax Act
    c. The Narcotic Control Act
    d. The Comprehensive Drug Abuse Prevention and Control Act

16-18. _____ is a legal term that describes the area surrounding a residence that can reasonably be said to be a part of the residence for Fourth Amendment purposes.
    a. Innocent owner
    b. Open field
    c. Curtilage
    d. Abandoned property

16-19. Which of the following pieces of legislation made marijuana a federally prohibited controlled substance?
    a. The Boggs Act of 1951
    b. The Comprehensive Drug Abuse Prevention and Control Act
    c. The Marijuana Tax Act of 1937
    d. The Narcotic Control Act of 1956

16-20. Which of the following strategies focuses on reducing penalties for drug offenses, treating a drug-related offense similarly to a traffic offense?
    a. legalization
    b. decriminalization
    c. crop control
    d. interdiction

Fill-In

16-21. Illicit drug use that results in social, economic, psychological, or legal problems for the user is called _____.

16-22. _____ is the interception of drug traffic at the nation's borders.

16-23. A federal Cabinet-level position created during the Reagan presidency to organize federal drug-fighting efforts is called _____.

16-24. _____ is the redefinition of certain criminal behaviors into regulated activities, which become "ticketable" rather than "arrestable."

16-25. _____ is the authorized seizure of money, negotiable instruments, securities, or other things of value.

16-26. Title II of the Comprehensive Drug Abuse Prevention and Control Act of 1970, which established schedules classifying psychotic drugs according to their degree of psychoactivity, is called the _____.

16-27. The _____, passed in 1914, was the first major piece of federal antidrug legislation.

16-28. _____ refers to legislation that allows the federal seizure of assets derived from illegal enterprise.

16-29. A _____ is a chemical substance defined by social convention as bioactive or psychoactive.

16-30. _____ eliminates the laws and associated criminal penalties that prohibit the production, sale, distribution, and possession of a controlled substance.

Crossword Puzzle

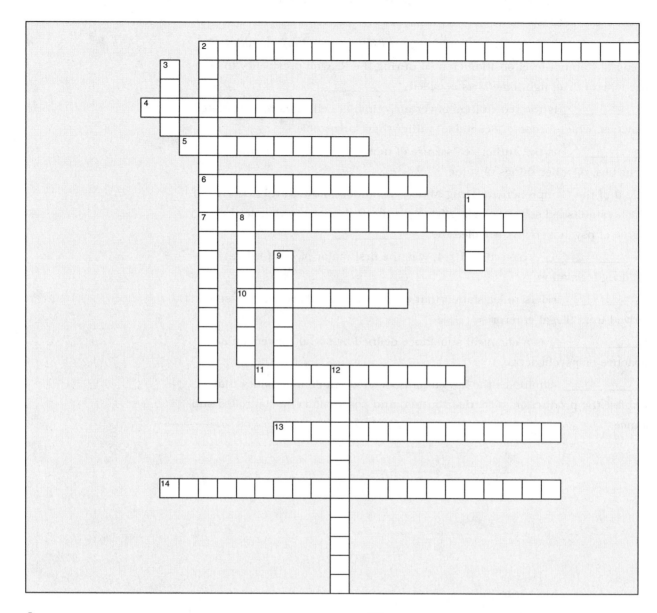

Across

2. Title II of the Comprehensive Drug Abuse Prevention and Control Act of 1970.
4. The legal term for the area near a residence.
5. The seizure of cash, instruments, and securities involved in a drug transaction.
6. Elimination of the laws and associated criminal penalties that prohibit the production, sale, distribution, and possession of a controlled substance.
7. Redefining criminal behaviors into regulated activities.
10. An alternative to traditional court processes for first-time substance abuse offenders.
11. The first major piece of federal antidrug legislation.
13. Converting illegally earned assets to some other form.
14. A chemical substance that affects cognition, feeling, and/or awareness.

Down

1. Federal statute that allows the federal seizure of assets derived from illegal enterprise.
2. A specifically defined bioactive or psychoactive chemical substance proscribed by law.
3. Any chemical substance defined by social convention as bioactive or psychoactive.
8. Examples include Ecstasy and GHB.
9. The popular name for the head of the Office of National Drug Control Policy.
12. The interception of drug traffic at the nation's borders.

Word Search Puzzle

```
L Y O Z T B S N C E I E R T E R O F Y I I D L N T C R I N I
E I T R L L C A C A E N R E E U T R C U N T N C S I E N L A
R I N A H E R B O E R E O N U R A D N R N O E S E O N S A N
A D P O A L R I R R H O T H E U A S C L U B D R U G R G O C
F A G S O C E I S G E D C R U E M I T I N S T O T S A I Z O
O D R P C C E A T G C D R L I A L I G S N S I I T N T D O N
D S I O C A I M O N E Y L A U N D E R I N G T D N A T U A T
A T I R L L T G Y G C A R D D G I S C P D D T C Z L A A C R
U U S G A A T U E R U T I E F R O F C R R S C I P P I M N O
S L R E S U G U R D L A N O I T A E R C E R L R S R O S A L
Z N E D E P O R E D O O H C S U U A R O D A N Y H S E S I L
O A I C I B E I C P L A R L L D R L T N N R C T C U R L D E
U I E S N Y R C C R A U D D S O T D Z I T H R I C D A I U D
D S C O L A R O T A B H C A T T E D M C O U N O Y B T S L S
U D N I I C T A N T B N Y L G E E I R A O E N E U C I T E U
G C E I R E R S N E I E D N P G R I C C T A T T E B I A G B
S A D E N E I T B I R U U N E C U T G R A R U I R C S U A S
M E N S I T O L G U G O G S E E I U I C A T D T R I I U L T
U U E U R T E R L E S T L D N V R P T I C L I T T O E R I A
C T P B C A A R E G A D D D E D N E G F I G H S A R O C Z N
A C E A Y E G R D G C R E S D A R A D U E A T H R H I I A C
T R D G R N T U I I U N U L L C T U S R R G E D O I O Z T E
A C L U P H L G C G C B D A L E I I O R U T A R U T G E I S
G D A R D O N E R U S T T C E O D S I N D G G L S T E R O A
D L C D R E L D R T C N I L M C R S U H I T C T I U A L N C
I R I S B G F R A T G C U O E N O T S E R C C Z N T A H R T
T U S D L E D N O A I E Z O N N E Y N O L A U D A D R T R I
S E Y U T Z C C N N Z A I M A O G O U O A L A R N R B U A E
G T H E R E N N S A C S R C G T S D C A C U G S R N U U C U
U O P U N N R L A R I C T B L G A A P I D E N D A S D T R A
```

Club Drug
Controlled Substance
Controlled Substances Act
Curtilage
Decriminalization
Drug
Drug Abuse
Drug Court
Drug Czar

Forfeiture
Harrison Act
Intediction
Legalization
Money Laundering
Physical Dependence
Psychoactive Substance
RICO
Recreational Drug User

chapter 17

Terrorism and Multinational Criminal Justice

LEARNING OBJECTIVES

After reading this chapter, you should be able to:

- Describe the nature of comparative criminal justice, and identify the potential benefits of, and problems inherent in, cross-cultural comparisons of crime

- Describe the main characteristics of the Chinese justice system

- Describe the principles that inform Islamic law

- Identify important international criminal justice organizations, and explain their role in fighting international crime

- Explain transnational crime, and explicate its possible relationship to terrorism

- Define terrorism, and identify two major types of terrorism

- Discuss the causes of terrorism and the U.S. government's attempts to prevent and control the spread of terrorism

- Explain why terrorism is a law enforcement concern and how it is a form of criminal activity

Chapter Summary

Thus far, the textbook has focused primarily on criminal justice in the United States. As you have discovered, the criminal justice process can be complex and confusing. However, the attention given to important criminal justice issues has provided the necessary foundation to cut through this complexity to develop a comprehensive understanding of the criminal justice system in the United States. Chapter 17 provides the opportunity to expand your understanding of these processes by first discussing the work of **comparative criminologists**. Comparative criminologists are interested in examining crime and criminal justice at a cross-national level. Chapter 17 provides considerable information on the Chinese and Islamic criminal justice systems. Chapter 17 also discusses **terrorism** in the United States.

The section on Chinese criminal justice begins by discussing the history of this system. Under Chairman Mao Tse-tung, the criminal justice system was very informal and it did not rely on criminal or procedural legal codes, lawyers, or officially designated prosecutors. After Tse-tung died, however, this system was significantly reformed. The Chinese justice system is built around four national offices: the Ministry of Public Security, the Supreme People's Court, the **People's Procuratorate**, and the Ministry of Justice. The *procuratorate*, a term frequently used to refer to agencies with powers and responsibilities similar to prosecutors in the United States, is responsible for supervising the administration of criminal justice throughout China. This section also describes each component of the Chinese criminal justice system. The official crime rate in China is low compared to that in the United States, and once someone is arrested, it is very likely that he or she will be convicted. Although the Chinese believe in swift and harsh punishment for the convicted, and there is widespread use of the death penalty, there is also a strong cultural commitment to reforming the offender.

Chapter 17 then explores Islamic criminal justice. The four primary sources of Islamic law are the *Koran*, the teachings of the Prophet Mohammed, the consensus of the clergy, and reason or logic. A key distinction of Islamic law is the difference between ***Hudud*** and ***Tazir*** crimes. ***Hudud* crimes** are serious violations of Islamic law and regarded as offenses against God. These crimes are essentially violations of "natural law," and the punishment for committing one is severe. In contrast, ***Tazir* crimes** are minor violations of Islamic law. These offenses are regarded as offenses against society, not God. The three levels of the Islamic court system are also discussed.

The next section of Chapter 17 focuses on international criminal justice organizations and **transnational** crime. This section describes the International Society of Criminology (ISC) and the role of the United Nations in criminal justice. It also describes the activities of INTERPOL and Europol. **INTERPOL** is an acronym for International Criminal Police Organization, an international law enforcement organization that began operations in 1946. **Europol** is the integrated police intelligence gathering and dissemination arm of the member nations of the European Union.

The final section of Chapter 17 discusses terrorism in the United States. Since the attacks on the World Trade Center and the Pentagon, terrorism has become a top-priority political and criminal justice issue. For example, significant legislation has been passed to improve the response to both **domestic** and **international** terrorism. Other types of terrorism discussed in this section include **cyberterrorism** and **narcoterrorism**. When considering how best to combat terrorism, the chapter discusses the role of the Department of Homeland Security. The chapter concludes with a discussion of **foreign terrorist organizations** and the future of international terrorism.

Key Concepts

Comparative Criminologist: One who studies crime and criminal justice on a cross-national level.

Cyberterrorism: A form of terrorism that makes use of high technology, especially computers and the Internet, in the planning and carrying out of terrorist attacks.

Domestic Terrorism: The unlawful use of force or violence by a group or an individual who is based and operates entirely within the United States and its territories without foreign direction and whose acts are directed at elements of the U.S. government or pop-

ulation. Source: Adapted from Federal Bureau of Investigation, *FBI Policy and Guidelines: Counterterrorism.* Web posted at http://www.fbi.gov/contact/fo/jackson/cntrterr.htm. Accessed March 4, 2002.

Ethnocentric: Holding a belief in the superiority of one's own social or ethnic group and culture.

European Police Office (Europol): The integrated police-oriented intelligence-gathering and dissemination arm of the member nations of the European Union.

Foreign Terrorist Organization (FTO): A foreign organization that engages in terrorist activity that threatens the security of U.S. nationals or the national security of the United States and that is so designated by the U.S. secretary of state.

Globalization: A process of social homogenization by which the experiences of everyday life, marked by the diffusion of commodities and ideas, can foster a standardization of cultural expressions around the world. Globalization involves the progressive erosion of the influence of nation-states and the rise in influence of global decision makers at both public and private levels. *Source*: Adapted from "Globalization," *Encyclopedia Britannica, 2003*. Encyclopedia Britannica Premium Service. Web posted at http://www.britannica.com/eb/article?eu=369857. Accessed July 23, 2003.

***Hudud* Crime:** A serious violation of Islamic law regarded as an offense against God. *Hudud* crimes include such behavior as theft, adultery, sodomy, alcohol consumption, and robbery.

Infrastructure: The basic facilities, services, and installations that a country needs to function. Transportation and communications systems, water and power lines, and institutions that serve the public, including banks, schools, post offices, and prisons, are all part of a country's infrastructure. *Source*: Adapted from Dictionary.com, Web posted at http://dictionary.reference.com/search?q=infrastructure. Accessed January 10, 2003.

International Criminal Police Organization (INTERPOL): An international law enforcement support organization that began operations in 1946 and today has 137 members.

International Terrorism: The unlawful use of force or violence by a group or an individual who has some connection to a foreign power, or whose activities transcend national boundaries, against people or property in order to intimidate or coerce a government, the civilian population, or any segment thereof, in furtherance of political or social objectives. *Source*: Adapted from Federal Bureau of Investigation, *FBI Policy and Guidelines: Counterterrorism.* Web posted at http://www.fbi.gov/contact/fo/jackson/cntrterr.htm. Accessed March 4, 2002.

Islamic Law: A system of laws, operative in some Arab countries, based upon the Muslim religion and especially the holy book of Islam, the Koran.

Mediation Committee: One of the civilian dispute-resolution groups found throughout China. Mediation committees successfully divert many minor offenders from the more formal mechanisms of justice.

Narcoterrorism: A political alliance between terrorist organizations and drug-supplying cartels. The cartels provide financing for the terrorists, who in turn provide quasi-military protection to the drug dealers.

Procuratorate: An agency in many countries with powers and responsibilities similar to those of a prosecutor's office in the United States. Also called *procuracy*.

***Tazir* Crime:** A minor violation of Islamic law that is regarded as an offense against society, not God.

Terrorism: A violent act or an act dangerous to human life in violation of the criminal laws of the United States or of any state committed to intimidate or coerce a government, the civilian population, or any segment thereof, in furtherance of political or social objectives. *Source*: Federal Bureau of Intelligence, Counterterrorism Section, *Terrorism in the United States, 1987* (Washington, D.C.: FBI, 1987).

Transnational Crime: Unlawful activity undertaken and supported by organized criminal groups operating across national boundaries.

Learning Tips

Cramming for Exams

Obviously "cramming" (trying to learn a tremendous amount in a short period) is not a desirable strategy, but if cramming is inevitable, follow these guidelines. Because you do not have time to learn everything, make a plan of attack. Instead of jumping into everything, decide what is most likely to be on the exam and concentrate on those items. Decide what is the most important material and recite it over and over. This method helps ingrain the material in your mind. And last, do not criticize yourself. It is hard to learn when you are constantly reminding yourself what you should have done.

Finals Week

Preparation for final exams is essential. Plan ahead by looking closely at your examination schedule. Be sure to give yourself enough time during finals week to prepare for every examination. It is important to stay focused and be sure to cover all the essential material, but try to relax as well. If you are stressed, it will be difficult to perform at your best.

CJ Today on the World Wide Web

Web links to organizations and agencies related to the material in Chapter 17 include:

WEBSITE TITLE	URL
Central and East European Law Initiative	http://www.abanet.org/ceeli/home.html
Chinalaw Web	http://www.qis.net/chinalaw
Justice Resources for England	http://arapaho.nsuok.edu/~dreveskr/eng.html-ssi
France: Criminal Justice Resources for France	http://arapaho.nsuok.edu/~dreveskr/fra.html-ssi
International Association of Women Police	http://www.iawp.org
International Centre for Criminal Law Reform and Criminal Justice Policy	http://www.icclr.law.ubc.ca
International Centre for the Prevention of Crime	http://www.crime-prevention-intl.org
International Court of Justice	http://www.icj-cij.org
International Criminal Justice References	http://www.uncjin.org
Japan: Criminal Justice Resources	http://arapaho.nsuok.edu/~dreveskr/jap.html-ssi
Scotland Yard (United Kingdom)	http://www.met.police.uk
World Factbook of Criminal Justice	http://www.ojp.usdoj.gov/bjs/abstract/wfcj.htm

Student Activities

Activity 1

Compare and contrast the Chinese and U.S. criminal justice systems. How is policing similar and different in these two countries? How are the court structures similar and different? Finally, compare and contrast the role of the defense attorney in the two systems.

REMEMBER

The framework used to think about criminal justice throughout the text involves balancing individual rights (i.e., the right of individuals to be protected from overzealous and intrusive government agents) against community interests (i.e., the right of society to feel secure from crime). Individual-rights advocates prefer to protect freedoms and liberties. Public-order advocates believe that the interests of society should take precedence over personal liberties. After reading Chapter 17, you can see that the framework is a little different in other countries. For example, the Chinese and Islamic systems lean significantly toward a public-order emphasis, and criminal justice in England is more midway between the two extremes.

_____

_____

_____

_____

_____

_____

Activity 2

Should some attempt be made to create a worldwide code of criminal behavior? Why or why not? What types of criminal behavior can be globally forbidden?

_____

_____

_____

_____

_____

_____

Activity 3

LIBRARY extra

Read the "National Strategy for Combating Terrorism," posted as **Library Extra 17–14**. What strategies directly involve the police, courts, and corrections components of the criminal justice systems? What strategies do you think are the most promising?

_____

_____

_____

_____

_____

Activity 4

LIBRARY extra

Choose a country not discussed in Chapter 17, and then research how criminal justice operates in that country using the Web and library resources. **Library Extra 17–1** is a good place to start. Gather information about policing, courts, and corrections in that country. Describe that criminal justice system in the space provided below.

_____

_____

_____

_____

_____

_____

Internet Activity

Visit the Talk Justice message boards at http://www.cybrary.info. Click on Begin and then log in in order to register as a new user (unless you have previously registered, in which case you can use your existing user name and password to enter the site). After creating a user name and a password, enter the message board area and look for the topic International Criminal Justice. Enter that board area and read what others have posted there. Write down some of the topics under discussion in that area. Choose a message of interest to you and post a reply. Check later (in a day or two) to see if others have responded to your posting.

_____

_____

_____

_____

_____

Distance Learning Activity

Visit the websites of criminal justice agencies located outside the United States. You can use any search engine to discover these agencies. In the space below, describe the major characteristics of the agencies from the country you selected. Assess the amount and type of criminal justice information posted on the World Wide Web for that country.

_____

_____

_____

_____

_____

Student Study Guide Questions

True or False

____ 17-1. Narcoterrorism is the act of "spiking" drugs to give them a more dangerous effect.

____ 17-2. Once you have been arrested for a crime in China, your chances of acquittal by the Chinese criminal courts are virtually nonexistent.

____ 17-3. After an execution in China, the offender's family is routinely ordered to pay for the cost of the bullet used to kill the offender.

____ 17-4. For all its apparent harshness, the Chinese justice system is based upon a strong cultural belief in personal reformation.

____ 17-5. Some Communist countries report only robberies and thefts that involve the property of citizens, since crimes against state-owned property fall into a separate category.

____ 17-6. Prison sentences in China do not allow possibility of parole.

____ 17-7. In Iran (under Islamic law), a person cannot be executed for any crime except murder or manslaughter.

____ 17-8. Terrorism is one form of transnational crime.

____ 17-9. International terrorism and foreign terrorism can be used interchangeably when describing international terrorist acts.

____ 17-10. The official recidivism rate for offenders in China is quite similar to the rate found in the United States.

Multiple Choice

17-11. The Chinese leader who resisted the use of bureaucratic agencies and relied heavily upon informal social control was
a. Deng Xiaoping.
b. Mao Ze-dong.
c. Hwa Zsunow.
d. Wan Kenobe.

17-12. Insurgents involved in the trafficking of narcotics are
a. money launderers.
b. mules.
c. narcoterrorists.
d. pseudoterrorists.

17-13. Using one's own culture as a benchmark against which to judge all other behavior patterns is
a. ethnocentrism.
b. Eurocentrism.
c. hypersensitivity.
d. fatalism.

17-14. What term is used in China to describe "thought reform through labor"?
a. laogai
b. jihad
c. procuratorate
d. mediation

17-15. All of the following are problems in the utilization of crime data from other countries except
a. differences in the definition of crime.
b. diverse crime-reporting practices.
c. lack of crimes to report.
d. political and other influences on the reporting of crime.

17-16. Most minor infractions of Chinese law are dealt with through the use of
a. arrests.
b. military intervention.
c. mediation committees.
d. stern warnings from a judge.

17-17. All of the following are considered *Hudud* crimes under Islamic law except
a. adultery.
b. drinking alcohol.
c. theft.
d. murder.

17-18. What term describes a new kind of terrorism emphasizing technological attacks?
a. Infoterrorism
b. Cyberterrorism
c. Technoterrorism
d. Infraterrorism

17-19. The police agency being created by members of the European Union to share crime information among European countries and INTERPOL is
   a. Europol.
   b. Outerpol.
   c. Francopol.
   d. Commonpol.

17-20. What country held the first international conference on criminology and criminal justice?
   a. England
   b. Germany
   c. United States
   d. Italy

Fill-In

17-21. A person who studies crime and criminal justice on a cross-national level is called a _____.

17-22. _____ is the belief that one's culture is superior to any other culture.

17-23. A political alliance between terrorist organizations and drug-supplying cartels is called _____.

17-24. _____ are Chinese civilian dispute-resolution groups designed to keep minor offenders out of the more formal mechanisms of justice.

17-25. Unlawful activity undertaken and supported by organized criminal groups operating across national boundaries is called _____.

17-26. _____ is a term used in many countries to refer to agencies with powers and responsibilities similar to those of U.S. prosecutors.

17-27. _____ is a process of social homogenization by which the experiences of everyday life, marked by the diffusion of commodities and ideas, can foster a standardization of cultural expressions around the world.

17-28. _____ is a form of terrorism that makes use of high technology, especially computers and the Internet, in the planning and carrying out of terrorist attacks.

17-29. The international law enforcement support organization that began operations in 1946 is called _____.

17-30. Minor violations of Islamic law that are offenses against society and against individuals, but not against God, are called _____.

Crossword Puzzle

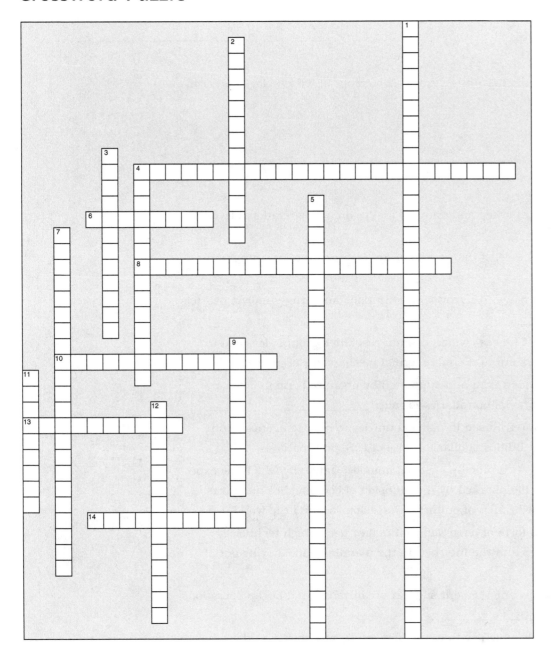

Across

4. One who studies crime and criminal justice on a cross-national level.
6. The type of terrorism by Timothy McVeigh, for example.
8. The integrated police-oriented intelligence-gathering and dissemination arm of the member nations of the European Union.
10. The basic facilities that a country needs to function.
13. A system of laws based upon the Muslim religion.
14. A minor violation of Islamic law.

Down

1. This organization has 137 members.
2. A process of social homogenization.
3. Holding a belief in the superiority of one's own social or ethnic group and culture.
4. Terrorism plus high technology.
5. A foreign organization that engages in terrorism.
7. The September 11th attacks are an example of this type of terrorism.
9. A serious violation of Islamic law.
11. One of the civilian dispute-resolution committees found throughout China.
12. When terrorists and drug cartels are linked.

Word Search Puzzle

```
N M S I R O R R E T L A N O I T A N R E T N I I R A G A I O
R E T C R C A N E T U A I L C I R T N E C O N H T E D R M A
P M E Y H I R M U O O O Z P E O R Z U A F Z O O D S I C R R
A O N T Z T E R R O R I S M G I O G L I O R R I C T O T R C
Z P N E T O C T O T S H L T Y E A M E I R T T S M M N A R E
O G O R R I E R P L D D M A T Z S R T M E T I S P E A N I N
N I B M I R M R O T C I I O O I I A I C I A T A I F D A M M
T I I A T N E M L A E E R A R N P O C R G R R R N T C R N R
E S U I I T O E O O R M R O S R R I A E N A C I O T L L R M
I N F R A S T R U C T U R E T N S C A M T I G R M N C E C T
E T T T C E A E A N R T W I O R E T I E T A O I R O I O I
R N E R T C R I A R E O A E T O T I V R R M T A I Z E T T R
G L I D I I O T I T C L I H O E R E T C R C M R O A A F R N
I E T A E E R L C E C I A T R R C O E L O E T I R I A T T I
T A O S E C O I M I U I M U A R O O I A R E T L S E I T N O
T S S R M N T I M C I W O U I I R T O N I H I I R O A I O O
O O T L R S A A N Z R V O M O I D G I O S C I I E T E L O I
O E A R E E L R D T I T I E I A L E A I T Y U A A E E A D M
I R T M R S T R C T E N O R R O E E M T O B O R T C O S S T
E A O N I R E R N O O R R U B A A G E A R E O H I N C E N I
E D I L R G O M I L T G P A E T S Z N N G R R T A N A R A I
M C R I O I N N O T N E L O O I D M C S A T T P I P G R R R
I G I R C R N G O I A I R E L I I C I N N E O M R I M T M R
R P G T R C I O N E Z S L R I R T I M A I R C C R A R A I G
C A O O C S T T O A A E R T O M A E O R Z R O R R S I E A M
D I I N T H M T T E O D T U M R C I N T A O T R I T R R I B
U O N O E C O I I T I N M A A I I T R I T R O E M O I P R M
D L A I R T O T S G C S I N S R E S B E I I U D M I N C E D
U R I E S N R R I H R O A N T I R N M S O S T M T I I O I R
H I G T U T R M I I Z T E I N T O R R O N M R R I O T I R I
```

Comparative Criminologist
Cyberterrorism
Domestic Terrorism
Ethnocentric
Europol
Foreign Terrorist Organization
Globalization
Hudud Crime
Infrastructure

INTERPOL
International Terrorism
Islamic Law
Mediation Committee
Narcoterrorism
Tazir Crime
Terrorism
Transnational Crime

chapter 18

The Future of Criminal Justice

chapter 100

OUTLINE

Introduction
Technology and Crime Control
Criminalistics: Past, Present, and Future
Technology and Individual Rights

LEARNING OBJECTIVES

After reading this chapter, you should be able to:

■ Describe the historical relationship between technological advances and social and cultural change

■ Explain the nature of high-technology crime, and list some forms that such crimes have taken in the past and that they might take in the future

■ Explain the important role that technology has played, and will continue to play, in the fight against crime and the quest for justice

■ Explain why laws defining criminal activity must change to keep pace with advancing technologies

■ Provide an overview of criminalistics, and explain how evolving technology contributes to advances in that field

■ Identify the threats to individual rights inherent in the ever-increasing use of advanced technology

Chapter Summary

The final chapter of the textbook focuses on issues critical to the future of the criminal justice system as it adapts to social, political, and cultural changes in society. In addition, as the level of technological sophistication in society grows and expands, regulating and responding to crimes that result from these changes become the responsibility of the criminal justice system.

The chapter begins with a discussion of various types of **technocrimes**. For example, it discusses **biocrime** and **cybercrime**. Biocrimes are those perpetrated through the use of some biologically active substance. Changes in technology have also provided opportunities to commit new types of crime. Any crime perpetrated through the use of computer technology is referred to as cybercrime. Offenders who hack computers, pirate software, engage in information piracy, destroy or manipulate data, or use computer technology to carry out theft of services are all committing cybercrimes.

Technological innovation is an important tool the criminal justice system uses to respond to crime. For example, the field of **criminalistics** has a long and distinguished history. The text provides some early examples of the use of criminalistics with a discussion of the system of personal identification created by Alphonse Bertillon, the use of fingerprints to identify suspects, and the reliance on **ballistics**, **forensic anthropology**, **forensic entomology**, and voiceprint identification.

Chapter 18 also describes emerging technologies in criminalistics. Perhaps the most significant scientific advance in the last decade is the development of **DNA profiling**. DNA profiling is the use of biological residue found at the scene of a crime for genetic comparisons aiding the identification of criminal suspects. DNA profiling has been used by law enforcement to identify suspects but also has assisted accused persons. For example, in a National Institute of Justice report titled *Convicted by Juries, Exonerated by Science*, researchers describe 28 cases of defendants who were released from prison after DNA tests established their innocence. Other emerging technologies discussed in Chapter 18 include online clearinghouses, computer-aided investigations, and computer-based training.

The last section of Chapter 18 focuses on technology and individual rights. It focuses on the clash between fighting crimes committed with new technology and individual rights.

Key Concepts

Augmented Reality (AR): The real-time and accurate overlay of digital information on a user's real-world experience, through visual, aural, and/or tactile interfaces. The computer readouts superimposed on the visual fields of the fictional cyborgs in the various *Robocop* and *Terminator* movies provide an example. *Source*: Thomas J. Cowper and Michael E. Buerger, *Improving Our View of the World: Police and Augmented Reality Technology* (Washington, D.C.: Federal Bureau of Investigation, 2003). Web posted at http://www.fbi.gov/publications/realitytech/realitytech.pdf. Accessed October 7, 2003.

Ballistics: The analysis of firearms, ammunition, projectiles, bombs, and explosives.

Biocrime: A criminal offense perpetrated through the use of biologically active substances, including chemicals and toxins, disease-causing organisms, altered genetic material, and organic tissues and organs. Biocrimes unlawfully affect the metabolic, biochemical, genetic, physiological, or anatomical status of living organisms.

Biometrics: The science of recognizing people by physical characteristics and personal traits.

Bioterrorism: The intentional or threatened use of viruses, bacteria, fungi, or toxins from living organisms to produce death or disease in humans, animals, or plants. *Source*: Centers for Disease Control and Prevention, *Bioterrorism: An Overview*. Web posted at http://www.bt.cdc.gov/documents/PPTResponse/laboverview.pdf. Accessed August 5, 2003.

Computer Crime: Any crime perpetrated through the use of computer technology. Also, any violation of a federal or state computer-crime statute. Also called *cybercrime*.

Computer Virus: A computer program designed to secretly invade systems and either modify the way in which they operate or alter the information they store. Viruses are destructive software programs that may effectively vandalize computers of all types and sizes.

Criminalist: A police crime-scene analyst or laboratory worker versed in criminalistics.

Criminalistics: The use of technology in the service of criminal investigation; the application of scientific techniques to the detection and evaluation of criminal evidence.

***Daubert* Standard:** A test of scientific acceptability applicable to the gathering of evidence in criminal cases.

DNA Profiling: The use of biological residue found at the scene of a crime for genetic comparisons in aiding the identification of criminal suspects.

Expert System: Computer hardware and software which attempts to duplicate the decision-making processes used by skilled investigators in the analysis of evidence and in the recognition of patterns which such evidence might represent.

Forensic Anthropology: The use of anthropological principles and techniques in criminal investigation.

Forensic Entomology: The study of insects to determine issues such as a person's time of death.

Hacker: A computer hobbyist or professional, generally with advanced programming skills. Today, the term *hacker* has taken on a sinister connotation, referring to hobbyists who are bent on illegally accessing the computers of others or who attempt to demonstrate their technological prowess through computerized acts of vandalism.

Identity Management: The comprehensive management and administration of a user's individual profile information, permissions, and privileges across a variety of social settings. *Source*: Adapted from Entrust, Inc., "Secure Identity Management: Challenges, Needs, and Solutions," Web posted at http://www.entrust.com, p. 1. Accessed August 5, 2003.

Malware: Malicious computer programs like viruses, worms, and Trojan horses.

Protected Computer: Under federal law, a computer exclusively for the use of a financial institution or the U.S. government, or, in the case of a computer not exclusively for such use, used by or for a financial institution or the U.S. government; or which is used in interstate or foreign commerce or communication.

Smart Card: A plastic card or similar device, containing a computer chip and other sources of nonalterable information (such as a hologram or a laser-encoded memory strip), that is used to provide highly secure personal identification.

Software Piracy: The unauthorized duplication of software or the illegal transfer of data from one storage medium to another. Software piracy is one of the most prevalent computer crimes in the world.

Technocrime: A criminal offense that employs advanced or emerging technology in its commission.

Weapon of Mass Destruction (WMD): A chemical, biological, and nuclear weapon that has the potential to cause mass casualties.

Key Cases

Daubert v. *Merrell Dow Pharmaceuticals, Inc.*: This case revised the criteria for the admissibility of scientific evidence by rejecting the "general acceptance" test set in *Frye* v. *United States*. This case determined that admissibility of scientific evidence would be based on Rule 402 of the Federal Rules of Evidence (*Daubert* v. *Merrell Dow Pharmaceuticals, Inc.*, 509 U.S. 579, 113 S.Ct. 2786 [1993]).

Frye v. *United States*: Created the "general acceptance" standard to determine the relevance of a test or procedure to the scientific community (*Frye* v. *United States*, 54 App. D.C. 46, 47, 293 F. 1013, 1014 (1923).

Holt v. *Sarver*: In this case the Court defined cruel and unusual punishment to be that which is "shocking to the conscience of reasonably civilized people" (*Holt* v. *Sarver*, 309 F.Supp. 362 [E.D. Ark. 1970]).

Reno v. *ACLU*: The Supreme Court upheld a lower court's ruling invalidating enforcement provisions of the Communications Decency Act. This rule accorded Internet content the same level of constitutional protection afforded print media (*Reno* v. *ACLU*, 117 S.Ct. 2329 [1997]).

Learning Tips

Service Learning

A good way to see the issues and ideas you learned in action is to volunteer at a criminal justice agency or arrange an internship. Many criminal justice agencies have internship programs for students to get hands-on experience. These experiences will enhance your understanding of criminal justice and will expose you to possible career opportunities.

Long-Term Learning of Criminal Justice

I hope you have enjoyed learning about the criminal justice system this semester. After you have had time to relax and catch up on your sleep during the semester break, think back to some of the issues that were most interesting to you. Fall and summer breaks provide perfect opportunities to read about the topics you enjoyed the most. Often, in the text or in the footnotes, two or three of the key books in the relevant area are mentioned. Explore criminal justice further. Go to the library and read some of these materials. You will be surprised how much you learned this semester.

CJ Today on the World Wide Web

Web links to organizations and agencies related to the material in Chapter 18 include:

WEBSITE TITLE	URL
Criminal Justice Policy Foundation	http://www.cjpf.org
International Centre for the Prevention of Crime	http://www.crime-prevention-intl.org
Justice Fellowship	http://www.justicefellowship.org
National Center for Policy Analysis	http://www.ncpa.org
The Center for Policy Alternatives	http://www.cfpa.org
The Future of DNA Evidence	http://www.ojp.usdoj.gov/nij/dna/welcome.html
Cybercrime Page	http://www.cybercrime.gov
Court Technology Laboratory	http://www.ncsc.dni.us/ncsc/ctl/ctl_main.htm
International Association of Crime Analysts	http://www.iaca.net

REMEMBER

Technological crimes, such as data destruction and software piracy, are difficult to investigate. One factor that contributes to the difficulty is the decentralized structure of policing in the United States, which is discussed in Chapter 5. Remember that federal, state, local, and private law enforcement agencies respond to crime incidents. Because of the nature of cybercrimes, it is apparent that federal and private law enforcement agencies will be the primary agencies responsible for dealing with them.

Student Activities

Activity 1

How much privacy are you willing to give up in the fight against crime? Would you be willing to be under constant video surveillance if it meant a 40% or 50% reduction in violent crime? Where would you draw the line to protect individual rights?

_____

_____

_____

_____

_____

_____

Activity 2

Throughout history, police have claimed that if they were just given the proper tools, they could really do something about crime. For example, law enforcement officials at the turn of the century argued that as soon as the police force became "motorized," they would be able to apprehend offenders with ease. The same claim was made for mobile radios, machine guns, mobile data terminals, cellular phones, and so forth. In some cities, equipping a police car with all of the electronic equipment and special features police claim as essential to their effectiveness costs nearly as much as the car itself! Do you think technology will ever be able to give police departments the edge they have been looking for in the fight against crime? Will the reactive nature of policing mean that cops will always be at least one step behind the offenders, or will police eventually get ahead of the offenders in the fight against crime?

_____

_____

_____

_____

_____

_____

Activity 3

What role do juries play in the court system? Will advances in technology make it easier for juries to arrive at decisions that represent the "truth"? Should technology be used to eliminate juries from the criminal justice system? Why or why not?

_____

_____

_____

_____

_____

_____

Activity 4

Visit **Web Extra 18–3**. This link provides an opportunity to learn more about biological and chemical terrorism. In the space below, summarize the materials posted at this link. In your analysis, be sure to describe efforts to respond to biological and chemical terrorism.

WEB extra

_____

_____

_____

_____

_____

_____

Distance Learning Activity

Write a short essay in the space below addressing how the criminal justice system can respond more effectively to crime in the United States. The following websites should be helpful: (1) Criminal Justice Policy Foundation: http://www.cjpf.org; (2) National Center for Policy Analysis: http://www.ncpa.org; and (3) the Center for Policy Alternatives: http://www.cfpa.org.

_____

_____

_____

_____

_____

_____

Student Study Guide Questions

True or False

_____ 18-1. One of the most prevalent computer crimes is the unauthorized duplication of copyrighted software.

_____ 18-2. Fingerprinting, which became widespread as a crime-fighting technique in the late 1800s, was the first nearly foolproof method of identification available to investigators.

_____ 18-3. Modern criminalistics depends heavily on ballistics, which involves the reconstruction of the likeness of a decomposed or dismembered body.

_____ 18-4. The "Pakistani Brain" and "Michelangelo" are the nicknames of two international terrorist bombing attacks.

_____ 18-5. Malware refers to malicious computer programs, such as viruses and worms.

_____ 18-6. Fingerprinting is an early example of biometric technology.

_____ 18-7. Most countries have effective computer-crime legislation in effect.

_____ 18-8. Identity theft is one of the fastest growing crimes in the United States.

_____ 18-9. Smart cards are tools used by criminalists to identify illegal credit card users.

_____ 18-10. It is impossible to share fingerprint data between automated fingerprint identification systems.

Multiple Choice

18-11. The _____, formerly known as the Technology Assessment Program Information Center (TAPIC), performs yearly assessments of key technological needs and opportunities facing the justice system.
   a. Law Enforcement Assistance Administration (LEAA)
   b. National Law Enforcement Technology Center (NLETC)
   c. Office of Law Enforcement Organization (OLEO)
   d. International Technology Protection Program (ITPP)

18-12. The case of _Daubert_ v. _Merrell Dow Pharmaceuticals_ proved to be important in the acceptance of _____ in criminal trials.
   a. DNA profiles
   b. computer-enhanced images
   c. fingerprints
   d. serial killer profiles

18-13. How many states have yet to fully accept DNA evidence in criminal trials?
   a. 1
   b. 24
   c. 12
   d. 4

18-14. Who coined the term "DNA fingerprints"?
   a. Alphonse Bertillon
   b. Michael Bloomberg
   c. Alec J. Jeffreys
   d. Henry Faulds

18-15. Which of the following is an example of malware?
   a. viruses
   b. worms
   c. Trojan horses
   d. All of the above

18-16. The constitutional amendment most concerned with equal protection under the laws is the _____.
   a. Eighth
   b. Fourteenth
   c. Fourth
   d. Fifth

18-17. According to the Computer Crime and Security Survey, how many large businesses and government agencies detected security-related breaches in 2002?
   a. 20
   b. 50
   c. 75
   d. 90

18-18. What constitutional amendment pertains most directly to the issue of gun control?
   a. First
   b. Second
   c. Fourth
   d. Fifth

18-19. As society becomes more dependent on computers, the damage potential of viruses will likely _____.
   a. increase
   b. decrease
   c. stay the same
   d. be unpredictable; we have no way of knowing

18-20. A computer that is the property of the federal government or a financial institution, or is located in a state other than the one in which the criminal perpetrator is operating, is classified as a _____.
   a. federated computer
   b. institutionalized computer
   c. protected computer
   d. interstate compact computer

Fill-In

18-21. _____ is another name for computer crime, or crime involving the use of computers.

18-22. _____ is the use of a blood sample or other residue found at the scene of a crime for genetic comparisons in aiding the identification of criminal suspects.

18-23. _____ are computer software models that attempt to replicate the decision-making processes used by skilled investigators in the analysis of evidence.

18-24. A _____ is a destructive computer code designed to vandalize computers.

18-25. _____ is the application of anthropological principles and techniques to a criminal investigation.

18-26. A _____ is a computer hobbyist who illegally accesses the computers of others to demonstrate technological superiority.

18-27. _____ refers to the study of insects to determine such matters as the time of death.

18-28. The application of scientific techniques to the detection and evaluation of criminal evidence is called _____.

18-29. The science of recognizing people by physical characteristics and personal traits is called _____.

18-30. _____ is the analysis of firearms, ammunition, bombs, and explosives.

Crossword Puzzle

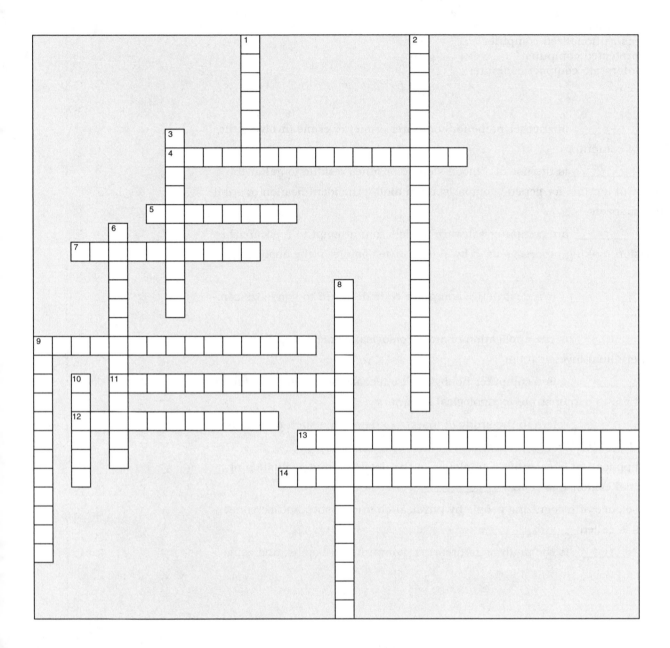

Across

4. Examples include *Robocop* and *Terminator*.
5. A criminal offense using biologically active substances.
7. To recognize people by physical characteristics and personal traits.
9. A test of scientific acceptability applicable to the gathering of evidence in criminal cases.
11. A computer program that invades another system to destroy it.
12. A police crime-scene analyst or laboratory worker versed in criminalistics.
13. Administration and control over a user's individual profile information.
14. Under federal law, a computer exclusively for the use of a financial institution or the U.S. government.

Down

1. Malicious computer programs.
2. The use of anthropological principles and techniques in criminal investigation.
3. The analysis of firearms, ammunition, projectiles, bombs, and explosions.
6. Also called cybercrime.
8. The study of insects to determine issues such as a person's time of death.
9. Scientific technique often used in rape cases.
10. A computer hobbyist.

Word Search Puzzle

```
R S I T A R R O R T E U C S I T I T D N E A T E T R N T S A
N R I N I I R U E O T P S S C I T S I L L A B N S T Y C L L
Y E L E U I G B M O L N D T M L U L E O E R E G E T S R E D
U C C M N E B T I I I E O R M M T T O I G I O O R N O E N M
R S E E S E O A R R O R T S E A G R M I C T D T R T C E W E
C C R G T M T F C M I E A O A L D E S R H A C K E R Y I I E
D M E A C M I H O B H D N T Y R S T C E N A I R A L N T N I
U N E N O R N O I T C U R T S E D S S A M F O N O P A E W I
I C S A K M C M B S U R E P H T R R C B U M N M A I I C C E
E R E M I R C R E T U P M O C R D A I T M E L O D R R O S E
U O I Y R Y D C Y M R R Y R S G R O C P A E I T S I A I I O
E N R T M V M A O G A U A S W B M G E T R O R N M R R N R Y
T T O I S I L P U R O A I L E E C R L M O T N I E E M M A I
F D E T I U S I S B M L R W T T C A O T D N N T T S B O L
C E E N I P R V E C E B O R C D E I E M R A R U P I O I M G
I T L E D M O I I M T R I P S S O C B S L N P D R M F L T H
T T R D T A I C V T R C T D O T B S H I O M L O U E T A C I
I P I I O T C R N R S N A S I R L M S N O O R A M T W E C I
A U G M E N T E D R E A L I T Y H T C C O R I A R S A N U A
F P S D S F C T S E U T S E A A I T D A E C T E E Y R T O R
T A T U R F A R E E R I U E M C N E N T E R R L O S E I T E
S M M N N A A T R P N L M P S A T D O A C I E I E T P R M N
M R A U S O C A R C E N R R M C N I A T C M S F M R I I E C
E E N E E A W T U S T R R E E O B M E R C I I E E E R E S S
M I W C I L U E R A S I M T M C C S T L D N S I W P A G E D
F M R O A I T S T A I R O I O I I L N R C A T N R X C N E T
T I M M T H I O L I M R N E N G C I I C A L R R E E Y I I C
Y I C Y B A S T E T P S I T E U E E I D F I N T U R P I F R
A I L T T H T E E A I U T T C R M C R E T S R G C D O A E R
M L O D N A P R O F I L I N G M A D T R I T M U O T I F C O
```

Augmented Reality	Expert System
Ballistics	Forensic Anthropology
Biocrime	Hacker
Biometrics	Identity Management
Bioterrorism	Malware
Computer Crime	Protected Computer
Computer Virus	Smart Card
Criminalist	Software Piracy
Criminalistics	Technocrime
Daubert Standard	Weapon of Mass Destruction
DNA Profiling	

Answers to Odd-Numbered Questions

Chapter 1

- 1-1. False
- 1-3. False
- 1-5. True
- 1-7. False
- 1-9. False
- 1-11. d
- 1-13. d
- 1-15. c
- 1-17. d
- 1-19. a
- 1-21. public-order advocates
- 1-23. Herbert Packer
- 1-25. criminal justice nonsystem
- 1-27. social justice
- 1-29. bail

Chapter 2

- 2-1. False
- 2-3. True
- 2-5. False
- 2-7. False
- 2-9. True
- 2-11. d
- 2-13. a
- 2-15. e
- 2-17. b
- 2-19. d
- 2-21. forcible rape
- 2-23. date rape
- 2-25. hate crimes

- 2-27. cyberstalking
- 2-29. motor vehicle theft

Chapter 3

- 3-1. True
- 3-3. True
- 3-5. True
- 3-7. False
- 3-9. False
- 3-11. d
- 3-13. c
- 3-15. d
- 3-17. a
- 3-19. d
- 3-21. Henry McKay
- 3-23. Sigmund Freud
- 3-25. Robert Merton
- 3-27. Cesare Lombroso
- 3-29. deviance

Chapter 4

- 4-1. True
- 4-3. False
- 4-5. False
- 4-7. True
- 4-9. False
- 4-11. a
- 4-13. c
- 4-15. c
- 4-17. d
- 4-19. d

- 4-21. civil law
- 4-23. *M'Naghten* rule
- 4-25. *Durham* rule
- 4-27. jurisprudence
- 4-29. *mens rea*

Chapter 5

- 5-1. True
- 5-3. True
- 5-5. False
- 5-7. False
- 5-9. False
- 5-11. c
- 5-13. b
- 5-15. c
- 5-17. c
- 5-19. d
- 5-21. Kansas City Preventive Patrol Experiment
- 5-23. Statute of Winchester
- 5-25. Minneapolis Domestic Violence Experiment
- 5-27. directed patrol
- 5-29. Kansas City Gun Experiment

Chapter 6

- 6-1. False
- 6-3. False
- 6-5. True
- 6-7. False
- 6-9. True

6-11. d
6-13. d
6-15. c
6-17. a
6-19. a
6-21. watchman
6-23. strategic policing
6-25. span of control
6-27. staff operations
6-29. service

Chapter 7

7-1. False
7-3. False
7-5. False
7-7. True
7-9. False
7-11. d
7-13. b
7-15. b
7-17. c
7-19. a
7-21. *U.S.* v. *Leon*
7-23. *Aguilar* v. *Texas*
7-25. *Warden* v. *Hayden*
7-27. *Terry* v. *Ohio*
7-29. *Mapp* v. *Ohio*

Chapter 8

8-1. True
8-3. False
8-5. False
8-7. False
8-9. True
8-11. d
8-13. c
8-15. d
8-17. d
8-19. c
8-21. problem police officer
8-23. use of force
8-25. biological weapon
8-27. police corruption
8-29. *Bivens* action

Chapter 9

9-1. True
9-3. False
9-5. True
9-7. True
9-9. False
9-11. b
9-13. d
9-15. d
9-17. c
9-19. d
9-21. bailiff
9-23. change of venue
9-25. trial de novo
9-27. appellate jurisdiction
9-29. expert witness

Chapter 10

10-1. True
10-3. False
10-5. True
10-7. True
10-9. True
10-11. c
10-13. d
10-15. b
10-17. c
10-19. b
10-21. circumstantial evidence
10-23. peremptory challenge
10-25. first appearance
10-27. perjury
10-29. rules of evidence

Chapter 11

11-1. False
11-3. True
11-5. False
11-7. False
11-9. False
11-11. e
11-13. c
11-15. b
11-17. b
11-19. a
11-21. presentence investigation
11-23. rehabilitation
11-25. indeterminate sentencing
11-27. determinate sentencing
11-29. aggravating circumstances

Chapter 12

12-1. False
12-3. True
12-5. True
12-7. False
12-9. True
12-11. d
12-13. b
12-15. a
12-17. b
12-19. a
12-21. general conditions
12-23. revocation hearing
12-25. home confinement
12-27. shock incarceration
12-29. community service

Chapter 13

13-1. False
13-3. False
13-5. False
13-7. False
13-9. False
13-11. c
13-13. c
13-15. b
13-17. b
13-19. a
13-21. Pennsylvania system
13-23. workhouse (bridewell)
13-25. state-use system
13-27. warehousing
13-29. justice model

Chapter 14

14-1. True
14-3. False
14-5. False
14-7. True
14-9. True
14-11. a
14-13. c
14-15. a
14-17. c
14-19. b
14-21. prison argot
14-23. *Cruz* v. *Beto*
14-25. balancing test
14-27. hands-off doctrine
14-29. civil death

Chapter 15

15-1. False
15-3. False
15-5. False
15-7. False

15-9. False
15-11. d
15-13. c
15-15. a
15-17. d
15-19. c
15-21. delinquent child
15-23. opportunity
15-25. *parens patriae*
15-27. juvenile petition
15-29. neglected child

Chapter 16

16-1. False
16-3. True
16-5. False
16-7. False
16-9. False
16-11. b
16-13. b
16-15. d

16-17. a
16-19. a
16-21. drug abuse
16-23. drug czar
16-25. forfeiture
16-27. Harrison Act
16-29. drug

Chapter 17

17-1. False
17-3. True
17-5. True
17-7. False
17-9. False
17-11. b
17-13. a
17-15. c
17-17. d
17-19. a
17-21. comparative criminologist
17-23. narcoterrorism

17-25. transnational crime
17-27. globalization
17-29. INTERPOL

Chapter 18

18-1. True
18-3. False
18-5. True
18-7. False
18-9. False
18-11. b
18-13. d
18-15. d
18-17. d
18-19. a
18-21. cybercrime
18-23. expert systems
18-25. forensic anthropology
18-27. forensic entomology
18-29. biometics

The Constitution of the United States

WE THE PEOPLE of the United States, in Order to form a more perfect Union, establish Justice, insure domestic Tranquility, provide for the common defence, promote the general Welfare, and secure the Blessings of Liberty to ourselves and our Posterity, do ordain and establish this CONSTITUTION for the United States of America.

Article I.

SECTION 1. All legislative Powers herein granted shall be vested in a Congress of the United States, which shall consist of a Senate and House of Representatives.

SECTION 2. The House of Representatives shall be composed of Members chosen every second Year by the People of the several States, and the Electors in each State shall have the Qualifications requisite for Electors of the most numerous Branch of the State Legislature.

No Person shall be a Representative who shall not have attained to the Age of twenty-five Years, and been seven Years a Citizen of the United States, and who shall not, when elected, be an Inhabitant of that State in which he shall be chosen.

Representatives and direct Taxes shall be apportioned among the several States which may be included within this Union, according to their respective Numbers, which shall be determined by adding to the whole Number of free Persons, including those bound to Service for a Term of Years, and excluding Indians not taxed, three fifths of all other Persons. The actual Enumeration shall be made within three Years after the first Meeting of the Congress of the United States, and within every subsequent Term of ten Years, in such Manner as they shall by Law direct. The Number of Representatives shall not exceed one for every thirty Thousand, but each State shall have at Least one Representative; and until such enumeration shall be made, the State of New Hampshire shall be entitled to chuse three, Massachusetts eight, Rhode-Island and Providence Plantations one, Connecticut five, New York six, New Jersey four, Pennsylvania eight, Delaware one, Maryland six, Virginia ten, North Carolina five, South Carolina five, and Georgia three.

When vacancies happen in the representation from any State, the Executive Authority thereof shall issue Writs of Election to fill such Vacancies.

The House of Representatives shall chuse their Speaker and other Officers; and shall have the sole Power of Impeachment.

SECTION 3. The Senate of the United States shall be composed of two Senators from each State, chosen by the Legislature thereof for six Years; and each Senator shall have one Vote.

Immediately after they shall be assembled in Consequence of the first Election, they shall be divided as equally as may be into three Classes. The Seats of the Senators of the first Class shall be vacated at the Expiration of the second Year, of the second Class at the Expiration of the fourth Year, and of the third Class at the Expiration of the sixth Year, so that one third may be chosen every second Year; and if Vacancies happen by Resignation, or otherwise, during the recess of the Legislature of any State, the Executive thereof may make temporary Appointments until the next Meeting of the Legislature, which shall then fill such Vacancies.

No Person shall be Senator who shall not have attained to the Age of thirty Years, and been nine Years a Citizen of the United States, and who shall not, when elected, be an Inhabitant of that State for which he shall be chosen.

The Vice President of the United States shall be President of the Senate, but shall have no Vote, unless they be equally divided.

The Senate shall chuse their other Officers, and also a President pro tempore, in the absence of the Vice President, or when he shall exercise the Office of President of the United States.

The Senate shall have the sole Power to try all Impeachments. When sitting for that Purpose, they shall be on Oath or Affirmation. When the President of the United States is tried, the Chief Justice shall preside: And no Person shall be convicted without the Concurrence of two thirds of the Members present.

Judgment in Cases of Impeachment shall not extend further than to removal from Office, and disqualification to hold and enjoy any Office of honor, Trust, or Profit under the United States: but the Party convicted shall nevertheless be liable and subject to Indictment, Trial, Judgment and Punishment, according to Law.

SECTION 4. The Times, Places and Manner of holding Elections for Senators and Representatives, shall be prescribed in each State by the Legislature thereof; but the Congress may at any time by Law make or alter such Regulations, except as to the Place of chusing Senators.

The Congress shall assemble at least once in every Year, and such Meeting shall be on the first Monday in December, unless they shall by law appoint a different Day.

SECTION 5. Each House shall be the Judge of the Elections, Returns and Qualifications of its own Members, and a Majority of each shall constitute a Quorum to do Business; but a smaller Number may adjourn from day to day, and may be authorized to compel the Attendance of absent Members, in such Manner, and under such Penalties as each House may provide.

Each House may determine the Rules of its Proceedings, punish its Members for disorderly Behaviour, and, with the Concurrence of two thirds, expel a Member.

Each House shall keep a Journal of its Proceedings, and from time to time publish the same, excepting such Parts as may in their Judgment require Secrecy; and the Yeas and Nays of the Members of either House on any question shall, at the Desire of one fifth of those Present, be entered on the journal.

Neither House, during the Session of Congress, shall, without the Consent of the other, adjourn for more than three days, nor to any other Place than that in which the two Houses shall be sitting.

SECTION 6. The Senators and Representatives shall receive a Compensation for their Services, to be ascertained by Law, and paid out of the Treasury of the United States. They shall in all Cases, except Treason, Felony and Breach of the Peace, be privileged from Arrest during their Attendance at the Session of their respective Houses, and in going to and returning from the same; and for any Speech or Debate in either House, they shall not be questioned in any other Place.

No Senator or Representative shall, during the Time for which he was elected, be appointed to any civil Office under the Authority of the United States, which shall have been created, or the Emoluments whereof shall have been encreased during such time; and no Person holding any Office under the United States, shall be a Member of either House during his Continuance in Office.

SECTION 7. All Bills for raising Revenue shall originate in the House of Representatives; but the Senate may propose or concur with Amendments as on other Bills.

Every Bill which shall have passed the House of Representatives and the Senate, shall, before it become a Law, be presented to the President of the United States; If he approve he shall sign it, but if not he shall return it, with his Objections to that House in which it shall have originated, who shall enter the Objections at large on their Journal, and proceed to reconsider it. If after such Reconsideration two thirds of that

House shall agree to pass the Bill, it shall be sent, together with the Objections, to the other House, by which it shall likewise be reconsidered, and if approved by two thirds of that House, it shall become a Law. But in all such Cases the Votes of both Houses shall be determined by Yeas and Nays, and the Names of the Persons voting for and against the Bill shall be entered on the Journal of each House respectively. If any Bill shall not be returned by the President within ten Days (Sundays excepted) after it shall have been presented to him, the Same shall be a Law, in like Manner as if he had signed it, unless the Congress by their Adjournment prevent its Return, in which Case it shall not be a Law.

Every Order, Resolution, or Vote to which the Concurrence of the Senate and House of Representatives may be necessary (except on a question of Adjournment) shall be presented to the President of the United States; and before the Same shall take Effect, shall be approved by him, or being disapproved by him, shall be repassed by two thirds of the Senate and House of Representatives, according to the Rules and Limitations prescribed in the Case of a Bill.

SECTION 8. The Congress shall have Power to lay and collect Taxes, Duties, Imposts and Excises, to pay the Debts and provide for the common Defence and general Welfare of the United States; but all Duties, Imposts and Excises shall be uniform throughout the United States;

To borrow Money on the credit of the United States;

To regulate Commerce with foreign Nations, and among the several States, and with the Indian Tribes;

To establish an uniform Rule of Naturalization, and uniform Laws on the subject of Bankruptcies throughout the United States;

To coin Money, regulate the Value thereof, and of foreign Coin, and fix the Standard of Weights and Measures;

To provide for the Punishment of counterfeiting the Securities and current Coin of the United States;

To establish Post Offices and post Roads;

To promote the Progress of Science and useful Arts, by securing for limited times to Authors and Inventors the exclusive Right to their respective Writings and Discoveries;

To constitute Tribunals inferior to the supreme Court;

To define and punish Piracies and Felonies committed on the high Seas, and Offences against the Law of Nations;

To declare War, grant Letters of Marque and Reprisal, and make Rules concerning Captures on Land and Water;

To raise and support Armies, but no Appropriation of Money to that Use shall be for a longer Term than two Years;

To provide and maintain a Navy;

To make Rules for the Government and Regulation of the land and naval Forces;

To provide for calling forth the Militia to execute the Laws of the Union, suppress Insurrections and repel Invasions;

To provide for organizing, arming, and disciplining the Militia, and for governing such Part of them as may be employed in the Service of the United States, reserving to the States respectively, the Appointment of the Officers, and the Authority of training the Militia according to the discipline prescribed by Congress;

To exercise exclusive Legislation in all Cases whatsoever, over such District (not exceeding ten Miles square) as may, by Cession of particular States, and the Acceptance of Congress, become the Seat of the Government of the United States, and to exercise like Authority over all Places purchased by the Consent of the Legislature of the State in which the Same shall be, for the Erection of Forts, Magazines, and Arsenals, dock-Yards, and other needful Buildings;—And

To make all Laws which shall be necessary and proper for carrying into Execution the foregoing Powers, and all other Powers vested by this Constitution in the Government of the United States, or in any Department or Officer thereof.

SECTION 9. The Migration or Importation of such Persons as any of the States now existing shall think proper to admit, shall not be prohibited by the Congress prior to the Year one thousand eight hundred and eight, but a Tax or duty may be imposed on such Importation, not exceeding ten dollars for each Person.

The privilege of the Writ of Habeas Corpus shall not be suspended, unless when in Cases of Rebellion or Invasion the public Safety may require it.

No Bill of Attainder or ex post facto Law shall be passed.

No Capitation, or other direct, Tax shall be laid, unless in Proportion to the Census or Enumeration herein before directed to be taken.

No Tax or Duty shall be laid on Articles exported from any State.

No Preference shall be given by any Regulation of Commerce or Revenue to the Ports of one State over those of another: nor shall Vessels bound to, or from, one State, be obliged to enter, clear, or pay Duties in another.

No Money shall be drawn from the Treasury, but in Consequence of Appropriations made by Law; and a regular Statement and Account of the Receipts and Expenditures of all public Money shall be published from time to time.

No Title of Nobility shall be granted by the United States: And no Person holding any Office of Profit or Trust under them, shall, without the Consent of the Congress, accept of any present, Emolument, Office, or Title, of any kind whatever, from any King, Prince, or foreign State.

SECTION 10. No State shall enter into any Treaty, Alliance, or Confederation; grant Letters of Marque and Reprisal; coin Money; emit Bills of Credit; make any Thing but gold and silver Coin a Tender in Payment of Debts; pass any Bill of Attainder, ex post facto Law, or Law impairing the Obligation of Contracts, or grant any Title of Nobility.

No State shall, without the consent of the Congress, lay any Imposts or Duties on Imports or Exports, except what may be absolutely necessary for executing it's inspection Laws: and the net Produce of all Duties and Imposts, laid by any State on Imports or Exports, shall be for the Use of the Treasury of the United States; and all such Laws shall be subject to the Revision and Control of the Congress.

No State shall, without the Consent of Congress, lay any Duty of Tonnage, keep Troops, or Ships of War in time of Peace, enter into any Agreement or Compact with another State, or with a foreign Power, or engage in War, unless actually invaded, or in such imminent Danger as will not admit of delay.

Article II.

SECTION 1. The executive Power shall be vested in a President of the United States of America. He shall hold his Office during the Term of four Years, and, together with the Vice President, chosen for the same Term, be elected, as follows

Each State shall appoint, in such Manner as the Legislature thereof may direct, a Number of Electors, equal to the whole Number of Senators and Representatives to which the State may be entitled in the Congress: but no Senator or Representative, or Person holding an Office of Trust or Profit under the United States, shall be appointed an Elector.

The Electors shall meet in their respective States, and vote by Ballot for two persons, of whom one at least shall not be an Inhabitant of the same State with themselves. And they shall make a List of all the Persons voted for, and of the Number of Votes for each; which List they shall sign and certify, and transmit sealed to the Seat of the Government of the United States, directed to the President of the Senate. The President of the Senate shall, in the Presence of the Senate and House of Representatives, open all the Certificates, and the Votes shall then be counted. The Person having the greatest Number of Votes shall be the President, if such Number be a Majority of the whole Number of Electors appointed; and if there be more than one who have such Majority, and have an equal Number of Votes, then the House of Representatives shall immediately chuse by Ballot one of them for President; and if no Person have a Majority, then from the five highest on the List the said House shall in like Manner chuse the President. But in choosing the President, the Votes shall be taken by States, the Representation from each State having one Vote; A quorum for this Purpose shall consist of a Member or Members from two thirds of the States, and a Majority of all the States shall be necessary to a Choice. In every Case, after the Choice of the President, the Person having the greatest Number of Votes of the Electors shall be the Vice President. But if there should remain two or more who have equal Votes, the Senate shall chuse from them by Ballot the Vice President.

The Congress may determine the Time of chusing the Electors, and the Day on which they shall give their Votes; which Day shall be the same throughout the United States.

No person except a natural born Citizen, or a Citizen of the United States, at the time of Adoption of this Constitution, shall be eligible to the Office of President; neither shall any Person be eligible to that Office who shall not have attained to the Age of thirty five Years, and been fourteen Years a Resident within the United States.

In Case of the Removal of the President from Office, or of his Death, Resignation, or Inability to discharge the Powers and Duties of the said Office, the same shall devolve on the Vice President, and the Congress may by Law provide for the Case of Removal, Death, Resignation or Inability, both of the President and Vice President, declaring what Officer shall then act as President, and such Officer shall act accordingly, until the Disability be removed, or a President shall be elected.

The President shall, at stated Times, receive for his Services, a Compensation, which shall neither be encreased nor diminished during the Period for which he shall have been elected, and he shall not receive within that Period any other Emolument from the United States, or any of them.

Before he enter on the Execution of his Office, he shall take the following Oath or Affirmation:—"I do solemnly swear (or affirm) that I will faithfully execute the Office of President of the United States, and will to the best of my Ability, preserve, protect and defend the Constitution of the United States."

SECTION 2. The President shall be Commander in Chief of the Army and Navy of the United States, and of the Militia of the several States, when called into the actual Service of the United States; he may require the Opinion in writing, of the principal Officer in each of the executive Departments, upon any subject relating to the Duties of their respective Offices, and he shall have Power to grant Reprieves and Pardons for Offenses against the United States, except in Cases of Impeachment.

He shall have Power, by and with the Advice and Consent of the Senate, to make Treaties, provided two thirds of the Senators present concur; and he shall nominate, and by and with the Advice and Consent of the Senate, shall appoint Ambassadors, other public Ministers and Consuls, Judges of the supreme Court, and all other Officers of the United States, whose Appointments are not herein otherwise provided for, and which shall be established by Law: but the Congress may by Law vest the Appointment of such inferior Officers, as they think proper, in the President alone, in the courts of Law, and in the Heads of Departments.

The President shall have Power to fill up all Vacancies that may happen during the Recess of the Senate, by granting Commissions which shall expire at the End of their next Session.

SECTION 3. He shall from time to time give to the Congress Information of the State of the Union, and recommend to their Consideration such Measures as he shall judge necessary and expedient; he may, on extraordinary Occasions, convene both Houses, or either of them, and in Case of Disagreement between them, with Respect to the Time of Adjournment, he may adjourn them to such Time as he shall think proper; he shall receive Ambassadors and other public Ministers; he shall take Care that the Laws be faithfully executed, and Shall Commission all the Officers of the United States.

SECTION 4. The President, Vice President and all civil Officers of the United States, shall be removed from Office on Impeachment for, and Conviction of, Treason, Bribery, or other high Crimes and Misdemeanors.

Article III.

SECTION 1. The judicial Power of the United States, shall be vested in one supreme Court, and in such inferior Courts as the Congress may from time to time ordain and establish. The Judges, both of the supreme and inferior Courts, shall hold their Offices during good Behavior, and shall, at stated Times, receive for their Services, a Compensation, which shall not be diminished during their Continuance in Office.

SECTION 2. The judicial Power shall extend to all Cases, in Law and Equity, arising under this Constitution, the Laws of the United States, and Treaties made, or which shall be made, under their Authority;—to all Cases affecting Ambassadors, other public Ministers and Consuls;—to all Cases of admiralty and maritime Jurisdiction;—to Controversies to which the United States shall be a Party;—to Controversies between two or more States;—between a State and Citizens of another State;—between citizens of different States;—between Citizens of the same State claiming Lands under Grants of different States, and between a State, or the Citizens thereof, and foreign States, Citizens or Subjects.

In all Cases affecting Ambassadors, other public Ministers and Consuls, and those in which a State shall be Party, the supreme Court shall have original Jurisdiction. In all the other Cases before mentioned, the supreme Court shall have appellate Jurisdiction, both as to Law and Fact, with such exceptions, and under such Regulations as the Congress shall make.

The Trial of all Crimes, except in Cases of Impeachment, shall be by Jury; and such Trial shall be held in the State where the said Crimes shall have been committed; but when not committed within any State, the Trial shall be at such Place or Places as the Congress may by Law have directed.

SECTION 3. Treason against the United States, shall consist only in levying War against them, or in adhering to their Enemies, giving them Aid and Comfort. No Person shall be convicted of Treason unless on the Testimony of two Witnesses to the same overt Act, or on Confession in open Court.

The Congress shall have Power to declare the Punishment of Treason, but no Attainder of Treason shall work Corruption of Blood, or Forfeiture except during the Life of the Person attainted.

Article IV.

SECTION 1. Full Faith and Credit shall be given in each State to the public Acts, Records, and judicial Proceedings of every other State. And the Congress may by general Laws prescribe the Manner in which such Acts, Records and Proceedings shall be proved, and the Effect thereof.

SECTION 2. The Citizens of each State shall be entitled to all Privileges and Immunities of Citizens in the several States.

A Person charged in any State with Treason, Felony, or other Crime, who shall flee from Justice, and be found in another State, shall on Demand of the executive Authority of the State from which he fled, be delivered up, to be removed to the State having Jurisdiction of the Crime.

No Person held to Service or Labour in one State, under the Laws thereof, escaping into another, shall, in Consequence of any Law or Regulation therein, be discharged from such Service or Labour, but shall be delivered up on Claim of the Party to whom such Service or Labour may be due.

SECTION 3. New States may be admitted by the Congress into this Union; but no new State shall be formed or erected within the Jurisdiction of any other State; nor any State be formed by the Junction of two or more States, or parts of States, without the Consent of the Legislatures of the States concerned as well as of the Congress.

The Congress shall have Power to dispose of and make all needful Rules and Regulations respecting the Territory or other Property belonging to the United States; and nothing in this Constitution shall be so construed as to Prejudice any Claims of the United States, or of any particular State.

SECTION 4. The United States shall guarantee to every State in this Union a Republican Form of Government, and shall protect each of them against Invasion; and on Application of the Legislature, or of the Executive (when the Legislature cannot be convened) against domestic Violence.

Article V.

The Congress, whenever two thirds of both Houses shall deem it necessary, shall propose Amendments to this Constitution, or, on the Application of the Legislatures of two thirds of the several States, shall call a Convention for proposing Amendments, which, in either Case, shall be valid to all Intents and Purposes, as Part of this Constitution, when ratified by the Legislatures of three fourths of the several States, or by Conventions in three fourths thereof, as the one or the other Mode of Ratification may be proposed by the Congress; Provided that no Amendment which may be made prior to the Year One thousand eight hundred and eight shall in any Manner affect the first and fourth Clauses in the Ninth Section of the first Article; and that no State, without its Consent, shall be deprived of its equal Suffrage in the Senate.

Article VI.

All Debts contracted and Engagements entered into, before the Adoption of this Constitution, shall be as valid against the United States under this Constitution, as under the Confederation.

This Constitution, and the Laws of the United States which shall be made in Pursuance thereof; and all Treaties made, or which shall be made, under the Authority of the United States, shall be the supreme Law of the Land; and the Judges in every State shall be bound thereby; any Thing in the Constitution or Laws of any State to the Contrary notwithstanding.

The Senators and Representatives before mentioned, and the Members of the several State Legislatures, and all executive and judicial Officers, both of the United States and of the several States, shall be bound by Oath or Affirmation, to support this Constitution; but no religious Test shall ever be required as a Qualification to any Office or public Trust under the United States.

Article VII.

The Ratification of the Conventions of nine States shall be sufficient for the Establishment of this Constitution between the States so ratifying the Same.

Articles in Addition to, and Amendment of, the Constitution of the United States of America, Proposed by Congress, and Ratified by the Legislatures of the Several States, Pursuant to the Fifth Article of the Original Constitution.

Amendment I. (1791)

Congress shall make no law respecting an establishment of religion, or prohibiting the free exercise thereof; or abridging the freedom of speech, or of the press; or the right of the people peaceably to assemble, and to petition the Government for a redress of grievances.

Amendment II. (1791)

A well regulated Militia, being necessary to the security of a free State, the right of the people to keep and bear Arms, shall not be infringed.

Amendment III. (1791)

No Soldier shall, in time of peace be quartered in any house, without the consent of the Owner, nor in time of war, but in a manner to be prescribed by law.

Amendment IV. (1791)

The right of the people to be secure in their persons, houses, papers, and effects, against unreasonable searches and seizures, shall not be violated, and no Warrants shall issue, but upon probable cause, supported by Oath or affirmation, and particularly describing the place to be searched, and the persons or things to be seized.

Amendment V. (1791)

No person shall be held to answer for a capital, or otherwise infamous crime, unless on a presentment or indictment of a Grand Jury, except in cases arising in the land or naval forces, or in the Militia, when in actual service in time of War or public danger; nor shall any person be subject for the same offence to be twice put in jeopardy of life or limb; nor shall be compelled in any criminal case to be a witness against himself, nor be deprived of life, liberty, or property, without due process of law; nor shall private property be taken for public use, without just compensation.

Amendment VI. (1791)

In all criminal prosecutions, the accused shall enjoy the right to a speedy and public trial, by an impartial jury of the State and district wherein the crime shall have been committed, which district shall have been previously ascertained by law, and to be informed of the nature and cause of the accusation; to be confronted with the witnesses against him; to have compulsory process for obtaining Witnesses in his favor, and to have the Assistance of Counsel for his defense.

Amendment VII. (1791)

In Suits at common law, where the value in controversy shall exceed twenty dollars, the right of trial by jury shall be preserved, and no fact tried by a jury, shall be otherwise reexamined in any Court of the United States, than according to the rules of the common law.

Amendment VIII. (1791)

Excessive bail shall not be required, nor excessive fines imposed, nor cruel and unusual punishments inflicted.

Amendment IX. (1791)

The enumeration of the Constitution, of certain rights, shall not be construed to deny or disparage others retained by the people.

Amendment X. (1791)

The powers not delegated to the United States by the Constitution, nor prohibited by it to the States, are reserved to the States respectively, or to the people.

Amendment XI. (1798)

The Judicial power of the United States shall not be construed to extend to any suit in law or equity, commenced or prosecuted against one of the United States by Citizens of another State, or by Citizens or Subjects of any Foreign State.

Amendment XII. (1804)

The Electors shall meet in their respective states and vote by ballot for President and Vice-President, one of whom, at least, shall not be an inhabitant of the same state with themselves; they shall name in their ballots the person voted for as President, and in distinct ballots the person voted for as Vice-President, and they shall make distinct lists of all persons voted for as President, and of all persons voted for as Vice-President, and of the number of votes for each, which lists they shall sign and certify, and transmit sealed to the seat of the government of the United States, directed to the President of the Senate;—The President of the Senate shall, in the presence of the Senate and House of Representatives, open all the certificates and the votes shall then be counted;—The person having the greatest number of votes for President, shall be the President, if such number be a majority of the whole number of Electors appointed; and if no person have such majority, then from the persons having the highest numbers not exceeding three on the list of those voted for as President, the House of Representatives shall choose immediately, by ballot, the President. But in choosing the President, the votes shall be taken by states, the representation from each state having one vote; a quorum for this purpose shall consist of a member or members from two-thirds of the states, and a majority of all the states shall be necessary to a choice. And if the House of Representatives shall not choose a President whenever the right of choice shall devolve upon them, before the fourth day of March next following, then the Vice-President shall act as President, as in the case of the death or other constitutional disability of the President. The person having the greatest number of votes as Vice-President, shall be the Vice-President, if such number be a majority of the whole number of Electors appointed, and if no person have a majority, then from the two highest numbers on the list, the Senate shall choose the Vice-President; a quorum for the purpose shall consist of two-thirds of the whole number of Senators, and a majority of the whole number shall be necessary to a choice. But no person constitutionally ineligible to the office of President shall be eligible to that of Vice-President of the United States.

Amendment XIII. (1865)

SECTION 1. Neither slavery nor involuntary servitude, except as a punishment for crime whereof the party shall have been duly convicted, shall exist within the United States, or any place subject to their jurisdiction.

SECTION 2. Congress shall have power to enforce this article by appropriate legislation.

Amendment XIV. (1868)

SECTION 1. All persons born or naturalized in the United States, and subject to the jurisdiction thereof, are citizens of the United States and of the State wherein they reside. No State shall make or enforce any law which shall abridge the privileges or immunities of citizens of the United States; nor shall any State deprive any person of life, liberty, or property, without due process of law; nor deny to any person within its jurisdiction the equal protection of the law.

SECTION 2. Representatives shall be apportioned among the several States according to their respective numbers, counting the whole number of persons in each State, excluding Indians not taxed. But when the right to vote at any election for the choice of electors for President and Vice-President of the United States, Representatives in Congress, the Executive and Judicial officers of a State, or the members of the Legislature thereof, is denied to any of the male inhabitants of such State, being twenty-one years of age, and citizens of the United States, or in any way abridged, except for participation in rebellion, or other crime, the basis of representation therein shall be reduced in the proportion which the number of such male citizens shall bear to the whole number of male citizens twenty-one years of age in such State.

SECTION 3. No person shall be a Senator or Representative in Congress, or elector of President and Vice-President, or hold any office, civil or military, under the United States, or under any State, who, having previously taken an oath, as a member of Congress, or as an officer of the United States, or as a member of any State legislature, or as an executive or judicial officer of any State, to support the Constitution of the United States, shall have engaged in insurrection or rebellion against the same, or given aid or comfort to the enemies thereof. But Congress may by a vote of two-thirds of each House, remove such disability.

SECTION 4. The validity of the public debt of the United States, authorized by law, including debts incurred for payment of pensions and bounties for services in suppressing insurrection or rebellion, shall not be questioned. But neither the United States nor any State shall assume or pay any debt or obligation incurred in aid of insurrection or rebellion against the United States, or any claim for the loss or emancipation of any slave; but all such debts, obligations and claims shall be held illegal and void.

SECTION 5. The Congress shall have power to enforce, by appropriate legislation, the provisions of this article.

Amendment XV. (1870)

SECTION 1. The right of citizens of the United States to vote shall not be denied or abridged by the United States or by any State on account of race, color, or previous condition of servitude.

SECTION 2. The Congress shall have power to enforce this article by appropriate legislation.

Amendment XVI. (1913)

The Congress shall have power to lay and collect taxes on incomes, from whatever source derived, without apportionment among the several States, and without regard to any census or enumeration.

Amendment XVII. (1913)

The Senate of the United States shall be composed of two Senators from each State, elected by the people thereof, for six years; and each Senator shall have one vote. The electors in each State shall have the qualifications requisite for electors of the most numerous branch of the State legislatures.

When vacancies happen in the representation of any State in the Senate, the executive authority of such State shall issue writs of election to fill such vacancies: *Provided*, That the legislature of any State may empower the executive thereof to make temporary appointments until the people fill the vacancies by election as the legislature may direct.

This amendment shall not be so construed as to affect the election or term of any Senator chosen before it becomes valid as part of the Constitution.

Amendment XVIII. (1919)

SECTION 1. After one year from the ratification of this article the manufacture, sale, or transportation of intoxicating liquors within, the importation thereof into, or the exportation thereof from the United States and all territory subject to the jurisdiction thereof for beverage purposes is hereby prohibited.

SECTION 2. The Congress and the several States shall have concurrent power to enforce this article by appropriate legislation.

SECTION 3. This article shall be inoperative unless it shall have been ratified as an amendment to the Constitution by the legislatures of the several States, as provided in the Constitution, within seven years from the date of the submission hereof to the States by the Congress.

Amendment XIX. (1920)

The right of citizens of the United States to vote shall not be denied or abridged by the United States or by any State on account of sex.

Congress shall have power to enforce this article by appropriate legislation.

Amendment XX. (1933)

SECTION 1. The terms of the President and Vice President shall end at noon on the 20th day of January, and the terms of Senators and representatives at noon on the 3d day of January, of the years in which such terms would have ended if this article had not been ratified; and the terms of their successors shall then begin.

SECTION 2. The Congress shall assemble at least once in every year, and such meeting shall begin at noon on the 3d day of January, unless they shall by law appoint a different day.

SECTION 3. If, at the time fixed for the beginning of the term of the President, the President elect shall have died, the Vice President elect shall become President. If a President shall not have been chosen before the time fixed for the beginning of his term, or if the President elect shall have failed to qualify, then the Vice President elect shall act as President until a President shall have qualified; and the Congress may by law provide for the case wherein neither a President elect nor a Vice President elect shall have qualified, declaring who shall then act as President, or the manner in which one who is to act shall be selected, and such person shall act accordingly until a President or Vice President shall have qualified.

SECTION 4. The Congress may by law provide for the case of the death of any of the persons from whom the House of Representatives may choose a President whenever the right of choice shall have devolved upon them, and for the case of the death of any of the persons from whom the Senate may choose a Vice President whenever the right of choice shall have devolved upon them.

SECTION 5. Sections 1 and 2 shall take effect on the 15th day of October following the ratification of this article.

SECTION 6. This article shall be inoperative unless it shall have been ratified as an amendment to the Constitution by the legislatures of three-fourths of the several States within seven years from the date of submission.

Amendment XXI. (1933)

SECTION 1. The eighteenth article of amendment to the Constitution of the United States is hereby repealed.

SECTION 2. The transportation or importation into any State, Territory, or possession of the United States for delivery or use therein of intoxicating liquors, in violation of the laws thereof, is hereby prohibited.

SECTION 3. This article shall be inoperative unless it shall have been ratified as an amendment to the Constitution by conventions in the several States, as provided in the Constitution, within seven years from the date of the submission hereof to the States by the Congress.

Amendment XXII. (1951)

SECTION 1. No person shall be elected to the office of the President more than twice, and no person who has held the office of President, or acted as President, for more than two years of a term to which some other person was elected president shall be elected to the office of the President more than once. But this Article shall not apply to any person holding office of President when this Article was proposed by the Congress, and shall not prevent any person who may be holding the office of President, or acting as President, during the term within which this Article becomes operative from holding the office of President or acting as President during the remainder of such term.

SECTION 2. The article shall be inoperative unless it shall have been ratified as an amendment to the Constitution by the legislatures of three-fourths of the several States within seven years from the date of its submission to the States by the Congress.

Amendment XXIII. (1961)

SECTION 1. The District constituting the seat of Government of the United States shall appoint in such manner as the Congress may direct:

A number of electors of President and Vice President equal to the whole number of Senators and Representatives in Congress to which the District would be entitled if it were a State, but in no event more than the least populous State; they shall be in addition to those appointed by the States, but they shall be considered, for the purposes of the election of President and Vice President, to be electors appointed by a State; and they shall meet in the District and perform such duties as provided by the twelfth article of amendment.

SECTION 2. The Congress shall have power to enforce this article by appropriate legislation.

Amendment XXIV. (1964)

SECTION 1. The right of citizens of the United States to vote in any primary or other election for President or Vice President, for electors for President or Vice President, or for Senator or Representative in Congress, shall not be denied or abridged by the United States or any State by reason of failing to pay any poll tax or other tax.

SECTION 2. The Congress shall have power to enforce this article by appropriate legislation.

Amendment XXV. (1967)

SECTION 1. In case of the removal of the President from office or of his death or resignation, the Vice President shall become President.

SECTION 2. Whenever there is a vacancy in the office of the Vice President, the President shall nominate a Vice President who shall take office upon confirmation by a majority vote of both Houses of Congress.

SECTION 3. Whenever the President transmits to the President pro tempore of the Senate and the Speaker of the House of Representatives his written declaration that he is unable to discharge the powers and duties of his office, and until he transmits to them a written declaration to the contrary, such powers and duties shall be discharged by the Vice President as Acting President.

SECTION 4. Whenever the Vice President and a majority of either the principal officers of the executive departments or of such other body as Congress may by law provide, transmit to the President pro tempore of the Senate and the Speaker of the House of Representatives their written declaration that the President is unable to discharge the powers and duties of his office, the Vice President shall immediately assume the powers and duties of the office as Acting President.

Thereafter, when the President transmits to the President pro tempore of the Senate and the Speaker of the House of Representatives his written declaration that no inability exists, he shall resume the powers and duties of his office unless the Vice President and a majority of either the principal officers of the executive department or of such other body as Congress may by law provide, transmit within four days to the President pro tempore of the Senate and the Speaker of the House of Representatives their written declaration that the President is unable to discharge the powers and duties of his office. Thereupon Congress shall decide the issue, assembling within forty-eight hours for that purpose if not in session. If the Congress, within twenty-one days after receipt of the latter written declaration, or, if Congress is not in session, within twenty-one days after Congress is required to assemble, determines by two-thirds vote of both Houses that the President is unable to discharge the powers and duties of his office, the Vice President shall continue to discharge the same as Acting President; otherwise, the President shall resume the powers and duties of his office.

Amendment XXVI. (1971)

SECTION 1. The right of citizens of the United States, who are eighteen years of age or older, to vote shall not be denied or abridged by the United States or by any State on account of age.

SECTION 2. The Congress shall have power to enforce this article by appropriate legislation.

Amendment XXVII. (1992)

No law, varying the compensation for the services of the Senators and Representatives, shall take effect, until an election of Representatives shall have intervened.